HISTORY OF R🎸CK

THE DEFINITIVE GUIDE TO ROCK, PUNK, METAL, AND BEYOND

Bath · New York · Singapore · Hong Kong · Cologne · Delhi
Melbourne · Amsterdam · Johannesburg · Auckland · Shenzhen

Contents

First published by Parragon in 2011

PARRAGON
Queen Street House
4 Queen Street
Bath BA1 1HE, UK

www.parragon.com

Copyright © Parragon Books Ltd 2011

Created and produced by JOLLANDS EDITIONS
Author MARK PAYTRESS
Design JC LANAWAY

ISBN 978-1-4454-3821-4

Printed in China

Introduction   6

1950s

Introduction   10
Time line   12
Artists and styles   18

1960s

Introduction   42
Time line   44
Artists and styles   50

1970s

Introduction   116
Time line   118
Artists and styles   124

1980s

Introduction **200**
Time line **202**
Artists and styles **208**

1990s

Introduction **252**
Time line **254**
Artists and styles **260**

2000s

Introduction **294**
Time line **296**
Artists and styles **302**

Glossary **317**
Index **318**
Acknowledgments **320**

Introduction

WHAT IS ROCK MUSIC? Frank Sinatra memorably once described it as "a loud-sounding aphrodisiac." Oddly enough, given Ol' Blue Eyes' lady-killing reputation, he wasn't in favor of it. Odder still, you'll probably find a reference to the velvet-voiced smoothie in here somewhere. That's because rock music, a term first coined to describe the emergence of grown-up pop during the late 1960s, has since become something of a catchall. For instance, neither Muddy Waters (R&B) nor Bob Marley (reggae), Notorious B.I.G. (hip hop), or Madonna (pop) are strictly rock artists, but all four have had a significant impact on the course of its development—which is why they are in this book.

Today, it is this all-inclusive, wide-angle definition of rock music that prevails. From its nonelectric origins in the country blues, to the antirock inclinations of post-punk and electronic music, the story of rock is inextricably interwoven with the course of popular music from the mid-twentieth

Rock has splintered in many directions since Elvis Presley (above) changed the face of pop culture in the mid-1950s—Jimi Hendrix's electric soundscapes, Rod Stewart's showmanship, Metallica's metal bluster, Kurt Cobain (opposite) hovering between Nirvana and despair, Björk's exoticism, Oasis's arrogant revivalism, and Eminem's complex wordplay. Elvis, that onetime scourge of civilized values, would be shocked!

century onward. It's hardly a straightforward journey either, with numerous subgenres and revivals further complicating the issue. I mean, try telling a latter-day R&B fan of Rihanna that the greatest R&B act was Muddy Waters—or the Rolling Stones, for that matter. And what does late 1970s post-punk genuinely have in common with the twenty-first-century variety? That's right. Very little. Don't worry: all will be explained...

Rock is "a loud-sounding aphrodisiac..."

This book is your indispensable guide to making sense of the most potent cultural force in recent decades. Organized in roughly chronological fashion, the book's narrative is neatly divided into eras, each with its own key artists and music areas. There are also sideways glances at relevant pop cultural fads and fashions, while an extensive time line provides an ever-moving thread that binds all the elements that make up the story of rock music together. In the words of the Grateful Dead, it's been a long, strange trip. And the journey is far from over yet. Welcome aboard!

Featuring

Hank Williams • Elvis Presley • Little Richard • Jerry Lee Lewis • Chuck Berry • Howlin' Wolf • Muddy Waters • Bo Diddley • Ray Charles • Johnny Cash • Buddy Holly

1950s

1950s: Introduction

IT WAS SUPPOSED TO HAVE been a decade of orderly reconstruction and material abundance, laying to rest the many hardships of the immediate postwar era with a consumption boom that would create an appliance-rich utopia of untroubled domesticity and the triumph of the American Dream. But President Truman's Fair Deal hadn't reckoned with rock 'n' roll, a rebel yell from Boom Town's dispossessed that between 1955 and 1957 actively shook the foundations of the Western world. Little wonder it was regarded as an intolerable act of treason by the guardians of picket-fence morality.

OPPOSITE *Cleveland-based radio DJ Alan Freed, "Mr Rock 'n' Roll," was the first to pick up on the potential of black urban R&B to cross over to the wider market. A mass outbreak of jukebox installation and jitterbug dancing duly followed.*

BELOW *Three appearances on The Ed Sullivan Show between September 1956 and January 1957 made Elvis Presley the most talked-about man in America—and established him as the hip-swiveling personification of rock 'n' roll.*

As the Cold War clicked into gear, and the world divided Hollywood-style into goodies and baddies, the emergence of rock 'n' roll created an enormous headache for the West. America had experienced moral panics before—over alcohol, sex in the cinema, and, in more recent times, Sinatra's exhibitionism and the flashy decadence of the (largely nonwhite) zoot-suit style boys. But nothing was as loudly threatening to the established order as rock 'n' roll, its so-called "jungle" primitivism soundtracking the instant desires of a rapidly emerging youth culture, while bringing the thorny issues of race and sexuality into mainstream public life. Elvis Presley was

Sounds of the decade

"Your Cheatin' Heart":
Hank Williams (1953)

"Rock Around the Clock":
Bill Haley & His Comets (1954)

"Blue Suede Shoes":
Carl Perkins (1956)

"Hound Dog":
Elvis Presley (1956)

"That'll Be the Day":
Buddy Holly & the Crickets (1957)

"Whole Lotta Shakin' Goin' On":
Jerry Lee Lewis (1957)

certainly no Frankie Laine, and the boisterous backbeat that transformed teenage girls into hysterical wrecks and caused oddly attired young men to lurk menacingly outside neon-lit movie theaters and jukebox-enhanced soda shops was an urgent challenge to the polite big-band swing that had prevailed for years.

Rock 'n' roll defined the decade, but its arrival, coupled with an exponential growth in the phonograph record industry, also prompted a surge of interest in other music from the subterranean underbelly. Urban rhythm and blues (R&B) and hillbilly music from the Southern United States flourished via specialist radio stations, and many independent record labels sprang up to meet demand. More refined circles focused on the politicized folk movement, popularized by Woody Guthrie, and cool jazz, epitomized by *Birth of the Cool* trumpeter Miles Davis.

At the core, though, remained the omnipresent crooners and balladeers, from wholesome rock 'n' roll opportunist Pat Boone to new Tin Pan Alley fabrications, such as Frankie Avalon and Ricky Nelson. By the end of the decade, these bobby-soxer teen idols had virtually routed rock 'n' roll with their own diluted version of the form. The rock revolution was over. Or so it seemed…

"Rumble":
Link Wray (1958)

"Johnny B. Goode":
Chuck Berry (1958)

"Summertime Blues":
Eddie Cochran (1958)

"What'd I Say":
Ray Charles (1959)

1950s: Time line

January 1950

Sam Phillips opens the Memphis Recording Service at 706 Union Avenue in Memphis, Tennessee. Later renamed Sun Studios, the location is widely recognized as the birthplace of 1950s rock 'n' roll.

The Sun label

August 1950

Canadian-born Hank Snow lands the first of seven country music No. 1 hits with "I'm Moving On," which stays at the top for a remarkable 21 weeks. The song will later be given a dramatic R&B makeover by the Rolling Stones.

January 1951

Husband-and-wife team Les Paul and Mary Ford record jazz standard "How High the Moon." Guitarist Paul throws in a range of electronic gimmicks—including overdubbing and an electric guitar solo—and the resulting single spends nine weeks at the top of the *Billboard* chart.

December 1951

Theatricality and teen-idol worship arrive early in the decade when both sides of Johnnie Ray's "Cry"/"The Little White Cloud that Cried" single land at Nos. 1 and 2 in the U.S. chart. Ray's demonstrative, scream-inducing act soon has him pegged as "the Cry Guy."

February 1952

Sam Phillips records blues harmonica player Little Walter for Sun Records, though the disc is canceled before release. Rufus Thomas's "Bear Cat," issued the following March, becomes the label's first R&B hit.

Sam Phillips

March 1952

What is quickly described as the first rock 'n' roll riot breaks out at Alan Freed's Moondog Coronation Ball in Cleveland Arena, Ohio, where opening act Paul Williams is greeted by a mass outbreak of fighting. Police promptly bring the event to a premature close.

December 1953

The Wild One, starring a mean and moody Marlon Brando, is released. As the leather-clad, shades-wearing biker Johnny Strabler, Brando creates a key male role model for aspiring rock 'n' roll miscreants.

January 1954

An all-black lineup, including the Drifters, the Clovers, Fats Domino, Big Joe Turner, and the Moonglows, perform to a mixed audience at Alan Freed's Rock 'n' Roll Jubilee Ball, held at St. Nicholas Arena, New York.

Johnny "Guitar" Watson

February 1954

Nineteen-year-old jump-blues prodigy Johnny "Guitar" Watson employs reverb and feedback on his astonishing guitar instrumental, "Space Guitar."

1950-1955

Jackie Brenston

March 1951

Jackie Brenston's "Rocket 88," an effervescent eulogy to a car recorded at Sun and backed by Ike Turner & the Kings of Rhythm, stakes a convincing claim as the first rock 'n' roll record. It is covered later in the year by white bandleader Bill Haley.

May 1951

Electric-blues guitarist John Lee Hooker, who came to prominence in 1948 with the magnificently hypnotic "Boogie Chillen," releases "Mad Man Blues"/"Boogie Now," his first single for the Chicago-based Chess label.

July 1951

Disc jockey, concert promoter, and self-styled "King of Rock 'n' Roll" Alan Freed broadcasts his first rhythm and blues radio show, "The Moondog House," from Cleveland, Ohio. In a bid to broaden the music's appeal, Freed—alias "Moondog"—starts using the term "rock and roll."

April 1952

Collector Harry Smith assembles a six-disc collection, the *Anthology of American Folk Music*, for Folkways Records. Comprising music originally issued between 1927 and 1932, the set becomes an enormous influence on the blues and folk music revivals.

August 1952

Big Mama Thornton records a raucous R&B song, "Hound Dog," backed by members of Johnny Otis's band. The composers are two white teenagers from Los Angeles, Jerry Leiber and Mike Stoller.

Big Mama Thornton

July 1953

Elvis Presley walks into the offices of Sun Records, and records two Ink Spots songs, "My Happiness" and "That's When Your Heartaches Begin." Impressed, company secretary Marion Keisker duly recommends the young truck driver to label boss Sam Phillips.

March 1954

Following the success of vocal groups the Orioles and the Dominoes, Bronx doo-wop quintet the Chords record "Sh-Boom," which gives them a Top 10 pop chart crossover hit.

December 1954

Backstage in Houston, while touring with Big Mama Thornton, R&B balladeer Johnny Ace shoots himself dead with a .22 revolver. Weeks later, his "Pledging My Love" tops the R&B chart.

February 1955

The latest song to be plucked from the R&B charts and transformed into a pop chart hit for a white act is the Moonglows' "Sincerely," given a sweet and brassy makeover by the McGuire Sisters.

The Moonglows

1950s: Time line

1955

February 1955

For the first time since its introduction in 1949, the 7-inch/18-cm 45 rpm disc outsells the 10-inch/25-cm 78. By the end of the decade, the heavy-duty shellac 78 will be rendered virtually obsolete.

March 1955

Blackboard Jungle, a juvenile delinquency movie set in the classroom and starring Glenn Ford, premieres in New York City. "(We're Gonna) Rock Around the Clock," rescued from a Bill Haley & His Comets B-side, plays over the opening credits. By early summer, the song becomes the first rock 'n' roll chart-topper.

April 1955

Contemporaneous with the growth of rock 'n' roll is "mambo fever," which peaks when Cuban bandleader Pérez Prado scores a No. 1 hit with "Cherry Pink (and Apple Blossom White)," and stays there for ten weeks.

Nat "King" Cole

1956

January 1956

After a long tradition of white singers poaching hits from the R&B listings, two Platters 45s, "Only You" and "The Great Pretender," triumph in the pop chart over a handful of cover versions.

April 1956

Hosted by Alan Freed, and premiered on the CBS Radio Network, *Rock 'n' Roll Dance Party* becomes the first nationally syndicated rock 'n' roll show. Later in the year, Freed pops up on Europe's Radio Luxembourg on Saturday nights.

April 1956

Racists rush the stage at an all-white Nat "King" Cole concert in Birmingham, Alabama, and the singer is assaulted by five men. The attack comes in the wake of the supremacist White Citizens' Council's request to boycott "bop and Negro music."

Rock Around the Clock

The Million Dollar Quartet

September 1956

Six months after its U.S. release, the movie *Rock Around the Clock* arrives in Britain, prompting scenes of hysteria and mayhem in theaters. In its wake, both Haley's "See You Later Alligator" and the title track return to the British singles chart.

November 1956

The piano-playing New Orleans boogie man Fats Domino scores his biggest transatlantic success with an uptempo take on the popular wartime hit, "Blueberry Hill." Its success prompts a riot at a North Carolina show where Fats is unceremoniously compelled to flee through a window.

December 1956

Elvis Presley, Jerry Lee Lewis, Carl Perkins, and Johnny Cash, alias "The Million Dollar Quartet," record an impromptu session of gospel songs and country music at Sun Studios. Ostensibly a Carl Perkins session, the others are apparently invited by Sam Phillips or else casually drop by.

1955-1957

May 1955

After closing a show in Jacksonville, Florida, with the words, "Girls, I'll see you backstage," Elvis Presley prompts a riot—the first of many hysteria-drenched moments for the man the press is calling "The Boppin' Hillbilly."

September 1955

James Dean, Hollywood's Porsche-driving loner and proverbial rebel without a cause, is dead. Weeks later, the Cheers' "Black Denim Trousers and Motorcycle Boots" charts, the first in a not always illustrious line of rock 'n' roll death discs.

Elvis with "Colonel" Tom Parker

November 1955

Just three months after taking on the role of special adviser to Elvis Presley, and a month after becoming his manager, the cigar-chomping onetime carnival hustler "Colonel" Tom Parker takes Presley from Sun to RCA Records in a deal worth $40,000.

Gene Vincent

June 1956

Limping rockabilly cult hero Gene Vincent scores the biggest hit of his career with the self-penned "Be-Bop-A-Lula," which is graced with a masterful, echo-drenched vocal.

June 1956

With no guitar to hold, and only the salacious "Hound Dog" to sing, Elvis Presley scandalizes elders with an electrifying, full-bodied performance on *The Milton Berle Show* that soon earns him the sobriquet "Elvis the Pelvis."

July 1956

Brenda Lee, the "Little Miss Dynamite" with the big voice, signs a deal with Decca Records and soon chalks up a series of country and rockabilly flavored 45s, including "Jambalaya" and "Sweet Nothin's."

Brenda Lee with Elvis, 1956

1957

January 1957

Based on a cellar-style beatnik hangout in Paris, the Cavern Club opens in Liverpool, northwest England. Though later known as a venue for skiffle and beat music, the first act through the doors is the Merseysippi Jazz Band.

February 1957

After touring Australia with Lavern Baker and Big Joe Turner, Bill Haley & His Comets become the first rock 'n' roll band to play Britain. Mobbed at London's Waterloo Station, Haley prompts a predictable round of riots at several shows, though some have doubts about a 31-year-old leading the rock 'n' roll charge.

March 1957

Buoyed by his extraordinary success and a lucrative Hollywood movie deal, Elvis Presley purchases a large piece of privacy in the form of an 18-room mansion south of Memphis, Tennessee. He calls it Graceland.

1950s: Time line

April 1957
Britain's skiffle boom, kicked off in 1956 by Lonnie Donegan's "Rock Island Line," peaks when his "Cumberland Gap" tops the British charts. The roots movement's London center of activities, Soho's 2-i's coffee bar, soon yields another homegrown hero, Tommy Steele.

Lonnie Donegan

June 1957
Sam Cooke breaks from the gospel tradition with the release of his first secular single. Widely regarded as a key moment in the development of soul, "You Send Me" tops both the R&B and pop charts.

July 1957
After teenage Liverpudlian skiffle enthusiasts the Quarrymen perform from the back of a truck, as part of the St. Peter's Church garden fete in Liverpool suburb Woolton, the watching Paul McCartney introduces himself to the band's guitarist, John Lennon. Three months later, the two future Beatles will share a stage for the first time.

March 1958
The Coasters record "Yakety Yak," the wittiest, most infectious, and successful of several hits written and produced for the Los Angeles-based vocal group by Jerry Leiber and Mike Stoller.

June 1958
RCA becomes the first major record company to introduce the stereo vinyl LP. Offering greater listening clarity, the new "living stereo" format is initially intended for classical music.

July 1958
Conway Twitty hits No. 1 on both sides of the Atlantic with his chest-beating ballad, "It's Only Make Believe." Some insist—incorrectly—that Twitty is a pseudonym for Elvis Presley.

The Big Bopper

January 1959
Detroit songwriter Berry Gordy forms Tamla Records in order to serve the Motor City's black talent. By the fall, the label has its first hit—Barrett Strong's "Money (That's What I Want)"—and an administrative HQ that Gordy christens Hitsville USA.

February 1959
Later immortalized as "The Day the Music Died," February 3, 1959, puts the lid on first-generation rock 'n' roll when Buddy Holly, Ritchie Valens, and the Big Bopper die in a plane crash in Iowa, midway through a three-week tour of the Midwest.

June 1959
The United States thirst for "Exotica"—music with a Latin or Polynesian twist—peaks when the Hawaii-based percussion maverick Martin Denny scores a huge hit with "Quiet Village," originally a hit for composer Les Baxter in 1952.

1957-1959

Paul Anka

August 1957

"Diana," a love-struck ballad written and sung by 16-year-old Paul Anka, hits No. 1 in Britain just days before enjoying similar success in the United States and his native Canada. His success will peak toward the end of the decade with four further Top 5 hits.

September 1957

Jack Kerouac's *On the Road* is published. A largely autobiographical work based on soul-searching travels across America, the book is a classic Beat Generation text and in turn inspires an anti-establishment social grouping known as beatniks.

October 1957

After the enormous success of "Bye Bye Love" earlier in the summer, the close-harmony duo the Everly Brothers score a second No. 1 hit with "Wake Up Little Susie"—which also confirms the brothers' success in Britain.

Everly Brothers

August 1958

After appearances in the movies *The Girl Can't Help It* (1956) and *Untamed Youth* (1957), up-and-coming rock 'n' roll guitarist Eddie Cochran hits the U.S. Top 10 with "Summertime Blues."

October 1958

Having made his chart debut in 1956 with "Please, Please, Please," James Brown returns to the R&B chart with a ballad, "Try Me." Over the next two decades, Brown will head the R&B charts on no fewer than 17 occasions.

December 1958

The Teddy Bears, a hitherto unknown vocal group from Los Angeles, hit the top spot for three weeks with a ballad, "To Know Him Is To Love Him." The song's author, and the group's prime mover, is future production genius Phil Spector.

July 1959

One of the century's most expressive singers, Billie Holiday, dies aged 44. A veteran of the jazz-club scene, Holiday nevertheless characterized herself in song as "Lady Sings the Blues," a testimony to her life of hardship.

Billie Holiday

August 1959

Miles Davis's *Kind of Blue* album, featuring John Coltrane and Cannonball Adderley on saxophones, is released. Largely improvised, while at the same time more melodious than Davis's previous hard-bop sound, it becomes a top-selling and hugely influential jazz album.

October 1959

Bronx-born vocal stylist Bobby Darin tops the charts on both sides of the Atlantic with a swinging version of Kurt Weill's Berlin theater song, "Mack the Knife." Despite a radio ban in the United States, Darin's classy reworking stays at No. 1 for nine weeks and later earns him a Grammy.

Hank Williams

THE LONESOME, LUSH VOICE of hillbilly music, hard-drinking Hank Williams also became the first live-fast, die-young corpse of a nascent rock culture, after his lifestyle-prompted death on New Year's Day 1953 at the age of 29.

Though Williams lacked the supposed Faustian pact with the devil that his Delta bluesman counterpart Robert Johnson had made before his premature death in 1938, the country man's influence on 1950s music was probably more tangible. And, covered by everyone from Presley and Dylan to Beck, Williams's relatively small but enduring catalog of songs continues to cast a lingering spell over popular music.

Hailing from the Alabama wilderness, minus an absent father but nursing a chronic back condition (said to have prompted his drinking and drug taking), Williams was hosting his own radio slot by his midteens. Influenced by Jimmie Rodgers and Roy Acuff, the singer's unreconstituted hillbilly sound, ably demonstrated on two dozen country chart hits between 1948 and 1951, was distinguished by the haunting quality of his voice, which personalized songs such as "I'm So Lonesome I Could Cry" and "Your Cheating Heart" to an often heartbreaking degree. Less remarked upon is Williams's role as the missing link between rural country music and rockabilly, as evidenced on 1947's "Move It On Over," a clear antecedent for Bill Haley's "(We're Gonna) Rock Around the Clock."

Hank Williams

Born: *September 17, 1923, Montgomery, Alabama*

Died: *January 1, 1953*

Years active: *1937–52*

Genre: *country/ hillbilly*

Key singles: *"I'm So Lonesome I Could Cry" (1949), "Your Cheating Heart" (1953)*

Key albums: Moanin' the Blues *(1952)*, Memorial Album *(1953)*

LEFT *Hank Williams (in signature white hat) at the height of his fame, posing for a promotional photo with his band the Drifting Cowboys at the studios of WSM Radio, Nashville.*

Sun Records, Memphis

IT'S NO EXAGGERATION to say that Sam Phillips's Sun Records was the Memphis-based midwife to 1950s rock 'n' roll. It was at Phillips's Memphis Recording Service in March 1951 that Jackie Brenston recorded "Rocket 88," widely acknowledged as the first rock 'n' roll song. It was at the same premises that Elvis Presley strolled in one hot Saturday afternoon in July 1953 and taped a demo that laid the foundation for a history-making two-year relationship with the label. And it was on January 1, 1956, that Sun released rockabilly pioneer Carl Perkins's "Blue Suede Shoes," arguably the song that best captures the gritty one-upmanship of rock 'n' roll culture.

ABOVE *"That's All Right" launched the career of Elvis Presley and put Sun Records on the map upon its release in 1954.*

BELOW *Sam Phillips (center left) with his most famous discovery. Presley released five singles on Sun.*

When onetime radio DJ Phillips opened his recording facility in 1950, it was to reflect the biracial aspects of Memphis's musical culture, with Phillips soon leasing masters of black R&B (artists such as Brenston and Howlin' Wolf) to the Chicago-based Chess Records. After Presley's enormous success, Phillips concentrated on white rock 'n' rollers, including rockabilly rebels Perkins and Jerry Lee Lewis, country rebel Johnny Cash and—with less success—Roy Orbison. After losing Elvis Presley to RCA late in 1955, Sun's stock slowly fell, and when Phillips moved premises in February 1961, it was confirmation that Sun's golden age had long passed.

Rock 'n' roll

ROCK 'N' ROLL EXPLODED in the face of postwar austerity, divided generations, and ushered in an era of boisterous rebellion through style and sound. A cultural revolution that shocked and shook the world, it marked the arrival of an accelerated way of living: neon-lit, rich in finger-snapping attitude, and rejoicing in a heady whiff of sex and subversion.

The spectacular arrival of Elvis Presley as an international phenomenon during 1955 marked a neat dividing line between the pre- and post-rock 'n' roll eras, and there is no doubt that popular music and its audience underwent a significant transformation between 1950 and 1959. But though it seemed that rock 'n' roll emerged fully formed, and with neither precedent nor context, the reality was quite different.

ABOVE RIGHT *Rock 'n' roll's arrival prompted many cash-in movies, such as Shake, Rattle and Rock! (1956), with Fats Domino and Big Joe Turner.*

RIGHT *Also from 1956, Rock, Rock, Rock! shoehorned numerous artists into its flimsy plot and featured Alan Freed playing himself.*

5 Top rock 'n' roll artists

Little Richard: "Tutti-Frutti" (1955)
Elvis Presley: "Heartbreak Hotel" (1956)

Fats Domino: "Blueberry Hill" (1956)
Jerry Lee Lewis: "Whole Lotta Shakin' Goin' On" (1957)

Eddie Cochran: "Summertime Blues" (1958)

ABOVE *The death of guitar virtuoso Eddie Cochran after an automobile crash in April 1960 robbed rock 'n' roll of its potential savior. His "C'mon Everybody," "Somethin' Else," and "Summertime Blues" were exultant hymns to the hopes and anxieties of youth.*

The term "rock 'n' roll," with its suggestions of sex and spiritual rapture, had been incorporated into song titles since the 1930s, though it was only in 1951, when DJ Alan Freed utilized it to give a new, color-blind impetus to rhythm and blues music, that it entered into popular parlance. The influences that acted on the style, though, ranged much wider than that – blues from the Mississippi Delta region (1920s), hillbilly/country music (1930s), gospel, and jazz all played a part in the creation of 1950s rock 'n' roll. More immediately influential was the growth of boogie-woogie and jump blues from New Orleans and Kansas City, and the howl of electric blues emanating out of Chicago.

Roy Brown's "Good Rocking Tonight" (1948), Fats Domino's "The Fat Man" (1949), and Jackie Brenston's "Rocket 88" (1951) all have competing claims to be the first rock 'n' roll record. But it was the emergence of Elvis Presley from the Sun Studio in Memphis during 1954 and 1955 that gave focus and direction to rock 'n' roll. His earliest sides, split neatly between bluesy takes on country songs ("Blue Moon of Kentucky") and countrified blues ("That's All Right," "Good Rockin' Tonight"), virtually defined southern-style rock 'n' roll – although Little Richard (gospel), Chuck Berry (blues), and various doo-wop vocal outfits stretched the parameters way beyond a simple rockabilly beat.

Elvis Presley

IN JULY 1953, a shy, truck-driving teenage misfit from Memphis, Tennessee, breezed into the offices of Sun Records and mumbled, "I don't sound like nobody." Within two years, the young man from lonely street had become an international phenomenon, a figurehead for sonic intoxication and the embodiment of a no-compromise attitude that, six decades later, still defines the outer parameters of rock music. That was Elvis Presley, "King of Rock 'n' Roll" and bona fide twentieth-century icon.

Possessing a voice that confounded racial typecasting, and a lasciviously loose-limbed stage presence that caused acute consternation once "Elvis the Pelvis" hit American television screens in 1956, Presley was an entirely new type of performer. Untethered and untrained, this sexualized riot of individualism exposed the surface calm of postwar culture to the giddying glare of subversion. Being denounced as depraved by the custodians of moral fortitude only further endeared Presley to teenagers, who greeted his early paeans to sex ("Hound Dog"), style ("Blue Suede Shoes"), and malevolent solitude ("Heartbreak Hotel") as manifestos for an entirely new way of living.

"Rhythm is something you either have or don't have"

ABOVE He didn't, in his own words, "sound like nobody." But at least as important to Presley's appeal was the look, a pop world equivalent of Marlon Brando's outlaw biker in the movie The Wild One.

FAR RIGHT *Within months of his spectacular rise to fame, Presley was screen-testing for Paramount. Love Me Tender, the first of 33 feature films, is regarded as one of his more satisfying efforts.*

RIGHT *The televised and hugely successful "Comeback Special" in 1968 reunited Elvis with his rock 'n' roll roots.*

LEFT *Barely a year after his hips had outraged a nation, Elvis was swaying them with abandon for Hollywood in 1957's Jailhouse Rock.*

Yet despite pouring all that raw, repressed instinct into song, mama's boy Elvis was always more entertainer than revolutionary. Sensing his commercial potential as early as 1956, Hollywood cast him as an on-screen hero, and after a two-year spell in the U.S. Army, devoured his soul over the course of 33 feature films.

A 1968 television "Comeback Special" found Presley back in leather and re-engaging with his roots, prompting a renaissance both in the studio and on stage. It didn't last. Lost in Las Vegas, and maudlin to the point of despair, Presley—overweight and overdressed in a now iconic series of jewel-encrusted jumpsuits—sang himself to an early, endless sleep with a crushing repertoire of heartbreaker ballads and routine medleys of his former glories. When, on August 16, 1977, the story broke that the King was dead, many—including John Lennon—felt as if they'd lost Elvis years earlier.

Elvis Presley

Born: *January 8, 1935, Tupelo, Mississippi*
Died: *August 16, 1977*

Years active: *1954–77*
Genres: *rock 'n' roll, rockabilly, country, R&B, blues, gospel*

Key singles: "Heartbreak Hotel" (1956), "Hound Dog" (1956)

Key albums: Elvis Presley (1956), From Elvis in Memphis (1969)

Little Richard

THE ONLY ROCK 'N' ROLL IDOL ever to truly match the hysteria of a hyped-up 1950s audience was Little Richard. The spectacle of this diminutive man with the gravity-defying pompadour and pencil-thin mustache pumping out sparkling notes at the high end of a piano was electrifying enough. But when the era's most flamboyant performer let loose a histrionic barrage of whelps and whooahs ("A-wop-bop-a-loo-lop-a-lop-bam-boom!" he shrieked on his 1955 breakthrough, "Tutti-Frutti"), it was clear that the abandon and showmanship of rock 'n' roll had crossed another threshold.

ABOVE *Little Richard acting the part in a scene from the 1956 movie,* The Girl Can't Help It, *featuring his title track.*

One of the most successful rock 'n' rollers, notching up seven U.S. Top 20 hits between 1955 and 1958 (including "Long Tall Sally," "Rip It Up," and "Good Golly, Miss Molly"), Georgia-born Richard Penniman made his first recordings as early as 1951. More significantly, though encouraged to emulate Ray Charles and Fats Domino, he'd taken his cue from flamboyant pianist Esquerita and female gospel singers, such as Mahalia Jackson.

It was to the realm of the sacred that Little Richard returned in October 1957, after an epiphany while on tour in Australia. Feted by the Beatles and the Rolling Stones during comeback tours of Britain in 1962 and 1963, he reconciled rock 'n' roll and the Bible and was later cited by James Brown and Otis Redding as key in the development of funk and soul.

Little Richard

Born: *December 5, 1932, Macon, Georgia*

Years active: *1951 to present*

Genres: *rock 'n' roll, R&B, gospel, soul*

Key singles: *"Tutti-Frutti" (1955), "Lucille" (1957)*

Key albums: *Here's Little Richard (1957), Little Richard (1958)*

LEFT *Both brilliant and controversial, Little Richard has been an enduring influence on funk, soul, and showmanship.*

Jerry Lee Lewis

JERRY LEE LEWIS wasn't the only conflicted rock 'n' roller—but no one contested the battle between licentiousness and the Good Lord with such devastating consequences as this piano-trashing wildcat from Louisiana. It's all there on his biggest hit, "Great Balls of Fire," a hymn to sexual heat delivered in the manner of a possessed evangelical staring eternal damnation in the face. Lewis admitted as much as he laid down the song at Sun Studios. "How can the devil save souls?" he asked Sam Phillips, arguing that the song was too sinful for him to play. "I got the devil in me!"

The combative rockabilly bad boy did himself few favors. Arriving for a British tour in May 1958, news leaked out that he'd married his third wife, Myra, when she was just 13. The tour was quickly canceled, Lewis was blacklisted by radio stations on his return home, and the man responsible for one of the defining rock 'n' roll hits, 1957's "Whole Lotta Shakin' Goin' On," was seemingly consigned to history. Instead, after enjoying a belated British welcome in the mid-1960s, he switched his attentions to the country music of his youth—though events in his personal life, marked by the deaths of two wives and two sons, various gun-toting incidents, and an enduring love affair with the whiskey bottle, have done little to quell his outlaw image. The biopic *Great Balls of Fire!* (1989), starring Dennis Quaid, reaffirmed Lewis's place in history.

BELOW *"The Killer," poised to leap to his feet during a 1957 performance of "Whole Lotta Shakin' Goin' On."*

Jerry Lee Lewis

Born: *September 29, 1935, Ferriday, Louisiana*
Years active: *1954 to present*

Genres: *rock 'n' roll, rockabilly, country*

Key singles: *"Whole Lotta Shakin' Goin' On" (1957), "Great Balls of Fire" (1957)*

Key albums: High School Confidential *(1958)*, Live at the Star Club, Hamburg *(1964)*

Chuck Berry

ACCORDING TO JOHN LENNON, the name is synonymous with rock 'n' roll. His music has provided the backbone for the Rolling Stones' entire career. And on any given night, bands the world over still perform his songs in bars crammed with crowds that can recite every word. That man—nay, legend—is Chuck Berry, architect of the quintessential rock 'n' roll tune, who patented the defining rock-guitar lick and whose lyrics brought a poetic elegance to the twentieth century's most immediate and expressive art form. He was by no means the first, nor the most successful, figure in rock 'n' roll, but he is possibly the most important.

Hailing from St. Louis, Missouri, Berry announced his arrival in 1955 with a burst of twisted, overamped guitar notes and a furiously insistent backbeat. The song was "Maybellene," and in its wake came an impeccable string of soundalike hits—"Roll Over Beethoven," "School Day," "Rock and Roll Music," "Sweet Little Sixteen," "Johnny B. Goode" among them—each one a euphoric, irresistible endorsement of the new music and the self-contained world of the teenage audience that lapped it up. Berry's two-string staccato intros, crucial moves in the lexicon of guitar phraseology, were complemented by Johnnie Johnson's equally influential barroom boogie-woogie piano fills.

Berry was less fleet-footed in his personal life, following a spell in jail for armed robbery in his late teens with another in 1962 for transporting an underage girl across state lines. Freed the following year, he discovered that his beat-boom disciples across the Atlantic—and, closer to home, the Beach Boys—had drawn much inspiration from him. But with no particular place for an aging rock hero to go, he turned his attentions to the nostalgia concert circuit, before enjoying a surprise success in 1972 with the innuendo-laden "My Ding-a-Ling." Berry still tours regularly, a living legend accompanied by pickup bands, feeding scraps of his genius to audiences that lap up the occasional duckwalk and, of course, those archetypal rock 'n' roll licks.

LEFT *Chuck Berry's duckwalk is almost as famous as his riffs. Here he is in 1964 seeking to upstage James Brown and the Rolling Stones on the TAMI Show.*

RIGHT *Until a health scare in January 2011, Berry has been a compulsive, if sometimes perfunctory, live performer.*

Chuck Berry

Born: *October 18, 1926, St. Louis, Missouri*

Years active: *1955 to present*
Genre: *rock 'n' roll*

Key singles: *"Rock and Roll Music" (1957), "Johnny B. Goode" (1958)*

Key albums: After School Session *(1957),* Chuck Berry On Stage *(1963)*

Rhythm and blues

BETWEEN 1946 AND 1948, there was a shift in the use of the pejorative term "race records" in favor of the more descriptive rhythm and blues (soon abbreviated to R&B). This coincided with a general shift in North American black music, where fast-paced boogie-woogie rhythms and the use of amplified instruments, especially guitars, were enjoying greater prominence. In African-American communities, such as New Orleans, St. Louis, and Kansas City, strongholds of boogie-woogie and jump blues, the emphasis was more on piano and saxophones. In Chicago, where numerous Delta blues musicians had migrated since the 1930s, the guitar and the harmonica were more prevalent. In sum, black music was beginning to make itself heard beyond the fringes of Middle America.

This richly tapestried diaspora was reflected on a number of record labels that emerged during the 1940s—Specialty and Imperial (both Los Angeles), King (Cincinatti), Savoy (New Jersey), Chess (Chicago), and Atlantic (New York)—all energizing the newly reclassified rhythm and blues record sales chart. Established big-band and jump-blues artists, such as T-Bone Walker, Louis Jordan, Big Joe Turner, and Wynonie Harris were slowly usurped by a new generation—

from Johnny Otis, who scored several R&B chart No. 1s during 1951, Fats Domino, and Little Richard to ballsy Big Mama Thornton and Atlantic's pop-inclined Ruth Brown.

However, it was the electrified blues coming out of Chicago that proved so crucially influential on the future course of rock. Several of the most prominent performers—Howlin' Wolf, Muddy Waters, Willie Dixon, John Lee Hooker,

BELOW *Jimmy Reed's inimitable style of electric blues was a huge influence on the Rolling Stones during their R&B purist days.*

5 Top rhythm and blues artists

Big Joe Turner: *"Shake, Rattle and Roll"* (1954)	Bo Diddley: *"Bo Diddley"* (1955)	John Lee Hooker: *"Boom Boom"* (1961)
Muddy Waters: *"Hoochie Coochie Man"* (1954)	Howlin' Wolf: *"Spoonful"* (1960)	

and Jimmy Reed—originated from the Mississippi Delta and had their roots in the deep country blues of the 1920s and 1930s. Possessing a more melancholy streak than the piano and sax-led rhythm and blues from other parts of the country, Chicago blues later provided the basis for the British rhythm and blues boom in the 1960s, the Rolling Stones in particular basing their early repertoire on Bo Diddley, Jimmy Reed, and Chuck Berry numbers.

ABOVE *Bandleader and pianist Johnny Otis in 1957 bringing some rock 'n' roll showmanship to his act.*

RIGHT *The 1955* Rhythm and Blues Revue *included jazz crossover acts, such as Nat "King" Cole.*

Howlin' Wolf

THE MOST DISTINCTIVE VOICE in electric blues came, unsurprisingly, from a tall, massively built man who was already in his forties before rock 'n' roll cast new light on his work and that of his Mississippi-raised contemporaries. To describe it as gravelly is only the half of it and, by the time Wolf reached Chicago, where he recorded at Chess Studios with some of the windy city's finest—notably pianist Otis Spann, guitarist Hubert Sumlin, and bassist/songwriter Willie Dixon—the Wolf-fronted combo cooked up the toughest sound in all America.

Born Chester Burnett in southwest Mississippi, Wolf was tutored in guitar by Charley Patton, took his vocal cue from yodeling country singer Jimmie Rodgers, and had wound up in Memphis by the late 1940s, where he briefly recorded for Sun Records. By 1954, Wolf had relocated to Chicago, where he recorded the best work of his career, including the ghostly howl of "Moanin' at Midnight" and the deliciously syncopated "Forty-Four." Several of these ended up on his self-titled 1962 album, alongside a handful of Willie Dixon numbers— "Wang Dang Doodle," "Little Red Rooster," "Smokestack Lightning," and "Back Door Man"—all later staples of the beat and blues booms. Wolf's own "Killing Floor," released in 1966, was covered by Jimi Hendrix and inspired Led Zeppelin's "The Lemon Song." Most extraordinary of all was Captain Beefheart's wholesale lifting of Wolf's vocal style.

"I don't play anything but the blues..."

Howlin' Wolf

Born: *June 10, 1910, White Station, Mississippi*

Died: *January 10, 1976*

Years active: *mid-1930s to 1976*

Genres: *blues, R&B*

Key singles: *"Smokestack Lightning" (1956), "Spoonful" (1960)*

Key albums: *Moanin' in the Moonlight (1959), Howlin' Wolf (1969)*

LEFT *A towering presence, both physically and musically, Howlin' Wolf had a voice to match. His repertoire was plundered by many during the early and late 1960s blues booms.*

Muddy Waters

THE LINK BETWEEN the great Delta bluesmen, such as Son House and Robert Johnson, and rock giants Jimi Hendrix, Led Zeppelin, and the Rolling Stones (who took their name from a 1950 Waters song), Muddy Waters personified the electric blues of Chicago's south side during the late 1940s and 1950s.

Born McKinley Morganfield, Waters took his epithet from the Mississippi Delta mudbanks and his distinctive slide-guitar playing from Robert Johnson, whom he had seen perform in his native Clarksdale. In 1943, as part of the great black migration, Waters relocated to urban Chicago, where he quickly switched to electric guitar on account of the noise levels in the city's south-side clubs and bars. In 1946, he began recording for the Chess brothers' Aristocrat label, which by the end of the decade had evolved into Chess Records.

Early Waters classics such as "I Can't Be Satisfied," "Rollin' and Tumblin'," and "Rollin' Stone" were followed in the early 1950s by more robust material, including "Hoochie Coochie Man," "I Just Want to Make Love to You," and "You Need Love," all Willie Dixon compositions that were later covered by the British blues-boom bands who feted him. Fame had come to Waters late, but a series of awards handed out toward the end of his life confirmed his key role in the development of rock music.

Muddy Waters

Born: April 4, 1915, Rolling Fork, Mississippi

Died: April 30, 1983

Years active: 1941–83

Genres: blues, R&B

Key singles: "Rollin' Stone" (1948), "Hoochie Coochie Man" (1954)

Key albums: Best of Muddy Waters (1957), At Newport 1960 (1960)

LEFT Muddy Waters (center, with guitar) performing in 1966 for Canadian television. Willie Dixon (with upright bass), who wrote numerous Chicago blues classics, remains something of an unsung legend.

Bo Diddley

AS COOL AND CONVINCING as most American R&B artists sounded to their young admirers in Britain, there was no getting around the generational divide. But the music of Bo Diddley, from its vaguely threatening if instantly recognizable "Diddley beat" to his sweet-toned voice, had a maraca-driven urgency to it that seemed to transcend both time and geography. As Diddley wails and moans over the quintessential three-note Chicago riff of "I'm a Man," there's a tribal-like primitivism about the performance that seems to take the song way back, down the Mississippi of Diddley's childhood through the Caribbean and to the heart of Africa.

Bo Diddley

Born: *December 30, 1928, McComb, Mississippi*

Died: *June 2, 2008*

Years active: *1943–2008*

Genres: *R&B, rock 'n' roll*

Key singles: *"Bo Diddley" (1955), "Who Do You Love" (1956)*

Key albums: *Bo Diddley (1957), Go Bo Diddley (1959)*

Unlike Waters and Wolf, Diddley spent much of his youth in Chicago, his family having moved there when he was six. But, being significantly younger than both, he didn't start recording there until 1954. Unsurprisingly, it was seeing the similarly rhythm-driven John Lee Hooker that prompted Diddley to take his music seriously, though the success of his first single, "Bo Diddley," would prompt plenty more self-referentiality when he hit his prolific peak during the late 1950s/early 1960s.

Though lionized by the British beat-boomers, Diddley's songs—from "Diddy Wah Diddy" (Captain Beefheart) to "Who Do You Love" (Quicksilver)—were equally coveted by the psychedelic jam bands of the late 1960s. He was, as many insist, "The Originator."

RIGHT *Bo Diddley holds his trademark customized rectangular Gretsch guitar, while Norma-Jean Wofford, alias "the Duchess," parades an early 1960s space-age model. Bo and his band were cherished for their primal "Diddley beat."*

Ray Charles

DUBBED "THE GENIUS" due to his ability to roll so many influences into his work, Ray Charles started out imitating blues pianist Charles Brown, before shifting to country music at the height of his career in the early 1960s. But it's for his remarkable transition during the 1950s that Charles is best remembered—an era that began with a handful of minor R&B hits and ended with the crossover success of the irresistible floor shaker, "What'd I Say."

Georgia-born, blind by the age of seven, and by his late teens deprived of both parents, Ray Charles played his way out with an elegant piano style and vocal cues taken from Nat "King" Cole. After joining Atlantic Records in 1952, the grief-filled inflections of gospel music began to usurp his hitherto gentle vocal style while his piano playing—as evidenced on the 1955 hit "I Got a Woman"—seemed to owe a greater debt to New Orleans-style jump blues.

After the success of 1959's "What'd I Say," Charles began the 1960s with another pop crossover chart-topper, "Hit the Road Jack," before the transatlantic triumph of the country cover, "I Can't Stop Loving You." The constant in Ray Charles's career, though, remained his voice—a hugely expressive instrument widely regarded as the first voice of soul.

Ray Charles

Born: September 23, 1930, Albany, Georgia

Died: June 10, 2004

Years active: 1947–2004

Genres: jazz, R&B, rock 'n' roll, gospel, soul, country

Key singles: "I Got a Woman" (1954), "What'd I Say" (1959)

Key albums: The Genius of Ray Charles (1959), Ray Charles in Person (1960)

Rockabilly

THERE'S A FINE LINE between rock 'n' roll and rockabilly, but it's not as indistinct as one might imagine. Essentially, rockabilly is blue-eyed rock 'n' roll. If the gospel influence underlies R&B, then it's country music that provides rockabilly's missing link.

BELOW *Bill Haley, pictured here with his Comets on British television in the mid-1960s, began his career singing country and western material.*

Country music provides rockabilly's missing link

The roots of rockabilly can be traced back to 1920s hillbilly singer Jimmie Rodgers, the so-called father of country music whose "blue yodel" and use of blues-derived chord progressions betrayed a clear blues influence on his work. Likewise, Bill Monroe's bluegrass style revealed that the two forms were by no means mutually exclusive.

It was at Sam Phillips's Sun Studio in the early 1950s that the hillbilly influence on rock 'n' roll was most clearly felt. Elvis Presley's habit of recording one blues and one country song for each of his five Sun singles was just the most obvious manifestation of a stylistic and multicultural mingling that proved the dominant force throughout popular music in the 1950s. With conventional country and western music in a honky-tonk rut, Presley's early reputation as "The Hillbilly Cat" provided a possible way out. Instead, it was the "rock" rather than the "billy" aspect of rockabilly—notable for its echoed voice, slap-bass, and amplified guitar—that prevailed, and country music had to wait until late in the decade before a new, pop-friendly Nashville sound brought the genre alive and kicking into the realm of the contemporary.

With Elvis Presley duly installed as "The King of Rock 'n' Roll," it was fellow Sun artist Carl Perkins, who began his career performing highly charged versions of Hank Williams songs, who stepped into the role of "King of Rockabilly." Less well known, but equally convincing, were the Johnny Burnette Trio, fronted by two amateur boxing enthusiasts whose tough, hiccup-voiced "Train Kept A-Rollin'" rivals Perkins's "Blue Suede Shoes" as the quintessential rockabilly song. Probably the most notable exception to the color code is Chuck Berry's first hit, 1955's "Maybellene," where the backbeat is far closer to rockabilly than to rhythm and blues.

ABOVE LEFT *Elvis Presley might now be most associated with "Blue Suede Shoes," but it was rockabilly king Carl Perkins who wrote the song and first took it into the charts early in 1956.*

ABOVE RIGHT *The Johnny Burnette Trio—Johnny is far left—cooked up some mean rockabilly riffs, none better than on "The Train Kept A-Rollin'," later covered by the Yardbirds and Led Zeppelin.*

5 Top rockabilly artists

Bill Haley: *"(We're Gonna) Rock Around the Clock"* (1954)

Elvis Presley: *"Mystery Train"* (1955)

Carl Perkins: *"Blue Suede Shoes"* (1956)

Gene Vincent: *"Race With the Devil"* (1956)

Johnny Burnette Trio: *"The Train Kept A-Rollin'"* (1956)

Johnny Cash

ONCE TOO EASILY TYPECAST as the wild card of country music, Johnny Cash grew in stature during the 1990s, with a remarkable late-career renaissance that found him interpreting contemporary material from various genres as if it were his own. Despite a career that had been dogged by drug abuse and run-ins with the law, Cash's strongest cards were a style that eschewed country-music convention and a warm, laconic voice, which reflected the deep spirituality that underpinned his seemingly chaotic exterior.

Legend who refused to toe the line

When Cash auditioned at Sun in 1954, he was favoring gospel-inspired material. Within a year, he'd stepped up the pace with "Hey Porter," and it was the freight-train rhythm of 1956's "I Walk the Line" that brought him his first crossover success. Moving to Columbia in 1958, Cash capitalized on his outlaw image with two prison concerts in the late 1960s, tempered by the occasional novelty tune, such as "A Boy Named Sue" and "Jackson," the latter a duet with wife June Carter.

Cash was unceremoniously dropped by Columbia in the 1980s, but his mid-1990s return at the behest of producer Rick Rubin prompted a magnificent late flourish, which was never bettered than on "Hurt," his reinvention of a deathly Nine Inch Nails song.

Johnny Cash

Born: *February 26, 1932, Kingsland, Arkansas*

Died: *September 12, 2003*

Years active: *1955–2003*

Genres: *country, rockabilly, rock 'n' roll, gospel*

Key singles: *"Folsom Prison Blues" (1955), "I Walk the Line" (1956)*

Key albums: Sings the Songs that Made Him Famous *(1958),* At San Quentin *(1969)*

BELOW *Johnny Cash, pictured with wife June Carter Cash in 1979, was the country legend who refused to toe the line.*

Buddy Holly

IN THE 18 MONTHS between mid-1957 and winter 1958, Buddy Holly, a shy, bespectacled young man with a hiccup in his voice, enjoyed a series of hits that unified the spirit of rock 'n' roll with the melodic sensibility that was coming back into fashion. But Holly's success was precarious. After the chart-topping success of "That'll Be the Day" in 1957, and the Top 10 achievement of the follow-up, "Peggy Sue," the audience for rock 'n' roll was plummeting. Yet, within a matter of years, when most 1950s rock 'n' rollers were regarded as passé, Holly's cachet had become second to none.

That the boy from Lubbock, Texas, had perished tragically at the age of 22, in an air crash that also claimed the lives of Richie Valens and the Big Bopper, certainly had something to do with it. But while the Beatles had worn leather and sweated buckets in Hamburg, their songwriting—and that of their beat-boom imitators—owed far more to Holly's harmonious, high school-flavored rock-a-pop sound than it did to the outré rock 'n' roll of the mid-1950s. The Shadows wore his specs and aped his Fender guitar style. At the other end of the spectrum, the Rolling Stones made manifest the primal urge that lurked within "Not Fade Away." Above all, it was Holly's auteurist desire to master every element of his work—from songwriting to arranging and producing—that perhaps has proved his most enduring legacy.

RIGHT *Ostensibly an unlikely rock 'n' roll icon, Buddy Holly was a remarkably skillful songwriter, who, after his death, proved a significant influence on, among others, Paul McCartney.*

Buddy Holly

Born: *September 7, 1936, Lubbock, Texas*
Died: *February 3, 1959*

Years active: *1956–59*
Genres: *rock 'n' roll, rockabilly*

Key singles: *"That'll Be the Day" (1957), "Peggy Sue" (1957)*

Key albums: The "Chirping" Crickets *(1957)*, Buddy Holly *(1958)*

Rock 'n' roll—the backlash

FOR EVERY ENTHUSIASTIC quiff-sporting teenager, there were long scowling lines of social conservatives young and old who raged hard at rock 'n' roll's intrinsic breaching of the racial divide, balked at the libidinous drives inherent in its rhythms, and feared that Communist subversion lay at the heart of the new music. And let's not forget that, despite rock 'n' roll's deafening volume, the desire for anodyne pop had hardly gone away. That's why, in 1955, Pat Boone's sanitized take on "Ain't That a Shame" was still outselling Fats Domino's version.

After three wild years, between 1955 and 1957, rock 'n' roll began to wane during 1958. When it was revealed at the start of his May 1958 tour of Britain that 22-year-old Jerry Lee Lewis's third wife Myra had been 13 at the time of their marriage, the singer was hounded out of the country—only to discover that back home his records had been blacklisted and TV and concert bookings all but dried up. Coming two months after Elvis Presley had been drafted into the U.S. Army, and seven after Little Richard's decision to forsake rock 'n' roll for God, the Lewis controversy was a serious blow to the cause. Further bad news emerged during 1959 when "Mr. Rock 'n' Roll" Alan Freed was embroiled in a payola scandal (see opposite) and, later in the year, Chuck Berry was charged with transporting a minor over state lines. Rock 'n' roll was in the dock—and up stepped Frankie Avalon, Ricky Nelson, and the bobby-soxer balladeers to turn temperatures down again.

TOP *Jerry Lee Lewis, pictured in May 1958 with third wife and second cousin Myra in New York after returning home from a scandalized Britain.*

ABOVE *In light of the scandals blighting rock 'n' roll, new clean-cut bobby-soxer acts, such as Ricky Nelson, were actively promoted.*

Alan Freed—and payola

IF ELVIS PRESLEY IS THE KING, and Sam Phillips the kingmaker, then Alan Freed must surely be the high priest of rock 'n' roll. For in 1951, two years before Presley walked through the doors of Sun Records, DJ Freed was already spreading the news. Though the expression "rock and roll" had been in use since the 1920s, usually in reference to sex, Freed would use it to describe the uptempo R&B records he played on his Moondog House show for the Cleveland-based radio station WJW. A genuine enthusiast for what he called "The Big Beat," Freed would invariably play the black artists' original rather than the more anodyne white remake, while tapping out the rhythm on a telephone book.

Freed's role grew exponentially. At the end of 1951 he began promoting live shows, with the Moondog Coronation Ball at the Cleveland Arena on March 21, 1952, commonly regarded as the first-ever rock 'n' roll concert. By the mid-1950s, this undeniably middle-aged character popped up regularly playing himself in rock 'n' roll movies. But Freed's influence began to unravel when ABC canceled his television show in 1957 after receiving complaints because a black artist, Frankie Lymon, was seen dancing with a white female member of the audience. The following year Freed was arrested on a charge of incitement to riot after complaining loudly about police handling at a show. And when the payola scandal broke in 1959, the bogeyman of Middle America was in the dock, and subsequently found guilty of accepting illegal payments in exchange for promoting records. A broken man, Freed drank himself to an early death in 1965, aged 43.

"This is Alan Freed...and this is rock and roll."

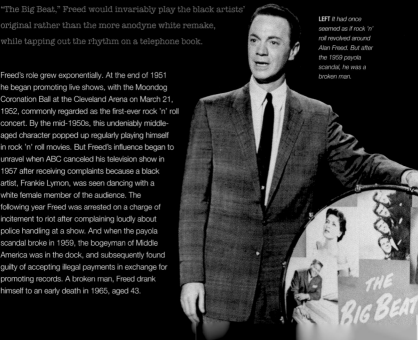

LEFT *It had once seemed as if rock 'n' roll revolved around Alan Freed. But after the 1959 payola scandal, he was a broken man.*

THE BIG BEAT

Featuring

James Brown • The Beach Boys • The Beatles • The Rolling Stones • The Kinks • The Animals • The Who • Bob Dylan • The Byrds • Ravi Shankar • Otis Redding • Aretha Franklin • Jefferson Airplane • Grateful Dead • The Doors • The Velvet Underground • Jimi Hendrix • Cream • The Band • The Monkees • Jackson 5 • Janis Joplin • Santana • Frank Zappa • Captain Beefheart

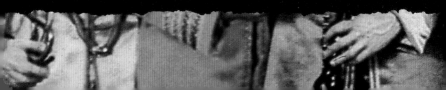

1960s

1960s: Introduction

IT WAS THE DECADE that went Day-Glo. From its inauspicious start, with popular music locked firmly in the jaws of the established entertainment industry, the "Swinging Sixties" erupted in a joyful riot of sound and color. It was both the heartbeat and the battering ram for the postwar baby boomers eager to shake out the last vestiges of austerity and assert their individuality.

At the center of this cultural revolution were the Beatles, four likely lads from Liverpool, whose transformation from suit-wearing harmonizers at the height of the mid-1960s beat boom to fatigued, flower-power idealists by 1969 mirrored the era's early hopes and bitter fade-out. The Beatles' success brought pop center stage: their clarion call was answered by thousands of aspiring musicians, and their ambition and desire to evolve ushered in the great Rock Revolution of the late 1960s.

Cultural forces, such as the newfound earning power and confidence of youth, contributed to this. So too did advances in technology. During the early part of the decade, musicians would simply replicate their

BELOW The Beatles' Sgt Pepper's Lonely Hearts Club Band LP, released in 1967, ushered in a new rock era.

ABOVE Poster design reflected the changes, with the functional R&B package-tour style giving way to abstract graphics for psychedelic stars such as Jimi Hendrix (far right).

Sounds of the decade

"Telstar":
The Tornados (1962)

"She Loves You":
The Beatles (1963)

"Like a Rolling Stone":
Bob Dylan (1965)

"(I Can't Get No) Satisfaction":
The Rolling Stones (1965)

"River Deep—Mountain High":
Ike & Tina Turner (1966)

"Reach Out (I'll Be There)":
The Four Tops (1966)

stage act on disc. With the development of multitrack recording facilities, sound-altering devices, such as phasing and the wah-wah pedal, and stereo sound, the quarter-inch tape became a canvas. After the Beatles' 1967 album, *Sgt Pepper*, musicians aspired to create art. A chasm opened up between "pop," where the primary concern was entertainment neatly packaged into three-minute songs, and "rock," piloted by groups such as Cream and the Jimi Hendrix Experience, privileging technique and innovation.

This change was reflected in the live musical experience. In the early 1960s, the package tour—where half a dozen artists would rattle out their hits in rapid-fire succession—was king. By the end of the decade, this had been eclipsed by the rock festival, tribal gatherings where musicians and audiences would "let it all hang out."

The 1960s remains a hallowed, totemic era for both fans and musicians. Over those ten years, popular music was transformed from something that was industry-led and strictly controlled to a vehicle for a cornucopia of free expression.

"Good Vibrations":
The Beach Boys (1966)

"All You Need Is Love":
The Beatles (1967)

"With a Little Help from My Friends":
Joe Cocker (1968)

"Something in the Air":
Thunderclap Newman (1969)

1960s: Time line

1960

March 1960
Two years after being inducted into the U.S. Army, Elvis Presley is discharged and returns from Germany to resume his career. But years later John Lennon will say: "He was never quite the same again."

April 1960
Cool and gifted rock 'n' roll guitar hero Eddie Cochran dies in a car crash in Chippenham, Wiltshire, England. Weeks later, the presciently titled "Three Steps to Heaven" is a posthumous No. 1 hit in Britain.

August 1960
The Beatles quit Liverpool for Germany, where they take up residency at Hamburg's Indra Club. The nucleus of John Lennon, Paul McCartney, and George Harrison cuts its teeth on a nightly repertoire of rock 'n' roll standards.

December 1961
The Marvelettes' "Please Mr. Postman" tops the U.S. charts, a first both for the all-girl group and for the Tamla label, paving the way for the label's subsequent success with the Supremes.

1962

January 1962
The release of blues veteran Howlin' Wolf's so-called *Rockin' Chair* album has a key influence on the British beat boom, with several songs finding their way into the homegrown R&B repertoire.

April 1962
Mick Jagger and Keith Richards meet aspiring slide-guitarist Brian Jones at West London blues haunt, the Ealing Club. Three months later, the Rollin' Stones debut at the Marquee Club.

1963

James Brown

March 1963
Country star Johnny Cash records the mariachi-flavored "Ring of Fire" in Nashville. A co-write with future wife June Carter, the single gives Cash the biggest success of his career.

April 1963
The Kingsmen, a little-known combo from Portland, Oregon, record "Louie Louie." By the end of the year, it's a U.S. novelty hit. Decades on, the song willl remain the quintessential garage-rock anthem.

May 1963
James Brown's *Live at the Apollo* album enjoys huge crossover success in the United States, bursting forth from the R&B chart to spend 66 weeks in *Billboard*'s pop listing.

1961

January 1961
Bob Dylan relocates to New York and visits the gravely ill folk-revival legend Woody Guthrie in hospital. Dylan vows to keep Guthrie's leftist humanitarian agenda alive.

October 1961
Chuck Berry goes on trial for transporting a minor across state lines and is sentenced to three years in prison. By the time he's freed, in 1963, Berry is the toast of the British R&B scene.

Chuck Berry

December 1961
The decade's first big dance craze shows no sign of waning as Chubby Checker's "The Twist" is released a second time, once again hitting the top slot in the United States.

Alexis Korner

June 1962
Alexis Korner's band Blues Incorporated record their influential *R&B from the Marquee* LP. The album becomes a landmark in the development of the British blues boom.

October 1962
The Beatles' "Love Me Do" is the group's first 45 with producer George Martin. Though only just scraping a Top 20 placing at home, it will be a different story in 1964, when it reemerges to top the U.S. charts.

December 1962
The Tornados' "Telstar" becomes the first single by a British group to top the U.S. charts. The instrumental, awash in space-age sound effects, is the brainchild of maverick producer Joe Meek.

The Beatles at the Cavern

July 1963
The surf music craze gets its first U.S. No. 1 hit with Jan & Dean's "Surf City," the most successful of the year's many surf-related 45s. The craze wanes after the bleach-blond duo's "Dead Man's Curve" death disc several months later.

August 1963
The Beatles perform their last gig at the Cavern Club and, later in the month, release their first anthem, "She Loves You." A mass outbreak of Beatlemania ensues.

November 1963
The assassination of U.S. President John F. Kennedy in Dallas, Texas, is perceived as an attack on both youth and hope. Popular music is poised to pick up the slack.

1960s: Time line

1964

January 1964
The title track from Bob Dylan's latest album, *The Times They Are A-Changin'*, captures the quickening pace of the decade and prompts his pop contemporaries to rethink their attitudes to songwriting.

February 1964
A reported 73 million people tune in to *The Ed Sullivan Show* for the first live appearance of the Beatles on American television. It heralds the start of a two-year "British Invasion."

The Rolling Stones

March 1964
"Would You Let Your Daughter Go with a Rolling Stone?" asks the British press, as London's answer to the Beatles position themselves as the bad boys of rhythm and blues.

The Who

May 1965
The Who's "Anyway Anyhow Anywhere" is distinguished by guitarist Pete Townshend's feedback-drenched solo, epitomizing the group's impressionistic, pop-art style and anticipating the electric storm to come.

June 1965
Inspired by his recent visit to Britain, Bob Dylan returns to New York and records a literate, electrified epic, "Like a Rolling Stone." A month later, he "goes electric" at the Newport Folk Festival. The Rock Revolution is born.

July 1965
The Velvet Underground record an 80-minute home demo that includes early versions of "Heroin" and "I'm Waiting for the Man." It will be over a decade before the band's drug-fixated, drone-rock genius is recognized.

April 1966
Time magazine coins a phrase that defines an era: "London: the Swinging City." The main thrust of Piri Halasz's article, though, is classlessness. "In London," she writes, "everyone parties with everyone else."

June 1966
Fronted by Frank Zappa, the Mothers of Invention release *Freak Out!*, a pioneering two-LP set that fuses avant-garde influences and pastiches of rock 'n' roll, beat music, and doo-wop.

Cream

July 1966
The release of John Mayall's *Blues Breakers with Eric Clapton* album coincides with a graffiti campaign that proclaims "Clapton Is God." However, the guitarist has already quit, joining forces with two other virtuosos in Cream.

1964-1966

July 1964

The Kinks record "You Really Got Me." Loosely based on the "Louie Louie" riff, its powerful chording and vocal intensity has since given it the status of a prototype heavy-metal record.

October 1964

"Baby Love" by all-woman Motown trio the Supremes becomes the first in a run of 12 No. 1 U.S. hit singles for the Diana Ross-fronted group.

The Supremes

1965

January 1965

The beat boom goes global as the Rolling Stones join Roy Orbison for a concert tour in Australia. Meanwhile, the Animals return for a second appearance on U.S. television's *The Ed Sullivan Show*.

1966

August 1965

The Beatles open their second U.S. concert tour with a record-breaking show at New York's Shea Stadium in front of 56,000 screaming fans.

The Four Tops

January 1966

The new psychedelic "wonder-drug" LSD is handed out freely at the Trips Festival in Longshoreman's Hall, San Francisco. Some 10,000 people are spellbound by light shows, poetry readings, and the Grateful Dead.

March 1966

John Lennon's observation that the Beatles are "more popular than Jesus" goes virtually unnoticed in Britain. Subsequently reprinted in the United States before the band's August tour, it prompts death threats and bonfires of Beatles discs.

August 1966

Already rejoicing in its "Sound of Young America" status, Motown goes one better with the Four Tops' "Reach Out I'll Be There." "Black Dylan," declares an effusive Phil Spector.

October 1966

The Beach Boys' latest 45, "Good Vibrations," is pop's first pocket symphony created from over 90 hours of recording sessions. It's a personal triumph for Brian Wilson, the band's producer-songwriter, perfectionist genius.

December 1966

Having announced their retirement from live performance, the Beatles enter Abbey Road Studios to begin work on what will become *Sgt Pepper's Lonely Hearts Club Band*. Its release the following June confirms the arrival of the new rock era.

1960s: Time line

1967

February 1967
A "Pop Stars and Drugs" headline in a British tabloid prompts a witch-hunt that results in jail sentences (subsequently quashed) for three Rolling Stones members later in the year.

March 1967
Two worlds collide when guitar-burning, acid-rock guru Jimi Hendrix tours Britain with housewives' favorites the Walker Brothers and crooner Engelbert Humperdinck.

Aretha Franklin

May 1967
Already poised to top the U.S. charts, Aretha Franklin's feminist take on Otis Redding's "Respect" is released in Britain. The song will earn Franklin a Grammy in February 1968.

1968

February 1968
The Beatles take off for an ashram in the foothills of the Himalayas in India to study Transcendental Meditation with the Maharishi. They return more confused than ever.

April 1968
After the assassination of civil rights leader Dr. Martin Luther King Jr., James Brown's Boston gig is televised the following night in a bid to quell rioting among the African-American community.

May 1968
Actor Richard Harris releases "McArthur Park," a seven-minute epic cloaked in mysterious symbolism. Its worldwide success suggests that psychedelic whimsy has now penetrated the middle-of-the-road market.

John Lennon and Yoko Ono

March 1969
After marrying in Gibraltar, John Lennon and his new wife Yoko Ono honeymoon in the Amsterdam Hilton, where the world's press is invited to their bedside to listen to their views on peace.

May 1969
San Francisco-based psychedelic soul act Sly & the Family Stone break through with their fourth album, *Stand!* The group confirms its newfound status with a dynamic performance at the Woodstock Festival in August.

July 1969
Rolling Stone founder member Brian Jones is found dead in his swimming pool. He is the first victim of rock-star excess— but by no means the last.

Brian Jones

June 1967

The first international pop festival takes place at Monterey in California. San Francisco's Janis Joplin, the Who, and Jimi Hendrix from London, Otis Redding from Memphis, and Ravi Shankar from India steal the show.

September 1967

Radio 1, the BBC's youth-orientated radio station, launches with the Move's "Flowers in the Rain" introduced by DJ Tony Blackburn. Also spinning the discs is John Peel, an early champion of the emerging underground rock groups.

October 1967

Hair, a "Tribal Love-Rock Musical," brings sexual permissiveness and an antiwar message to a theater in New York's East Village. By the end of the decade it plays to packed houses across the world.

Led Zeppelin

August 1968

The Doors' "Hello, I Love You" tops the U.S. singles chart, sells a million, and raises the band's profile in Britain, just in time for a concert appearance at London's Roundhouse in September.

November 1968

The Monkees flout their "pop puppet" reputation and commit career suicide with *Head*, a largely plotless feature film that seems tailor-made for acid heads, rather than the group's young fanbase.

January 1969

Ace session musician Jimmy Page's new group, Led Zeppelin, launch their career with an eponymous debut that eschews psychedelic excess in favor of a new hard-rock sound.

August 1969

Increasingly influenced by rock pioneers such as Jimi Hendrix, jazz legend Miles Davis records *Bitches Brew*, a hugely influential set of lengthy electric jams. Jazz-rock fusion is born.

November 1969

Elvis Presley returns to the top of the *Billboard* chart for the first time in five years with "Suspicious Minds," an epic arrangement and a soulful symbol of his late-1960s renaissance. It is his last-ever No. 1 single in the United States.

December 1969

Cult hippie leader Charles Manson and several of his so-called "Family" are charged with the murder of movie star Sharon Tate and six others. The curtain goes down on the Age of Aquarius.

James Brown

TAKING HIS CUES from Little Richard and Ray Charles, James Brown became a key figure in the transition from gospel to soul and, more important still, from R&B to funk. As the founding father of funk's super-syncopated, ever-propulsive groove, spun out across a string of extraordinary records from the mid-1960s to the early 1970s, Brown's influence on popular music has been immense. From krautrock to hip hop (a genre that sampled his records repeatedly), post-punk to contemporary R&B, the funked-up sound of James Brown has grown from an idiosyncratic beat largely associated with one man to an all-encompassing, floor-shaking revolution.

Brown's stature as a modern master goes even deeper than his groove. As the feverish frontman of the most urgent sounding R&B revue during the late 1950s and early 1960s, Brown—the self-styled "Hardest Working Man in Showbusiness"—saw his dance routines mimicked by Mick Jagger and his highly disciplined work ethic aped by Berry Gordy at Motown. Above all, Brown was gripped by a self-belief that was loudly exonerated in 1963 when, against record company advice, he financed *Live at the Apollo*, an extraordinary encapsulation of the James Brown stage show that won him huge crossover success, climaxing in 1965 with two huge hits, "Papa's Got a Brand New Bag" and "I Got You (I Feel Good)."

LEFT *James Brown, flanked by his Famous Flames vocal group and backing band, at the Apollo Theater in Harlem, New York, 1964. The previous year's* Live at the Apollo *has long been regarded as one of the finest concert performances on record.*

Soul Brother Number One

After the 1966 ballad, "It's a Man's Man's Man's Man's World," songs such as "Cold Sweat" (1967), "Funky Drummer" (1969), and "Get Up (I Feel Like Being a) Sex Machine" (1970), backed by the irrepressible J.B.'s, defined Brown's funk groove. Though more entrepreneur than civil rights activist, Brown's "blacker" sound, coupled with the arrival of disco, temporarily stalled his crossover appeal. This probably won him more kudos during the 1980s hip-hop boom, when politically conscious acts such as Public Enemy would happily juxtapose a Funky Drummer sample with the words of Malcolm X. Brown's main concern, as always, remained his impeccable showmanship. Before his death on Christmas Day 2006, he had spent much of the year touring the world.

RIGHT *James Brown has been a legend in black music circles since the late 1950s. During the 1960s, his influence widened. Mick Jagger aped his dance routine, while Brown's funky beat became a clubland fixture. His influence is now so pervasive that it is barely remarked on.*

James Brown

Born: *May 3, 1933, Barnwell, South Carolina*
Died: *December 25, 2006*

Years active: *1955–2006*
Genres: *R&B, soul, funk*

Key singles: *"Papa's Got a Brand New Bag" (1965), "Cold Sweat" (1967)*

Key albums: *Live at the Apollo (1963), Sex Machine (1970)*

Surf music

BETWEEN THE PASSING of first-generation rock 'n' roll and the emergence of the beat boom, only Californian surf music afforded a privileged place for the rock guitar. Though eventually eclipsed by the Beach Boys, whose multiple harmonies carried the Golden State's watery passions across the globe, initially surf was an instrumental phenomenon showcasing the kind of virtuoso playing that later became commonplace during the rock era.

ABOVE *By 1963, surf music was breaking out of its instrumental infancy. Vocal duo Jan & Dean enjoyed two years of beach-related hits—"Surf City" being the biggest.*

BELOW *The group's songwriter and musical genius Brian Wilson (far right) never learnt to surf, but that didn't stop the Beach Boys becoming the genre's golden boys.*

Sun-kissed girls and souped-up hot rods

Inspired by the guitar twang of Duane Eddy's "Rebel-Rouser" (1958) and the Ventures' "Walk Don't Run" (1960), guitarist Dick Dale emerged in 1961 with "Let's Go Trippin'," commonly regarded as the first surf instrumental. The following year's "Misirlou," based on a Greek rebel melody but performed by Dale at a furious pace and on one string, pushed the genre to the outer limits of reverb-enhanced excitement. Dale repeated his achievement with a stunning, staccato reworking of another early twentieth-century melody, the popular Jewish song "Hava Nagila."

The surf instrumental reached its peak when first the Chantays ("Pipeline") and then the Surfaris ("Wipe Out") became Top 10 hits during 1963. By the time of the Trashmen's bizarre 1964 cash-in, "Surfin' Bird," the surf craze had extended to embrace sun-kissed girls and souped-up hot rods, thanks largely to the Beach Boys' desire to compose an extended musical love letter to California. Having briefly tried their hand at surf instrumentals (covering "Misirlou" and "Let's Go Trippin'"), it was the emergence of Brian Wilson as a songwriter, coupled with the band's Four Freshmen-inspired love of harmony, that soon found them transcending—and diluting—the form.

Vocal duo Jan & Dean, who hit No. 1 in 1963 with "Surf City" (a co-write with Wilson), remained true to the style with a gently rolling wave of hits, including "Drag City," "The Little Old Lady from Pasadena," and the death disc "Dead Man's Curve," an eerie prophecy of the near death of Jan Berry in a car crash in 1966. Happily, he survived; surf music didn't.

TOP Dick Dale, master of the surf instrumental, poses for the cameras. His hit "Misirlou" was later revived for Quentin Tarantino's Pulp Fiction.

ABOVE The Surfaris' 1962 hit, "Wipe Out," remains one of surf music's most enduring recordings.

5 Top surf artists

Dick Dale: *"Misirlou" (1962)*
The Beach Boys: *"Surfin' USA" (1963)*

Chantays: *"Pipeline" (1963)*
The Surfaris: *"Wipe Out" (1963)*

Jan & Dean: *"Surf City" (1963)*

The Beach Boys

NO BAND BETTER ILLUSTRATES the competing drives of corny, escapist fun and tortured, art-wracked introspection that made the 1960s such an energetic and experimental decade than the Beach Boys. Pop rarely sounded as uncomplicated as it did on mid-1960s hits such as "Surfin' USA," "Fun, Fun, Fun," "I Get Around," and "Barbara Ann," each one a high-five celebration of the joys of Golden State teen life—surf, summer, girls, and cars. Having built their style on the vocal harmonies of the Four Freshmen and licks from the Chuck Berry songbook, the Beach Boys showed significant signs of development in 1965 with the deceptively sophisticated "California Girls," which confirmed them as America's best-possible answer to the Beatles.

That idea increasingly obsessed Brian Wilson, the group's falsetto-voiced bassist and songwriter, and eldest of the quintet's three brothers. Giving up live performances in a bid to pursue his ambitions, Wilson began to regard pop as an art form to rival classical music and as a platform for intense personal expression. The first and perhaps greatest outcome of his plunge into perfectionism was 1966's "Good Vibrations," the product of months in the studio, easily the most sophisticated record of its time, and, with its multilayered textures and odd shifts in style and structure, a harbinger of the rock era.

BELOW TOP *Clean-cut and color-coordinated, the 1962 Beach Boys—including, briefly, David Marks (right)—were a model of pop conformity.*

BELOW BOTTOM *The definitive mid-1960s lineup, shortly before Brian Wilson retired from touring: (left to right) Dennis Wilson, Al Jardine, Carl Wilson, Brian Wilson, Mike Love.*

A contemporaneous album, *Pet Sounds*, earned Wilson plaudits from everyone from Leonard Bernstein to Paul McCartney, and the prodigious Beach Boy set to work on his epic rock masterpiece, *Smile*. Not everyone in the band was convinced, and in May 1967, as psychedelia blossomed, the project was shelved and the mentally scrambled Brian Wilson increasingly withdrew from the band. Though fragments of *Smile* leaked out on subsequent albums, the Beach Boys' popularity waned until guitarist Carl Wilson engineered a move toward a more mature country-rock sound. Since then, the band—with ever-shifting personnel, sometimes including Brian—has traded on its early, party-hat vibe, while Brian Wilson has trodden the comeback trail happy in the knowledge that his genius has at last been recognized.

ABOVE *During 1966 and 1967, Brian Wilson remained studio-bound while working on two epic projects,* Pet Sounds *and the aborted* Smile. *This photograph—showing the band reflected in a mirror held by Wilson—captures the great man's growing detachment from his fellow Beach Boys.*

The Beach Boys

Formed: *Hawthorne, California*
Years active: *1961 to present*

Definitive lineup: *Brian Wilson, Mike Love, Carl Wilson, Dennis Wilson, Al Jardine*

Genres: *surf, pop, rock*
Key singles: *"I Get Around" (1964), "Good Vibrations" (1966)*

Key albums:
The Beach Boys Today! *(1965),* Pet Sounds *(1966)*

The Spector Sound

PHIL SPECTOR DIDN'T JUST DEAL in songs. He made *records*—vast mini-operas sculpted from layers of voices and instruments and loudly compressed into a series of remarkable pop 45s. At the peak of his influence (1962–66), this production perfectionist and so-called "Tycoon of Teen" was a virtual pop Wagner. His finely tuned "Wall of Sound" and auteurist—even autocratic—tendencies in the studio might have seemed faintly anachronistic by the mid-1960s, but Spector's dedication to the art of perfect pop anticipated rock's increasingly studio-bound tendencies as the decade progressed. In fact, so magnificently realized were Spector's twin peaks of production achievement—"You've Lost That Lovin' Feelin'" (Righteous Brothers, 1965) and "River Deep—Mountain High" (Ike & Tina Turner, 1966)— that, in terms of sheer grand-scale artistic vision, many of rock's subsequent self-conscious sonic ventures pale by comparison.

OPPOSITE ABOVE
The "Wall of Sound" production genius, in trademark dark glasses, overseeing a 1964 session flanked by engineer Larry Levine and session player Nino Tempo.

OPPOSITE BELOW *Spector conducts his session players, known collectively as "the Wrecking Crew," at a Gold Star recording session in 1965.*

BELOW *The Ronettes, whose lead singer Ronnie (right) later married Spector (1968–74), in the studio, 1963.*

The writer and co-performer behind the Teddy Bears' 1958 No. 1 hit, "To Know Him Is to Love Him," Spector picked up some production tricks from Duane Eddy producer Lee Hazlewood, formed his own Philles label late in 1961, and launched his so-called "Wall of Sound" a year later with the Crystals' chart-topping "He's a Rebel." The template—black female voices, ace session musicians, and production-line songwriting enveloped in a mist of reverb—yielded further hits, both for the Crystals ("Da Doo Ron Ron," "Then He Kissed Me") and the Ronettes ("Be My Baby," "Baby I Love You"). But the seemingly unthinkable failure of the 1966 Ike & Tina Turner masterpiece in the United States prompted the producer's temporary withdrawal from the business.

Beat boom

AFTER THE STRANGE HOWL of rock 'n' roll that had reached Britain from across the Atlantic had died down, in the late 1950s the country was awash in a new, more comfortable sound. Wholesome balladeers, such as Cliff Richard, Marty Wilde, and Helen Shapiro, crooned over finger-popping rhythms garnished with pizzicato strings and "yeh-yeh" backing vocals. But in the urban undergrowth, something stirred.

The skiffle boom, driven by the success of Lonnie Donegan's "Rock Island Line" in 1956, had energized a generation of aspiring rock 'n' rollers to take up guitars. A flourishing club and ballroom scene played host to numerous guitar-led bands, whose repertoire ranged from American rock 'n' roll (Chuck Berry and Buddy Holly being particular favorites) to dance crazes ("La Bamba," "The Twist") and show tunes ("Besame Mucho"). And on the fringes, in sweat-drenched cellars or dimly lit jazz clubs, a growing number of acts—from auto mechanic Cyril Davies to the studenty Rolling Stones—were performing their own take on American rhythm and blues. When the Beatles' sound took hold during 1963, prompting a nationwide search for guitar-wielding groups, the beat boom was born. There were plenty to choose from.

Unsurprisingly, Liverpool provided the early focus for the talent scouts, with the Beatles' boss Brian Epstein quickly bringing Gerry & the Pacemakers and the Searchers to national prominence. Manchester yielded the Hollies, Herman's Hermits, and Freddie & the Dreamers, while the Moody Blues (Birmingham), the Animals (Newcastle), and Them (Belfast) brought more robust sounds from around the country.

BELOW *Although Liverpool had been the epicenter of the 1963 beat boom, the reverberations were soon felt elsewhere. The Dave Clark Five, who topped the British charts at the end of the year with "Glad All Over," were standard-bearers for "the Tottenham Sound."*

London, where jazz clubs had been hosting rhythm and blues sessions since the late 1950s, was the center of the R&B boom, where far more emphasis was given to moodier, blues-derived material. The Rolling Stones were the most prominent of the new arrivals, and were soon being touted as a more subterranean alternative to the Beatles. But in terms of chart success, it was the much-fancied "Tottenham Sound" of the Dave Clark Five that initially looked most likely to topple the Beatles and "Merseybeat."

RIGHT *Less than a month before the release of their first British hit single, "Love Me Do," the Beatles headlined this night of aspiring Mersey stars.*

BELOW *While Liverpool's legendary beat-boom music venue, the Cavern, is most famously linked with the Beatles, club rivals Gerry & the Pacemakers were equally successful during 1963.*

LEACH ENTERTAINMENTS PRESENT

OPERATION BiG BEAT - 5TH

AT THE

TOWER BALLROOM NEW BRIGHTON
FRI. 14TH SEPT. 7·30 - 1·0 A.M.

FEATURING AN ALL STAR 6 GROUP LINE UP · STARRING THE NORTH'S TOP ROCK COMBO APPEARING AT 9:30 PROMPT

The BEATLES

RORY STORM AND THE **Hurricanes**

GERRY AND THE **PACEMAKERS**   THE **4 JAYS**

BILLY KRAMER AND THE **COASTERS**   **MERSEY BEATS**

5/-   ★ LICENSED BARS (UNTIL 11P.M.)

5 Top beat-boom artists

The Beatles: *"She Loves You" (1963)*

The Rolling Stones: *"Not Fade Away" (1964)*

The Animals: *"The House of the Rising Sun" (1964)*

The Kinks: *"You Really Got Me" (1964)*

The Who: *"My Generation" (1965)*

The Beatles

INITIALLY MERELY FIRST among equals in the 1963 Merseybeat boom, the Beatles transcended their provincial origins and even national success by becoming, during 1964, an international cultural phenomenon on a scale that eclipsed even Elvis Presley's arrival a decade earlier. That was probably due to the fact that, unlike rock 'n' roll, the Beatles were perceived as nonthreatening, with an appeal that crossed continents and generations, and whose ringing sound embodied all the cheery optimism of postwar progress and regeneration. It was, of course, a fragile peace. Within three years, religious fanatics in the Southern United States were burning Beatles records; by the end of the decade even their own fans greeted news of the band's split with some relief.

OPPOSITE TOP *The "Fab Four" pose at Abbey Road Studios before unveiling "All You Need Is Love" to an international audience via satellite.*

OPPOSITE BELOW *This 1964 shot, which graced the Beatles' "Twist and Shout" EP, captures all the joyful innocence of the early days of Beatlemania.*

BELOW *Between 1960 and 1962, the Beatles spent long periods in Germany, playing the Hamburg clubs and polishing up their act.*

Unlike the noble savages of 1950s rock 'n' roll, the Beatles were provincial and working class, a group of four roughly equal personalities rather than the manufactured, star-led acts of the pre-beat era, and their music was a pitch-perfect balance of Tin Pan Alley entertainment and youthful energy. All their early records, from "Love Me Do" (1962) to the hysteria-provoking "She Loves You" (1963), chime with the era's democratic instincts. Nowhere was this balance more brilliantly struck than on "I Want To Hold Your Hand" (1963), a classic beat-era clap-along, crammed with hooks and melodic twists, yet with a hint of grit in the voices.

By mid-decade, the Fab Four's collective imagination had been lit by drugs, Dylan, and technological developments. Assisted by producer George Martin, the Beatles grew more concerned with creativity than commercial considerations. The apotheosis of this was 1967's *Sgt Pepper's Lonely Hearts Club Band*, the one record that symbolized the emergence of the new rock era. A follow-up, the so-called "White Album," revealed that by 1968 the Beatles were less a group than four increasingly unhappy individuals. Paul McCartney's announcement in March 1970 that the band had split also signaled the end of an era.

The Beatles

Formed: *Liverpool, England*
Years active: *1960–70*

Definitive lineup: *John Lennon, Paul McCartney, George Harrison, Ringo Starr*
Genres: *pop, rock*

Key singles: *"She Loves You" (1963), "Penny Lane"/"Strawberry Fields Forever" (1967)*

Key albums: Rubber Soul *(1965),* Sgt Pepper's Lonely Hearts Club Band *(1967)*

Beatlemania!

THROUGHOUT 1963, the Beatles toured Britain incessantly, saw three successive 45s—"From Me To You," "She Loves You," and "I Want To Hold Your Hand"—spend 20 weeks at No. 1, performed for Queen Elizabeth II at the Royal Variety Performance, and saw out the year with the phrase "Aeolian cadence" ringing in their ears, thanks to London *Times* critic William Mann comparing their music to Mahler's. But the phrase on everyone's lips was "Beatlemania," which had entered general parlance in October as a catchall for the commercial, musical, and psychological hysteria generated by the four "Moptops" from Liverpool.

Initially, the United States had been resistant to the Beatles, just as it had been to British pop in general. The only group to have enjoyed transatlantic success in recent times had been Joe Meek protégés the Tornados, whose weird and wonderful "Telstar" topped the *Billboard* chart in 1962. But with the November 1963 assassination of President John F. Kennedy, the nation was in need of a lift. In December news of an outbreak of Beatlemania in America was quickly followed by the rush-release there of "I Want To Hold Your Hand." By the time the Beatles arrived in New York, on February 7, 1964, the song had already hit No. 1. Two days later, a record 73 million viewers witnessed the band's performance on *The Ed Sullivan Show*, and by April the entire nation was engulfed by Beatlemania, as the group's records filled the top five positions in the *Billboard* chart.

The most visible aspects of the phenomenon were the sight of hysterical crowds (usually girls) at the group's concerts, and a growing (usually male) penchant for bowl-cut hairstyles, collarless jackets, and Cuban-heeled boots. The fan worship was further stoked by the growth of a huge merchandising industry, which flogged all manner of magazines, posters, mugs, dolls, and even wigs and stockings to the more ardent enthusiasts. Musically, of course, the band's impact was greater still.

LEFT *After the massive success of "She Loves You" in 1963, Beatlemania in Britain soared, as these lucky ticket holders for a Beatles concert enthusiastically demonstrate.*

LEFT AND BELOW *On February 9, 1964, the Beatles made the first of three appearances on The Ed Sullivan Show. Here, George Harrison and Ringo Starr discuss their impact with the host. Those appearances prompted a mass outbreak of Beatlemania in the United States that lasted well into 1965.*

The Rolling Stones

THE STONES' CRAGGY RESILIENCE and super-lucrative longevity has almost eclipsed their real purpose—as the driving force for the 1960s rock revolution. In frontman Mick Jagger they possessed the most potent, perfect symbol of pop decadence, a rubber-lipped, rubber-limbed riposte to the postwar beefcake notion of masculinity. Better still, the Stones expressed the anxieties of their times in a run of extraordinary singles, none more perfect than 1965's "(I Can't Get No) Satisfaction," with Jagger's mocking vocal set against an insistent fuzztone riff, hinting at difficult times ahead. It was a huge advance for the callow copyists of 1963 whose heroes were the black bluesmen of Chicago.

RIGHT *Despite their well-publicized spats, songwriters Mick Jagger and Keith Richards have successfully steered the Stones into the twenty-first century, keeping their reputation virtually intact.*

BELOW *During the earliest months of their career, the surly Rolling Stones were marketed as the antidote to the more saccharine Beatles, though in truth both bands enjoyed similar lifestyle habits.*

After a series of drug busts during 1967, a dalliance with the occult, the death of founder member and gifted instrumentalist Brian Jones in 1969, and the breakup of rivals the Beatles, the Stones reemerged at the end of the decade as the self-styled "Greatest Rock 'n' Roll Band in the World." With vast tours and a jet-set lifestyle, the band rejoiced in the outré glamour of new rock aristos. Guitarist Keith Richards perfected his "living corpse" demeanor, and with new lead player Mick Taylor the group hit a peak in 1972 with *Exile on Main St.*, an expansive set that encompassed (and eclipsed) their many influences— from country and gospel to hard rock.

Since then, the Stones have weathered glam, disco, and punk, thanks to Jagger's keen ear for contemporary trends and Richards' continued allegiance to the gutteral riffs and gnarly reputation on which the band's legend rests.

The Greatest Rock 'n' Roll Band in the World

The Rolling Stones

Formed: *London, England*

Years active: *1962 to present*

Definitive lineup: *Mick Jagger, Keith Richards, Brian Jones, Charlie Watts, Bill Wyman*

Genres: *R&B, rock*

Key singles: *"(I Can't Get No) Satisfaction" (1965), "Jumpin' Jack Flash" (1968)*

Key albums: Beggars Banquet *(1968)*, Sticky Fingers *(1971)*, Exile on Main St. *(1972)*

The Kinks

PERHAPS THE MOST BRITISH of the beat-boom groups, the Kinks relied heavily on the keenly observed songwriting of frontman Ray Davies, never bettered than on the string of classy mid-1960s hits that peaked in 1967 with the elegiac "Waterloo Sunset." The elegance of this extraordinary run of 45s—from the languid, deconstructed R&B of 1965's "Set Me Free" to the music-hall satire of "A Well Respected Man" (1965), "Dedicated Follower of Fashion," and "Sunny Afternoon" (both 1966)—is all the more surprising given that the band's breakthrough hit, "You Really Got Me" (1964), is commonly regarded as the foundation stone of heavy metal. No other beat-era record focused the attention so heavily on the guitar, a distorted and loudly repetitive reworking of the Kingsmen's "Louie Louie" riff. Unsurprisingly, the Kinks cannibalized their own song for the equally hyperactive follow-up, "All Day and All of the Night" (1964).

The Kinks

Formed: *London, England*

Years active: *1964–96*

Definitive lineup: *Ray Davies, Dave Davies, Pete Quaife, Mick Avory*

Genres: *pop, rock*

Key singles: *"You Really Got Me" (1964), "Lola" (1970)*

Key albums: Face To Face *(1966),* The Kinks Are the Village Green Preservation Society *(1968)*

After the glories of their mid-1960s singles, a concept album of sorts, *The Kinks Are the Village Green Preservation Society* (1968), painted the group as faintly anachronistic. But a masterful return with "Lola" in 1970, which anticipated the sexual politics of the glam era, prompted a reinvention of the Kinks as a discerning rock band via a series of theatrical concept albums. Taking a hard-rocking live set out on the road eventually won over the hitherto elusive American market.

RIGHT *The Kinks in a television studio in August 1965 promoting their latest single, "See My Friends." The song was an early example of drone, almost acid rock, some two years before psychedelia took hold.*

The Animals

FOREVER ASSOCIATED with their transatlantic chart-topping breakthrough song, "The House of the Rising Sun," the Animals were the grittiest of the British R&B groups. Much of that reputation was down to the gravel-voiced frontman Eric Burdon, who embodied both the pain and the resilience of the best American blues singers, though the Animals' industrial northeast England origins also lent them a Chicago-like blue-collar authenticity. Deriving much of their live repertoire and album material from black America, the Animals were soon at loggerheads with their avowedly pop-motivated producer Mickie Most, who looked toward the Brill Building school of hit making for the group's singles.

This caused considerable friction within the band, as did the news that (thanks to a technical quirk) Alan Price, who played the distinctive organ part on "Rising Sun," was handed all the royalties on the arrangement. Price quit the band in mid-1965, taking his credit with him. There was a suitably moody, existential quality to later hits, such as "It's My Life" (1965) and "Don't Bring Me Down" (1966), but the band's creative contradictions could not be healed, and in September 1966 Burdon also quit.

Forming the New Animals, the tough Geordie relocated to San Francisco and reemerged as a leather-clad advocate of flower power, singing passionate odes to "San Franciscan Nights" (1967) and "Monterey" (1967) that bore little resemblance to the original band.

ABOVE *Frontman Eric Burdon (foreground) was perhaps the most convincing white British singer of the entire R&B boom, but the early success of "The House of the Rising Sun" tended to overshadow the Animals' career.*

The Animals

Formed:
Newcastle-upon-Tyne, England

Years active:
1962–69

Definitive lineup:
*Eric Burdon,
Alan Price,
Chas Chandler,
Hilton Valentine,
John Steel*

Genres: *R&B, pop, rock, psychedelia*

Key singles:
*"The House of the Rising Sun" (1964),
"It's My Life" (1965)*

Key albums:
*Animalisms (1966),
Winds of Change (1967)*

The British Invasion

THE BRITISH BEAT BOOM had been a group phenomenon largely built on a repertoire based on various American popular music styles—from rock 'n' roll and R&B via the girl groups and early Tamla. In February 1964, when the Beatles first touched down in New York, this music began to make its return journey. Over the next two years, hundreds of U.S.-worshipping hopefuls crossed the Atlantic in search of emulating the Beatles' success, though as the Rolling Stones discovered in June that year, cracking a country as vast and as disparate as the United States was quite different to achieving fame at home. Not every chart-bound British group found favor across the Atlantic.

Two No. 1s for Petula Clark ("Downtown" and "My Love"), as well as chart-topping success for Peter & Gordon, Chad & Jeremy, and Wayne Fontana & the Mindbenders, confirmed that the United States generally preferred their "invasion" to be of the more peaceable variety. But it was a different story out in the high schools and garages of the country's sprawling suburbia, where groups of bored teenagers preferred to beat out rudimentary versions of the more R&B-inclined British Invasion material. To an emerging generation of aspiring garage rockers, it was the moodier, more uptight Yardbirds, Kinks, Pretty Things, Who, Them, and Rolling Stones that marked the real British Invasion.

Alas, the chart revealed quite different heroes. Two of Britain's biggest successes Stateside, perhaps to the surprise of the British public (and of posterity), were the Dave Clark Five and Herman's Hermits. The former, which had the dubious distinction of being fronted by a drummer, accentuated a top-heavy beat while projecting an image that was more wholesome than the more individualistic and often caustic Beatles. The result was a remarkable run of seven Top 10 singles, including the chart-topping "Over and Over," during 1964 and 1965.

The similarly clean-cut and smiling Herman's Hermits had notched up an extraordinary run of nine Top 10 hits by spring 1966. By this time, though—after acts such as Manfred Mann and Peter & Gordon enjoyed U.S. No. 1 hits—the British Invasion had more or less run its course.

OPPOSITE BELOW *Favorites with the emerging U.S. garage-rock scene were the Yardbirds from Richmond, Surrey. This 1965 lineup, featuring Jeff Beck (right), found the band on a creative high.*

RIGHT *After topping the U.S. chart in 1965 with "Downtown," Petula Clark enjoyed a remarkable love affair with the American public—and an extraordinary run of hits.*

BELOW *The Beatles' August 1966 concert in San Francisco's Candlestick Park, which proved to be their last, marked the end of the British Invasion era.*

CANDLESTICK PARK

HERE COME THE BEATLES

MONDAY · AUGUST 29 · 8PM

THE CYRKLE   THE RONETTES   THE REMAINS

PLUS THREE OTHER ACTS TO BE DETERMINED

The Who

THE MOST STYLISH and artfully conscious of the beat-boom bands, the Who dressed to kill, swilled pills to thrill, and perfected the dispassionate gaze of the streetwise inner London ne'er-do-well. They also took mid-1960s pop to new levels of intensity with a series of magnificently taut and uptight singles that took off from where the Kinks had got to. Nothing, though, quite prepared the world for "Anyway Anyhow Anywhere," a Top 10 hit in summer 1965, which featured a magnificently unhinged, feedback-drenched instrumental middle section. According to guitarist and songwriter Pete Townshend, this remarkable, free-form passage was inspired by jazz pioneer Charlie Parker.

Surprisingly, the Who never achieved a chart-topping single, though in Britain at least the strutting, stuttering "My Generation" came closest late in 1965. The group reached a peak of sorts during 1966 and 1967 with a remarkable trilogy of singles—"Happy Jack," "Pictures of Lily," and "I Can See for Miles," an intoxicatingly tough and trippy classic that confirmed the arrival of a "heavier" rock era.

As ambitious as he was articulate, Townshend fulfilled his long-held desire to create a rock opera with 1969's *Tommy*, a two-LP set that took as its main themes child abuse, the perils of fame, and false prophets. That same year, the Who came of age at Woodstock, with the climactic "See Me, Feel Me" from *Tommy* becoming one of the festival's— and era's—defining moments.

By now a formidable stage act, as confirmed on 1970's *Live at Leeds*, the Who embraced the new decade with the synthesizer-enriched *Who's Next* (1971), which concluded with "Won't Get Fooled Again," a bitter indictment of the rock revolution. After revisiting their Mod days with 1973's *Quadrophenia*, the Who survived the losses of Keith Moon in 1978 and bassist John Entwistle in 2002 with live performances that still bristle with tension.

FAR LEFT AND LEFT *The Who took the Monterey Pop Festival by storm (far left) in June 1967. By the early 1970s, Roger Daltrey (left), a tough West Londoner, had become an iconic figure in the Robert Plant mold.*

RIGHT *Who songwriter and guitarist Pete Townshend remains one of pop's most articulate spokesmen. The man who once wrote, "Hope I die before I get old," is now in his mid-60s.*

The Who

Formed: *London, England*
Years active: *1964 to present*

Definitive lineup: *Roger Daltrey, Pete Townshend, John Entwistle, Keith Moon*
Genres: *pop, rock*

Key singles: *"My Generation" (1965), "I Can See for Miles" (1967)*

Key albums: The Who Sell Out *(1967),* Tommy *(1969)*

Bob Dylan

NO ONE DID MORE to liberate popular music from its perceived low cultural status than this young rock 'n' roll enthusiast from Duluth, Minnesota. After a brief flirtation with rock 'n' roll in the late 1950s, Dylan discovered the "truth" of folk music at university, dropped out, and headed to New York to meet his idol, protest singer Woody Guthrie. Between 1962 and 1964, he released four albums that bore out his stated desire to dedicate himself to Guthrie's legacy. But a chance hearing of the Animals' take on "The House of the Rising Sun" changed all that, and by 1965 Dylan was working with an electric rock band.

The result was the most influential trilogy of recordings in the transition from pop (or, indeed, folk) to rock. *Bringing It All Back Home* (1965) upped the lyricism and R&B quota. *Highway 61 Revisited* (also 1965), which kicked off with the epochal "Like a Rolling Stone," marks the apotheosis of Dylan's ramshackle-rock-meets-cut-glass-lyricism adventure. The two-LP *Blonde on Blonde* (1966) only served to maximize the heady effect.

LEFT *Dylan's conversion to electric rock alienated folk purists but marked a tipping point from the beat era to a new age of rock.*

ABOVE *Split down the middle between electric and folk sides,* Highway 61 Revisited *accelerated the potential of the pop record on its release in 1965.*

As Martin Scorsese's *No Direction Home* documentary attests, the mid-1960s Bob Dylan was a remarkable figure—a Chaplinesque man/myth wrapped in a prickly veil of self-assurance that left his British Invasion counterparts looking like schoolboys in comparison. Perhaps the intensity was too much to bear, for shortly after a tour of Britain in spring 1966—prompting an infamous cry of "Judas!" by an aggrieved folkie who resented Dylan's electrification—the poet-rocker disappeared following a mysterious motorcycle accident.

Returning in 1967 with *John Wesley Harding*, the new Dylan was more musically restrained if no less enigmatic. That set the tone for the rest of his career, where, down the decades, renewed creative flourishes (1975's *Blood on the Tracks*, 1997's *Time Out of Mind*) have often been undermined by a routine glibness to the actual sound of his records. In concert, though, the old, cantankerous Dylan is still very much alive, often reworking his catalog in such a way as to be virtually unrecognizable.

Prickly veil of self-assurance

Bob Dylan

Born: *May 24, 1941, Duluth, Minnesota*

Years active: *1961 to present*

Genres: *folk, protest, folk rock, singer-songwriter*

Key singles: *"Blowin' in the Wind" (1963), "Like a Rolling Stone" (1965)*

Key albums: Highway 61 Revisited *(1965)*, Blonde on Blonde *(1966)*

Protest—pop meets politics

ALTHOUGH FIRST-GENERATION rock 'n' roll was sometimes branded as un-American—even Communist—the biggest threat it posed was always cultural rather than political. Like the strong whiff of deviance that hung around the burgeoning, and overwhelmingly black, be-bop community, it was more concerned with individual expression than with any collective, politicized consciousness. The clearest musical demonstration of organized protest, which eventually fed into rock during the mid-1960s, was heard from the folk movement.

BELOW *Folksinger Woody Guthrie, who sang highly charged songs of solidarity, hope, and liberation, was the inspiration for Bob Dylan and in turn the entire pop-protest generation.*

Woodie Guthrie, whose instrument bore a sticker that read "This guitar kills fascists," was a huge influence on Bob Dylan, who tapped into the honesty and intent of Guthrie's class-based material, such as "This Land Is Your Land" and the Steinbeck-inspired "Tom Joad." Contemporary with Guthrie were the Weavers, featuring Pete Seeger, who co-wrote the quartet's most popular progressive anthem, "If I Had a Hammer." Emerging at the end of the 1940s, the Weavers soon found themselves blacklisted at the height of McCarthyism. Even Josh White, the African-American civil rights singer, who was a good friend of ex-President Roosevelt, found himself blacklisted and forced to migrate to London.

As McCarthyism faded, the civil rights and antinuclear protest movements took hold at the dawn of the 1960s. Young, committed, and gifted in the art of the sharply pointed lyric, Bob Dylan energized the new folk-protest movement with songs such as "Blowin' in the Wind" (1962), "Masters of War" (1963), and "The Lonesome Death of Hattie Carroll" (1964). Often appearing alongside him on marches was Joan Baez, who famously led the chorus for "We Shall Overcome" at Martin Luther King Jr.'s massive "March on Washington" in 1963. As protest peaked, Dylan's main rival in the United States was Phil Ochs, while in Britain, in 1965, Donovan scored a No. 1 with a version of Buffy Sainte-Marie's "Universal Soldier." After the success of "Eve of Destruction"—an opportunist hit by Barry McGuire in summer 1965—the high watermark of the protest song had passed.

LEFT *Initially saddled with the "British Dylan" tag, Donovan soon swapped the protest of "Catch the Wind" for psychedelia, exemplified by his 1966 hit, "Sunshine Superman."*

BELOW *Joan Baez and Bob Dylan, the king and queen of the folk-protest movement, performing at a Civil Rights rally in Washington in 1963.*

Motown—Hitsville USA

IF THERE WAS SUCH A THING as the American Beatles, then it wasn't a band but a record label—Berry Gordy's Tamla-Motown stable, operating out of Detroit. Assertive, joyful, and—as the company slogan had it—"The Sound of Young America," Motown (as it subsequently became known) was also an incredibly powerful force for black/white integration during an era that saw the civil rights campaign grow increasingly divided and embittered. Notching up an unrivaled 110 Top 10 hits in the United States between 1961 and 1971, the label soundtracked the 1960s every bit as much as the Beatles did, albeit in a production-line fashion that owed plenty to Phil Spector, both in terms of creating a signature sound and with regard to studio discipline.

Drawing its sound from gospel, R&B, and pop, Motown ran a tight musical and organizational ship. Its stars were carefully groomed in presentation and etiquette. Its songwriters—including the Holland/Dozier/Holland team, Ashford & Simpson, and early signing and Miracles frontman Smokey Robinson—were encouraged to keep it simple; and its studio musicians, the fabled Funk Brothers, rehearsed to an almost telepathic level of understanding.

After announcing itself to the world with the Miracles' "Shop Around" (No. 2, 1960) and the Marvelettes' "Please Mr Postman" (No. 1, 1961), Motown's route to mid-1960s singles-chart dominance came via the Supremes, fronted by Diana Ross. Emerging with "Baby Love" in 1964, the group scored 12 U.S. No. 1 hits during the decade, though arguably Stevie Wonder and Marvin Gaye were the real creative trailblazers, the latter enduring much friction with Gordy in a bid to get his best work (such as 1968's "I Heard It Though the Grapevine" and 1971's *What's Going On*) heard. The Temptations, too, were keen to embrace conscious, soulful pop with 1972's remarkable "Papa Was a Rollin' Stone," but by then Motown had decamped to Los Angeles and, despite the extraordinary success of Michael Jackson, never again quite recaptured its extended magical moment.

LEFT *Label boss Berry Gordy (at piano) leads a gathering of Motown hitmakers, including Smokey Robinson (back, center) and Stevie Wonder (second right).*

RIGHT *The Supremes, led by Diana Ross (center), the brightest stars in Gordy's empire.*

BELOW *After a string of successes during the early and mid-1960s, Marvin Gaye challenged the Motown hit factory later in the decade, prompting his best work.*

The Sound of Young America

Folk rock

IT WAS AN UNLIKELY HYBRID: folk, which positively reveled in an unvarnished, politicized, and invariably acoustic "authenticity," and pop, the upstart offspring of Tin Pan Alley, which sang loudly of romantic love and other youthful fancies. But by the mid-1960s, folk rock had eclipsed beat, R&B, and all those other subgenres and heralded the start of a new, more socially conscious pop era. The catalyst was Bob Dylan, lately turning his hand to beat-influenced electric rock, but the delivery boys were the Byrds, whose jangly 12-string, harmony-driven take on Dylan's "Mr. Tambourine Man" (1965) established a folk-rock template that would provide the basis for much new pop over the next two years.

RIGHT *Bob Dylan with the Byrds during their 1965 residency at Ciro's on Hollywood's Sunset Strip. Dylan was impressed by their band interpretation of "Mr. Tambourine Man."*

BELOW *The Mamas & the Papas, a Los Angeles-based vocal group led by John Phillips (right), became hit-making ambassadors for a blissed-out California during 1967.*

Dylan, who hated the term, nevertheless remained in the vanguard—though his summer 1965 watershed song, "Like a Rolling Stone," was probably closer to gospel-fired blues rock than folk rock. Both the Beatles ("You've Got To Hide Your Love Away") and the Rolling Stones ("Get Off Of My Cloud") had their Dylanesque moments, though the Searchers and the Animals were Britain's biggest contributors to the development of folk rock.

Among those roused into action by the Byrds were fellow West Coast ex-folkies Jefferson Airplane; the more R&B-inclined Love; the pop-oriented Turtles; New York jug band the Lovin' Spoonful; LA vocal harmony quartet the Mamas & the Papas; and the opportunist and extravagantly photogenic duo Sonny & Cher, whose beatnik apparel inspired the first whispers of an impending "hippie" movement.

Also emerging from the folk-rock boom was a new breed of singer-songwriters, including tortured teenage romantic Tim Buckley and Buffalo Springfield's Neil Young.

But the most successful folk-rock act of all were Simon & Garfunkel, whose thorny, decade-long career was transformed overnight in June 1965 when (Dylan's) producer Tom Wilson dubbed backing musicians onto a recent Paul Simon composition, "The Sounds of Silence." A No.1 in the United States that winter, the song set the pair on their way to becoming the era's most successful duo, peaking in 1970 with "Bridge Over Troubled Water."

ABOVE *Ostensibly a folk-duo, Simon & Garfunkel enjoyed huge success in the 1960s, transcending easy categorization.*

RIGHT *Bursting onto the international stage in 1965 with "I Got You Babe," Sonny & Cher were harbingers for the hippie look and lifestyle that became popular during 1967.*

5 Top folk-rock artists

The Byrds: *"Mr. Tambourine Man"* (1965)

Sonny & Cher: *"I Got You Babe"* (1965)

Simon & Garfunkel: *"The Sounds of Silence"* (1965)

The Mamas & the Papas: *"California Dreamin' "* (1965)

Donovan: *"Sunshine Superman"* (1966)

The Byrds

THE BYRDS WERE AMERICA'S most dramatic response to the British beat boom. Bringing a Beatles-inspired 12-string electric jangle to Bob Dylan's "Mr. Tambourine Man" and Pete Seeger's "Turn! Turn! Turn!," they pioneered folk rock, the pivot on which the pop and rock divide was delicately balanced. Unlike their British counterparts, the Byrds—with the exception of drummer Michael Clarke—were veterans of the coffee-house folk scene, and this was reflected in the band's penchant for pitch-perfect harmonies and open-chord guitar styles. This was stunningly realized on their debut single, "Mr. Tambourine Man" (1965), which topped the charts on both sides of the Atlantic and was inevitably followed by a second Dylan cover, "All I Really Want To Do."

Having brought folk rock to the world's attention, the Byrds then took a huge step toward psychedelic rock with "Eight Miles High" (1966). Something of an American response to the Who's "Anyway Anyhow Anywhere," "Eight Miles High" was more marijuana than amphetamine, more John Coltrane than Charlie Parker, more raga drone than feedback fury. But with the departure of first singer Gene Clark, then David Crosby, the budding space rockers failed to capitalize on their extraordinary sonic advances and by 1969 had retreated to the safety of a more harmonious country-rock style.

ABOVE With pop's balance of power shifting from London to California, the 1966-era Byrds epitomized pop elegance (top), having refined their earlier folk-rock image (above).

The Byrds

Formed:
Los Angeles, California

Years active:
1964–73

Definitive lineup:
Roger McGuinn, Gene Clark, David Crosby, Chris Hillman, Michael Clarke

Genres: *pop, rock, raga rock, country rock*

Key singles:
"Mr. Tambourine Man" (1965), "Eight Miles High" (1966)

Key albums:
Mr. Tambourine Man (1965), The Notorious Byrd Brothers (1968)

Ravi Shankar and raga rock

MID-1960S POP had been hewn from a variety of sources, from made-to-order Tin Pan Alley melodies to blues and folk songs forged from the gritty lives of the rural communities from which they sprang. Urban R&B, gospel, even jazz had also left their mark. But as pop was poised to take its epochal trip into the disorienting sound world of psychedelia, one final ingredient emerged, at once liberating pop from its chord-changing formalities and lending a pungent exoticism to its textures. This was the modal, drone style of Indian raga music, of distinctly Bohemian appeal in the West, until Byrds guitarist David Crosby introduced Beatle George Harrison to the music of sitar player Ravi Shankar toward the end of the Beatles' August 1965 U.S. tour.

BELOW Discovering his love of Indian music during the filming of Help! in 1965, George Harrison studied sitar under master musician Ravi Shankar, and introduced it into the Beatles' work.

Its influence was first heard in 1965 on a short run of British records—the Kinks' mantra-like "See My Friends," the faux-sitar riff on the Yardbirds' "Heart Full of Soul," and George Harrison's rudimentary sitar fumblings on the Beatles' "Norwegian Wood (This Bird Has Flown)." But it was the Byrds' "Eight Miles High" that took the drone effect into new sonic spaces, prompting a short-lived phrase, "raga rock." However, the sound endured. After Rolling Stone Brian Jones popularized the sitar on the band's 1966 single, "Paint It Black," emerging guitarists, such as Jefferson Airplane's Jorma Kaukonen and Quicksilver Messenger Service's John Cippolina, loudly embraced Eastern scales in their playing, bringing a further sense of sonic otherness to psychedelia's kaleidoscopic musical patchworks.

Garage rock

THE BEATLES-LED BRITISH INVASION of 1964–66 changed the face of contemporary America. It also turned thousands of suburban garages into no-go zones, as a generation of bored adolescents scratched out a rock 'n' rebellion of their own. Giving themselves names such as the Count Five or the Electric Prunes, these collegiate miscreants grew their hair and souped up their guitars. Sometimes, they'd even venture out as far as the high school hop, or release a no-hoper record via a local entrepreneur. The best, or perhaps the luckiest, might break through onto the national chart before returning just as quickly to Nowheresville. These were America's garage rock bands, who, though largely unloved during their 1965–66 heyday, created an aesthetic that would later form the basis for punk rock.

OPPOSITE TOP *San Jose's Count Five enjoyed 15 minutes of fame late in 1966, when "Psychotic Reaction" hit the Top 5 in the United States.*

RIGHT *The Electric Prunes' disorientating "I Had Too Much to Dream (Last Night)" remains a garage-rock perennial.*

BELOW *Taking their cues—and bowl haircuts—from British R&B, "Gloria" hit makers Shadows of Knight led the great American garage rock fightback.*

If the musical template was "Louie Louie," a 1963 U.S. hit for three-chord wonders the Kingsmen, the impetus for garage rock clearly came from the tougher R&B end of the British Invasion. Rolling Stone Mick Jagger was the voice to emulate, while bands such as the Kinks, the Yardbirds, and Them, with their crude, fuzzed-up riffs and "my girl gone done me bad" vibe, provided the musical inspiration. After Chicago's Shadows of Knight took a cracking version of Them's "Gloria" into the *Billboard* Top 10 early in 1966, the U.S. singles chart became a playground for angst-ridden adolescent upstarts. By now, the melodic niceties of early combos such as the Beau Brummels and Paul Revere & the Raiders had given way to a wild pre-psychedelic howl, best exemplified by the Count Five's "Psychotic

Reaction" and the Electric Prunes' "I Had Too Much to Dream (Last Night)." But things changed fast. The emergence in 1967 of grown-up psychedelia rendered these two- and three-minute bursts of suburban snottiness oddly anachronistic, and it wasn't until Elektra's trailblazing 1972 *Nuggets* compilation that the form—then known as punk rock—began to earn a belated respect.

5 Top garage-rock artists

The Kingsmen: *"Louie Louie" (1963)*
The Shadows of Knight: *"Gloria" (1966)*

The Electric Prunes: *"I Had Too Much To Dream (Last Night)" (1966)*
The 13th Floor Elevators: *"You're Gonna Miss Me" (1966)*

The Count Five: *"Psychotic Reaction" (1966)*

One-hit wonders

ONE-HIT WONDERS were those here today, gone tomorrow acts whose 15 minutes of fame somehow seemed to encapsulate pop at its most quintessentially honest. But what seemed at first glance to be a fleeting opportunist or novelty act could also, on occasion, mark the arrival of a new form of music for which the world was not entirely ready. Millie's "My Boy Lollipop," for example, was a huge transatlantic hit in 1964, and a first both for Island Records and for the bluebeat style. Though little was ever heard of Millie again (despite a couple of follow-up singles), both Island Records and Jamaican music went on to enjoy great success several years later.

The mid-1960s was a particularly fertile time for the one-hit wonder, especially in the United States, where a vast swathe of garage-rock combos, such as the Castaways and the Music Machine, raised their heads above the pop parapet for a single moment of glory before quietly fading into obscurity. Perhaps the most surprising one-off single successes came during the late 1960s and early 1970s, as rock began to split away from pop. Inevitably, the break wasn't clear-cut, as the singles-chart success of Vanilla Fudge ("You Keep Me Hangin' On," 1967) and Iron Butterfly ("In-A-Gadda-Da-Vida," 1968) in the United States, and the Crazy World of Arthur Brown ("Fire," 1968) in Britain, proved.

ABOVE *Leading hippie underground figure Arthur Brown made his British chart breakthrough in 1968 with the chart-topping "Fire!" It was to be his first and last hit.*

LEFT *Millie's bluebeat hit, "My Boy Lollipop," was a huge transatlantic success in 1964. The singer quickly returned to obscurity, but Jamaican music was here to stay.*

Star makers and Svengalis

IN THE 1950S, two management archetypes emerged. The cigar-chomping "Colonel" Tom Parker, who helped himself to a sizable portion of Elvis Presley's earnings, tended to busy himself with contracts. The suave British manager/impresario Larry Parnes, who created a stable of stars bearing names such as Marty Wilde, Vince Eager, and Billy Fury, took a more actively creative role. Pop continued to attract its fair share of hustlers and opportunists during the 1960s, though the success of the benign and mild-mannered Beatles' boss Brian Epstein presented a more acceptable face of the business of pop management.

In total contrast was the Rolling Stones' manager Andrew Loog Oldham. Younger than the band, and more mischievous too, it was the PR-savvy Oldham who engineered the band's "bad boy" image—feeding headlines to the press and writing scandalous sleeve notes for their album covers. One man who took this rabble-rousing approach even further, while at the same time embodying much of the Machiavellian 1950s archetype, was the Sex Pistols' manager Malcolm McLaren. Probably the most brilliant of them all, McLaren—a true believer in rock 'n' roll's insurrectionary potential—created the punk ideology almost single-handedly. Since punk's demise, with one or two notable exceptions, such as Creation Records boss Alan McGee, the rock manager has become little more than a conduit between an artist and their lawyers and accountants.

RIGHT Brian Epstein (top) and Andrew Loog Oldham (right) represented the two different faces of pop management during the 1960s. Epstein was gentlemanly and faintly paternalistic, while Oldham was younger and in many ways more outrageous and in his charges.

Soul

IT WAS RIGHT THERE in the work of Ray Charles, Little Richard, and James Brown during the 1950s, but soul—roughly where gospel meets R&B—was the defining sound of the black experience during the 1960s. Motown gave this emerging form its most popular face, especially later in the decade, when artists such as Marvin Gaye and the Temptations extricated themselves from the hit formula. But it was the deep, Southern soul sound that came out of the FAME Studios in Muscle Shoals, Alabama, the studio home of Memphis's Stax/Volt stable of stars, that delivered a purer version of the form. Given that the Stax engine room was manned by the mixed-race Booker T. & the M.G.'s, hit makers with club evergreen "Green Onions" (1962), that was somewhat ironic.

STAX
SOULSVILLE U.S.A.

The raw but elegant brilliance of the house band provided a perfect musical bed for a front line made in soul heaven—Otis Redding, Rufus Thomas and his daughter Carla, Sam & Dave, Eddie Floyd, and later Isaac Hayes and the Staple Singers. Despite Curtis Mayfield's sweet soul activities in Chicago, it was Stax that soon earned the reputation as the home of soul music. The first to break through was Otis Redding, the big-voiced, big-hearted "King of Soul," who won crossover success with gut-wrenching hits such as "I've Been Loving You Too Long" (1965) and his concert showstopper, "Try a Little Tenderness" (1966).

The Otis-penned "Sweet Soul Music," a huge, infectious hit for Arthur Conley in 1967, popularized the music further, though Redding's death in December 1967, just when he was in his prime, was a massive blow, which was followed by a breakdown in

Stax's relationship with distributor Atlantic Records the following year. However, Atlantic's own Aretha Franklin, who had already reworked Redding's "Respect" earlier that year, emerged during 1968 as the embodiment of soul, and with Sly & the Family Stone, Isaac Hayes, Marvin Gaye, and James Brown taking the form into new territories, soul was no longer a niche genre by the start of the 1970s.

ABOVE *Otis Redding (left) and Carla Thomas pose with label boss Jim Stewart, Rufus Thomas, and Booker T. Jones.*

OPPOSITE *Sam & Dave at the Stax studios with members of the Bar-Kays, guitarist Steve Cropper, and producer Isaac Hayes (left).*

5 Top soul artists

Sam Cooke: *"A Change Is Gonna Come"* (1964)

Otis Redding: *"Try a Little Tenderness"* (1966)
Sam & Dave: *"Hold On, I'm Comin' "* (1966)

Aretha Franklin: *"Respect"* (1967)
Marvin Gaye: *"I Heard It Through the Grapevine"* (1967)

Otis Redding

THE MOST DEMONSTRATIVE performer of his generation, Otis Redding was a charismatic, big-voiced presence, whose name remains synonymous with soul. Able to wring every last ounce of emotion from self-penned heart-tuggers, such as "I've Been Loving You Too Long" (1965) and "Ole Man Trouble" (1965), as well as whip Sam Cooke's "Shake" (1965) and the Rolling Stones' "(I Can't Get No) Satisfaction" (1965) into frenzied floor shakers, Redding was both auteur and interpreter.

Pitched somewhere between Little Richard, a fellow native of Macon, Georgia, and his hero Sam Cooke, Redding emerged in 1962 with "These Arms of Mine." Hitting his stride, the prolific Redding released six albums for Stax/Volt between 1964 and 1967, none with more impact than 1965's *Otis Blue*. Two tributes to the recently deceased Cooke were balanced by Redding's reworking of the Stones' "Satisfaction" and three of his own songs, the above-named pair plus "Respect," subsequently covered by Aretha Franklin.

Having written and produced Arthur Conley's massive 1967 summer hit, "Sweet Soul Music," and wowed the hippies at the Monterey pop festival, Redding's death, in a plane crash that December, came as he was poised to cross over into the international market. The posthumous No 1. success of the Summer of Love-flavored "(Sittin' on the) Dock of the Bay"—cowritten with Stax guitarist Steve Cropper—only hinted at where the big man was headed.

Otis Redding

Born:
September 9, 1941, Dawson, Georgia

Died:
December 10, 1967

Years active:
1960–67

Genres: *soul, R&B*

Key singles:
"I've Been Loving You Too Long" (1965), "(Sittin' on) the Dock of the Bay" (1968)

Key albums:
Otis Blue: Otis Redding Sings Soul *(1965)*, Live in Europe *(1967)*

LEFT *The irrepressible Otis Redding, who did more than anyone else to popularize soul music in the mid-1960s, found himself up against a new generation of acid-rock acts at the 1967 Monterey Pop Festival. He upstaged them.*

Aretha Franklin

OF ALL THE MANY REMARKABLE voices that emerged during the 1960s, none carried more emotional weight than Aretha Franklin's. A piano-playing prodigy and Baptist minister's daughter, Franklin—having grown up singing in her father's church—had a difficult voyage as she switched from sacred to secular material during the early years of the decade, recording a string of jazz-flavored records for Columbia. Meeting Atlantic producer Jerry Wexler in 1966 changed all that, and during 1967 and 1968 she released a remarkable run of nine U.S. hit singles that brought Southern soul (albeit mostly recorded in New York) center stage.

On the basis of on these records alone— which included the breakthrough "I Never Loved a Man (the Way I Love You)" (1967) and her feminist reworking of Otis Redding's "Respect" (1967)—Franklin thoroughly deserves her Queen of Soul epithet. And for the next half-dozen years, during which time she performed to rock crowds at San Francisco's Fillmore West and to a Baptist congregation in Los Angeles for her 1972 *Amazing Grace* album, Franklin continued to reign supreme.

The arrival of disco found Franklin struggling to maintain a profile, though an appearance in the 1980 movie *The Blues Brothers* (1980) led to mid-1980s collaborations with Eurythmics and George Michael (the chart-topping "I Knew You Were Waiting [For Me]"). Franklin's iconic status was enhanced further still when she sang at the 2009 inauguration of President Obama.

ABOVE *Aretha Franklin in June 1968, on stage at the Soul Together concert in New York. That same month, she made the cover of* Time *magazine.*

Aretha Franklin

Born: *March 25, 1942, Memphis, Tennessee*

Years active: *1956 to present*
Genres: *soul, R&B, gospel*

Key singles: *"Respect" (1967), "Chain of Fools" (1967)*

Key albums: Lady Soul *(1972)*, Amazing Grace *(1972)*

Acid rock

POP MOVED AT AN INCREDIBLE pace in the years after 1963, and, by 1967, a significant part of it was being more respectfully referred to as rock. That was due to a newfound sense of ambition on the part of musicians, further aroused by advances in technology and, from 1965, the growing popularity of the psychedelic wonder drug LSD. Initially developed by the U.S. military, lysergic acid diethylamide—known colloquially as "acid," not least for its mind-frying properties— dramatically altered consciousness. Inevitably, musicians desired to make music that reflected acid's derangement of the senses. Similarly, tripped-out audiences wanted to hear sounds that would best amplify their experiences.

OPPOSITE *Bathed in the liquid lights of an early Pink Floyd performance, frontman Syd Barrett would tease out volleys of psychedelic sound from his mirrored Telecaster guitar during the band's acid-rock heyday in 1966 and 1967.*

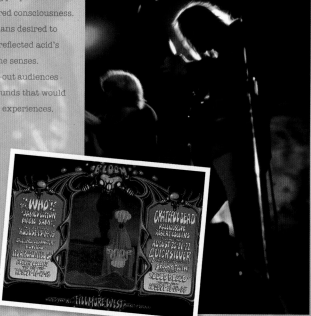

ABOVE RIGHT *Grateful Dead, whose gigs represented the acme of acid rock, at the Monterey Pop Festival in June 1967.*

RIGHT *Forthcoming attractions at promoter Bill Graham's legendary Fillmore West venue in San Francisco in August 1968 were the Who and local acid-rock luminaries Grateful Dead and Quicksilver Messenger Service.*

Dissolving into "freak-outs"

The heartbeat of acid rock reverberated out of San Francisco, the West Coast's Bohemian enclave, to which beatniks had been gravitating for years. That's where acid evangelist Ken Kesey held his "Acid Tests" during winter 1965–66, and where dozens of oddly named bands performed in clubs such as the Avalon and the Fillmore—where spiked Kool-Aid, rather than uncool booze, was served, and liquid light shows enhanced the sensation-seeking mood. Above all, there was sound.

The city's leading psychedelic bands— Grateful Dead, Jefferson Airplane, Quicksilver Messenger Service, Country Joe & the Fish, Big Brother & the Holding Company—let their songs dissolve into "freak-outs," lengthy passages that would crescendo before returning to the basic melody. Pop's old three-minute barrier was of little importance to the acid-rock iconoclasts.

Unlike the West Coast high-fliers, whose music was usually rooted in blues or folk, London-based psychedelia shared more with the contemporary classical art tradition (such as the early work of Pink Floyd), jazz improvisation (as favored by Soft Machine), or fantasy-driven innocence (the calling card of Tyrannosaurus Rex). And then, of course, there was the transatlantic Jimi Hendrix, whose explosive psychedelia was clearly rooted in the blues but aimed at somewhere else entirely.

5 Top acid-rock artists

Pink Floyd: *The Piper at the Gates of Dawn* (1967)

Jefferson Airplane: *After Bathing at Baxter's* (1967)

The Jimi Hendrix Experience: *Are You Experienced* (1967)

Country Joe & the Fish: *Electric Music For the Mind and Body* (1967)

Grateful Dead: *Anthem of the Sun* (1968)

Jefferson Airplane

THE EARLY COMMERCIAL success of "Somebody to Love" and the bolero-beat paean to LSD, "White Rabbit," both huge Summer of Love hits in 1967, tends to overshadow the bittersweet genius of San Francisco's premier acid-rock high-fliers. The striking beauty of singer Grace Slick belied a venomous vocal bite; the band's sublime, three-part harmonies often descended into stoned, onstage battle cries; and the electrifying runs of bassist Jack Casady and guitarist Jorma Kaukonen poured tripped-out, Eastern-scented oil over the fiery folk-rock veneer of the band's material.

Jefferson Airplane lived communally, were routinely busted for drugs, and played all of the major late-1960s festivals from Monterey to Woodstock. By the time of 1969's "Volunteers," the multifaceted psychedelia of albums such as *Crown of Creation* had acquired a more radical political dimension, though the band's "tear down the walls" battle cry ultimately fell on deaf ears.

As the counterculture fragmented, so too did the always temperamental and fractious band, which increasingly poured its energies into solo projects. The Airplane soldiered on until 1972, before splitting into two spin-off bands: Casady and Kaukonen's blues-based Hot Tuna and Slick and partner Paul Kantner's Jefferson Starship. The latter reemerged from the environs of San Francisco to enjoy surprise success during the mid-1970s in their new guise as FM-radio favorites.

BELOW *Jefferson Airplane could veer from flower-power pop to instrumentally charged acid rock, from Eastern textures to rootsy folk. Their sound was defined by the supercharged vocal interplay between Grace Slick (center) and Marty Balin (right).*

Jefferson Airplane

Formed: *San Francisco, California*

Years active: *1965–73*

Definitive lineup: *Grace Slick, Marty Balin, Paul Kantner, Jorma Kaukonen, Jack Casady, Spencer Dryden*

Genres: *acid rock*

Key singles: "Somebody to Love" (1967), "White Rabbit" (1967)

Key albums: Surrealistic Pillow (1967), Crown of Creation (1968)

Grateful Dead

THE ARCHETYPAL commune-dwelling rock group from San Francisco's hippified Haight-Ashbury district, the Grateful Dead's richly tapestried psychedelia—woven from folk, country, jazz, blues, rock 'n' roll, and experimental music—sounds like no other. At their best in concert, where they'd often play for four hours, it's the band's epic *Live/Dead* set (1969) that remains their masterpiece. "Dark Star," the side-long opener, illustrates perfectly the group's instrumental dexterity and near telepathic gift for flowing improvisation.

ABOVE *The band pose in San Francisco's hippie enclave of Haight-Ashbury in the mid-1960s, just prior to the breakout of flower power.*

While the band's late-1960s live recordings (including much of 1968's *Anthem of the Sun*) boast some of the era's most intense and intoxicating acid rock, the Dead's penchant for beards, harmonies, and country rock later earned them the reputation of "cosmic cowboys." *Workingman's Dead* (1970) was the first in a series of albums that posited the band as standard-bearers for a semistoned, posthippie lifestyle. However, 1975's *Blues for Allah* found them back in staggeringly inventive form. It didn't last, and after a dalliance with an FM radio-friendly sound on *Terrapin Station* (1977), the Dead survived as an alternative American institution, selling more T-shirts and merchandise than they ever did records. The death of guitarist Jerry Garcia, the band's spiritual guru, in August 1995, effectively marked the end of the band's long, strange trip—though the live albums, literally dozens of them, just keep coming.

Grateful Dead

Formed: *San Francisco, California*
Years active: *1964–95*

Definitive lineup: *Jerry Garcia, Bob Weir, Phil Lesh, Ron "Pigpen" McKernan, Bill Kreutzmann, Mickey Hart, Tom Constanten*

Genres: *acid rock, country rock*
Key singles: *"Dark Star" (1968), "Truckin' " (1970)*

Key albums: Live/Dead *(1969),* American Beauty *(1970)*

The Summer of Love

A COMBINATION OF POP, youth, and a reasonably tolerant postwar cultural establishment led to 1967's so-called Summer of Love. Since the previous fall, records such as the Beach Boys' "Good Vibrations," Donovan's "Sunshine Superman," and the Beatles' "Strawberry Fields Forever" had anticipated the 1967 buzzword, "psychedelic." So too had reports of the fashionable new way of life taking root in the Haight-Ashbury district of San Francisco—where commune-dwelling hippies shared love, LSD, and loud music.

By summer 1967, the world was awash with gentle, love-filled anthems—notably the Beatles' "All You Need is Love" and Scott McKenzie's "San Francisco (Be Sure To Wear Some Flowers in Your Hair)"—while fashion went Technicolor, "unisex," and exotic. But it wasn't all *Sgt Pepper*, "pass the joint," and peace signs. Three of the Rolling Stones faced jail sentences after a series of drug busts, and even San Francisco itself staged a "death of the hippie" ceremony that fall.

The Summer of Love's key moment was the Monterey Pop Festival in June. With an incredibly eclectic lineup, featuring Jimi Hendrix and the Who (representing London), Janis Joplin and Jefferson Airplane (San Francisco), the Mamas & the Papas and the Byrds (Los Angeles), Otis Redding (Memphis), and Ravi Shankar (India), Monterey caught the psychedelic era in full flow—before cliché and cynicism set in.

ABOVE In terms of blissful vibe and musical thrills, no pop festival ever quite matched June 1967's Monterey Pop Fesival.

RIGHT Two hippies line up at the intersection of Haight and Ashbury in San Francisco, marking the epicenter of the Summer of Love.

The Doors

BOTH MAGNIFICENT and messed up, Doors frontman Jim Morrison remains the embodiment of the romantic/tragic rock 'n' roll antihero. After a decade of deification during the 1980s, from myth-making biographies to Oliver Stone's movie *The Doors*, a backlash—intensified, perhaps, by the death of Kurt Cobain—has since threatened to overshadow the Doors' reputation. It shouldn't.

BELOW *Jim Morrison's often apocalyptic poetry and "Theater of Cruelty" stage routine gave a dark twist to the Doors' trippy music.*

Oozing sex and rebellion, Jim Morrison seemed a perfect, poetic Presley/Jagger hybrid for the psychedelic age. When the Doors broke big in summer 1967 with "Light My Fire," Morrison made the transition from Sunset Strip to the cover of *Hit Parader* with ease. The band, equally adept at three-minute bossa-nova rock ("Break On Through") and improvised, labyrinthine, death-drive psychodrama ("The End"), seemed poised to seduce a generation of pop enthusiasts into the risky thrills of the rock revolution.

The uneasy alliance didn't last long. Throwing himself headlong into the part of rock's great romantic, Morrison lost his head at gigs, and his mind through a ceaseless booze-and-drugs binge. By the time the band recorded their sixth album, *L.A. Woman*, the heavily bearded Morrison

had become gruff-voiced and bloated, which worked well on record but less so on his health. Within three months of the album's release, Morrison had died of a heart attack.

BELOW *Even standing in a field of flowers, the Doors were reluctant to relax their intense glare. Their work drew from a wide range of sources, including Berlin theater songs and psychoanalysis.*

The Doors

Formed: *Los Angeles, California*
Years active: *1965–73*

Definitive lineup: *Jim Morrison, Ray Manzarek, Robbie Krieger, John Densmore*

Genres: *acid rock, blues rock*
Key singles: *"Light My Fire" (1967), "Riders on the Storm" (1971)*

Key albums: The Doors *(1967),* L.A. Woman *(1971)*

The Velvet Underground

THOUGH THEIR IMPACT at the time was minimal, the Velvet Underground's legacy and influence on the subsequent course of rock have probably been second only to those of the Beatles. Eclectic enough on their debut album—*The Velvet Underground & Nico* (1967)—to take Dylan-like reportage to the dark end of the street ("Heroin") and to include a tender paean to the joys of "Sunday Morning" and eight minutes of feedback-drenched rock 'n' roll improvisation ("European Son"), the Velvet Underground stretched the bounds of rock without recourse to psychedelic gimmickry. In fact, though impeccably "underground," the Velvets were defiantly antipsychedelic.

Starting life as the house band at Andy Warhol's Factory, the band soundtracked S&M low life rather than acid-induced highs, preferred plastic pop art "Superstars" to commune-dwelling Californian hippie types, Neanderthal beats and viola drones over folk and blues "authenticity." Over a decade before punk, the Velvet Underground were the archetypal antigroup, drawing inspiration from a variety of untapped and seemingly illicit sources.

BELOW *Lou Reed, John Cale and Nico at a reunion show in Paris, 1972. The Velvet Underground started out as the house group at artist Andy Warhol's Factory art studio and ended up as a blueprint for punk and assorted dissident music movements.*

The house band at
Andy Warhol's Factory

At the root of their sound was the tension between the subversive pop of songwriter Lou Reed and the textured, instrumental approach of trained avant-gardist John Cale. Cementing the two iconoclasts together was drummer Maureen Tucker, who whacked her kit with mallets, eschewed cymbals, and underpinned the sound with poetic primitivism. The presence of European chanteuse Nico on the debut album enhanced the Velvets' impeccable misfit status further still.

A second album, January 1968's *White Light/White Heat*, boasted one of the most sonically challenging sides of vinyl ever, with side two's "I Heard Her Call My Name" (featuring a violent volley of guitar solos) followed by a magnificent 17-minute dirge, "Sister Ray." A self-titled 1969 third album, recorded after Cale's departure, foregrounded Reed's intimate songwriting, while the frontman's swansong, *Loaded* (1970), returned the group to something approaching conventional rock 'n' roll. David Bowie's enthusiasm in the early 1970s did much to enhance the band's reputation, and by 1977 the Velvets were widely regarded as the great progenitors of punk rock.

RIGHT *Lou Reed pictured in 1966 fronting the Velvet Underground at a dinner in New York. He later found crossover success with hits such as "Walk on the Wild Side" and "Perfect Day."*

BELOW *The classic lineup that recorded the* White Light/White Heat *album. Lou Reed is seated right. John Cale, seated left, quit shortly afterward, and the band changed direction dramatically.*

The Velvet Underground

Formed: *New York*
Years active: *1965–73, 1993*

Definitive lineup:
Lou Reed, John Cale, Sterling Morrison, Maureen Tucker

Genres: *rock, alternative rock*
Key singles: *"All Tomorrow's Parties" (1967), "White Light/White Heat" (1968)*

Key albums: The Velvet Underground & Nico *(1967)*, White Light/White Heat *(1968)*

Jimi Hendrix

ROCK BOASTS ITS FAIR SHARE of poets, prodigies, and geniuses, but it's entirely feasible that none can ever match the incomparably gifted Jimi Hendrix. A force of nature, forever adrift in his own creative cosmos, this shy ex-U.S. Army rookie from Seattle spent years on the black American club circuit before ex-Animals bassist-turned-manager Chas Chandler brought him over from New York to Swinging London in September 1966. Hendrix's R&B apprenticeship, supporting showmen such as Little Richard and the Isley Brothers, had served him well. Within weeks, Britain's burgeoning rock aristocracy— the Beatles, the Stones, and guitar gods Pete Townshend and Eric Clapton—were driven to even greater heights after witnessing Hendrix's extraordinary performances in and around London's Soho club scene.

RIGHT *Pairing Hendrix with British musicians, bassist Noel Redding (left) and drummer Mitch Mitchell (center), proved to be a masterstroke by manager Chas Chandler.*

ABOVE *Hendrix pulled out all the stops for his performance at Monterey in 1967— including setting fire to his guitar at the end of his set.*

The guitar, which Hendrix ritually humped and burned on stage, was his muse; the recording studio, which became a second home, a canvas. But it was on stage that Hendrix earned his reputation as the era's prime countercultural icon, making his international name at Monterey in June 1967 and crowning Woodstock with a feedback-drenched "Star-Spangled Banner" two years later. Later gigs, notably at the Isle of Wight Festival in August 1970, weeks before his death, could be erratic, as Hendrix struggled to break free from routine displays of showmanship and rattling out the hits. But, eternally lost in sound, especially during longer, newer numbers such as the antiwar epic "Machine Gun," he could still reach extraordinary heights.

Hendrix's biggest battle came in the studio where, having split the original Experience power trio early in 1969, he strove to create a new cosmic soul sound, which he dubbed "Sky Church Music." After 1968's two-LP set, *Electric Ladyland*, he spent much of his time musing on black consciousness and riding a roundabout of sexual and drug-inspired highs, in the hope of cracking his creative impasse. It proved a fast track to nowhere: his death on September 18, 1970, was the most tragic consequence of the hippie era's faith in total abandonment.

Jimi Hendrix

Born: *November 27, 1942, Seattle, Washington*
Died: *September 18, 1970*

Years active: *1964–70*
Genres: *acid rock, blues rock, blues, soul*

Key singles: *"All Along the Watchtower" (1968), "Voodoo Child (Slight Return)" (1970)*

Key albums: Are You Experienced *(1967),* Electric Ladyland *(1968)*

Cream

CREATED BY VIRTUOSOS from two of the most respected blues and jazz combos, John Mayall's Blues Breakers and the Graham Bond Organisation, Cream were a blues-rock supergroup trio, whose immense volume and lengthy instrumental jams set the agenda for much late-1960s rock.

The first of the rock supergroups

Formed by fiery drummer Ginger Baker, featuring a guitarist whose reputation had recently prompted (Eric) "Clapton Is God" graffiti in London, and fronted by firebrand bassist Jack Bruce, this awe-inspiring power trio started out performing high-octane versions of blues standards. Howlin' Wolf/Willie Dixon's "Spoonful," Muddy Waters' "Rollin' and Tumblin'," and Skip James's "I'm So Glad" all remained part of Cream's dynamic live set during the band's two-year existence. But it was after Jack Bruce teamed up with beat-inspired

poet Pete Brown that the group made a singles chart breakthrough with "I Feel Free" (1966) and "Strange Brew" (1967). Cream's biggest success in the United States was "Sunshine of Your Love," a hit in 1968 and a landmark in the emergence of the heavy-rock riff.

Essentially, Cream were an albums-market combo whose forte was live concerts. *Disraeli Gears* (1967) might have boasted a classic psychedelic cover, but it was on the band's live recordings that they were at their most explosive.

ABOVE *Jack Bruce (left), Ginger Baker (center), and Eric Clapton (right). Individually they were ferociously talented virtuosos. Collectively, Cream set new standards in rock.*

Cream

Formed: *London*
Years active: *1966–68, 2005*

Definitive lineup: *Eric Clapton, Jack Bruce, Ginger Baker*

Genres: *blues rock, acid rock*
Key singles: *"I Feel Free" (1966), "Badge" (1969)*

Key albums: Disraeli Gears *(1967)*, Wheels of Fire *(1968)*

The Band

ENJOYING AN INFLUENCE that far exceeded their commercial success, the Band were responsible for reversing the rush toward psychedelic gimmickry and virtuoso jamming, instead bringing rock "back home" to a form that privileged tradition and storytelling. Their summer 1968 debut, *Music from Big Pink*, built on the sepia ghosts of old-time gospel and the white rural styles of the American South, marked a remarkably subtle and sophisticated return to a pre-pop style of songwriting. The effect was instant. Within months, both the Beatles and the Rolling Stones had released back-to-basics-flavored albums, while Eric Clapton was moved to announce his departure from Cream and adopt a more rootsy approach.

The Band (then known as the Hawks) cut their teeth during the early 1960s backing Canadian rock 'n' roller Ronnie Hawkins, before joining Bob Dylan on his electrifying 1965 and 1966 tours. Dylan returned the favor, gifting the Band three songs (and providing the cover artwork) for *Big Pink*, though the group's self-titled follow-up confirmed that they—rather than Dylan— were more firmly installed in the driver's seat by 1969. Though the spell gradually wore off, especially by the time of 1973's lackluster covers set, *Moondog Matinee*, the all-star cast that turned out for "The Last Waltz," their November 1976 farewell gig at Winterland, San Francisco—filmed by Martin Scorsese—was a testament to the esteem in which the Band are held. Among the guests were Bob Dylan, Joni Mitchell, Eric Clapton, and Neil Young.

BELOW *In complete contrast to the kaleidoscopic colors and swirling sounds of psychedelia, the Band came on like officials from a nineteenth-century Wild West town, with a more sober sound to match.*

The Band

Formed: *Toronto, Canada*

Years active: *1964–76*

Definitive lineup: *Robbie Robertson, Levon Helm, Rick Danko, Richard Manuel, Garth Hudson*

Genres: *country rock*

Key singles: *"The Weight" (1968), "Rag Mama Rag" (1970)*

Key albums: Music from Big Pink *(1968),* The Band *(1969)*

The Monkees

THE BEACH BOYS were never quite the hysteria-driven answer to the Beatles that America wanted. The answer came in summer 1966 when, inspired by the zaniness of the Beatles' movie *A Hard Day's Night*, *The Monkees* was launched as a weekly television series about a fictional rock 'n' roll band. Within weeks, the "group" had two U.S. chart-topping singles ("Last Train to Clarksville" and "I'm a Believer") and the first of four No. 1 albums. However, the makers of the series hadn't reckoned with their individual ambitions.

With hit singles and albums coming thick and fast during 1967 as the group's popularity soared, the four Monkees—who had been cast from some 400 hopefuls – began to assert themselves. Guitarist Mike Nesmith went public about the fact that their records were generally the work of session musicians, while the brilliant and faintly bizarre Micky Dolenz-penned "Alternate Title" suggested that the band were becoming familiar with something rather stronger than bubblegum. Resentment grew to such a degree that, for much of 1968, the band presided over their own demise, with the reputation-blowing and psychedelic-inspired movie, *Head*. Two years later, with Nesmith following Peter Tork out of the group, it was all over.

The Monkees

Formed: *Los Angeles, California*

Years active: *1966–71, 1996–97, 2011*

Definitive lineup: *Davy Jones, Peter Tork, Michael Nesmith, Micky Dolenz*

Genres: *pop, bubblegum, rock*

Key singles: *"I'm a Believer" (1966), "Daydream Believer" (1967)*

Key albums: Pisces, Aquarius, Capricorn & Jones Ltd *(1967)*, Head *(1968)*

LEFT *Vaudeville, fake surrealism, you name it: the Monkees were game for anything in their hugely popular TV series. On record, the quartet soon wanted their say.*

Bubblegum

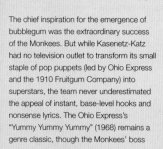

IN A SENSE, MOST SUCCESSFUL pop is "bubblegum," in that it rejoices in hummable hooks and melodies, is created in an artificial situation (the recording studio), and saturates people's lives for a month or two before giving way to the next three-minute flavor. But during 1968, when many musicians began to set their sights on the more challenging albums market, pop became prey to a new breed of producers. Aware that a teenage, even preteen market was eagerly expectant, the Kasenetz-Katz production team led the way with an unashamedly formulaic series of effervescent pop 45s.

The chief inspiration for the emergence of bubblegum was the extraordinary success of the Monkees. But while Kasenetz-Katz had no television outlet to transform its small staple of pop puppets (led by Ohio Express and the 1910 Fruitgum Company) into superstars, the team never underestimated the appeal of instant, base-level hooks and nonsense lyrics. The Ohio Express's "Yummy Yummy Yummy" (1968) remains a genre classic, though the Monkees' boss Don Kirshner hit back with the Archies, whose 1969 "Sugar, Sugar" was bubblegum perfection, in that its "stars" were television cartoon characters.

Though gifted auteurs, Swedish singing sensations ABBA enjoyed great success during the 1970s with what might be termed "adult bubblegum," while the mid-1990s girl-powered Spice Girls revived the cartoonlike personae and joyfully immediate sonic pleasures of vintage bubblegum.

TOP *Though Gorillaz have revived the idea of a virtual band for the twenty-first century, late 1960s fictional pop group the Archies got there first.*

ABOVE *Months after the heady highs of the Summer of Love, the Lemon Pipers scored a U.S. No. 1 with the wonderfully faddy "Green Tambourine."*

5 Top bubblegum artists

The Lemon Pipers: *"Green Tambourine" (1967)*

Ohio Express: *"Yummy Yummy Yummy" (1968)*
The Archies: *"Sugar Sugar" (1969)*

ABBA: *"Dancing Queen" (1975)*
Spice Girls: *"Wannabe" (1996)*

Jackson 5

MORE THAN A LITTLE mythmaking surrounded the Jackson 5's earliest days at Motown. Diana Ross discovered them, it was claimed, and several years were lopped off their collective ages. But that was nothing compared to the mythic heights later achieved by little Michael, the preteen singing, dancing sensation who was the Jackson 5's biggest asset. Between the twin myths was a remarkable run of successes, starting in 1969 with an unprecedented four consecutive *Billboard*-topping, bubblegum-soul 45s before fading after the irrepressible high of "Shake Your Body (Right to the Ground)" (1978), one of the most vibrant dance-floor cuts to emanate from the disco era.

Jackson 5

Formed: *Gary, Indiana*

Years active: *1964–89*

Definitive lineup: *Michael Jackson, Jackie Jackson, Jermaine Jackson, Tito Jackson, Marlon Jackson*

Genres: *pop, soul, disco, funk*

Key singles: *"I Want You Back" (1969), "Shake Your Body (Down to the Ground)" (1978)*

Key albums: *Third Album (1970), Maybe Tomorrow (1971)*

In typical showbiz fashion, father Joe Jackson mentored the singing brothers' early career, before a recommendation from Gladys Knight in 1968 earned them an audition for Motown. Within two years, after those back-to-back No. 1s—including the hyperactive "I Want You Back," "ABC," and "I'll Be There"— the Jackson 5 had usurped the Supremes as the label's favorite hit machine.

Inevitably, the naturally gifted Michael—still only 11 in 1970—was encouraged to pursue a simultaneous solo career: this wasn't particularly helpful to the quintet, which struggled to maintain its momentum. Quitting Motown for CBS mid-decade prompted that brief, explosive, late-1970s renaissance, but once Michael teamed up in 1979 with producer Quincy Jones for *Off the Wall*, his brothers rarely got a look-in.

LEFT *Part bubblegum soul, part post-psychedelic funksters, the late-1960s Jackson 5 became an instant phenomenon once they scored their first hit for Motown. That's Michael in the center.*

Brazilian Tropicália

WHILE THE MUSIC-FRONTED youth movements in Europe and North America represented a challenge to the old order by demanding ever-greater freedoms, in Brazil, which in 1964 had succumbed to a military government, more basic liberties were under threat. That made the emergence of the Tropicália—or Tropicalismo—movement all the more astonishing.

An eruption of art, poetry, theater, style, and sound from across the entire arts spectrum, Tropicália—originating in the country's Bahai state—found its most potent expression in music. Unlike the contemporaneous psychedelic movement sweeping the North Atlantic, Tropicália was motivated less by drugs than by a brave and flamboyant rejection of the political establishment. Inevitably, several of its leading figures ended up in jail.

Tropicália's first musical strike was Caetano Veloso's self-titled debut from 1968. Dressed in an impeccably psychedelic cover, the album was a kaleidoscopic mix of Western rock and Latino balladry, carried along by the giddy elegance of the bossa-nova beat.

BELOW *Gilberto Gil was a key figure in the Tropicália movement, entering politics in the late 1980s while continuing his music career.*

Contemporaries Os Mutantes ("the Mutants") were more radical still, their vocal harmonies soaring over dreamy psych arrangements and buzzing guitar breaks. Both acts, together with Gilberto Gil, Tom Zé, and Gal Costa, appeared on the collaborative 1968 set, *Tropicália: ou Panis et Circencis*.

Happily, more than three decades after the brutal suppression of Tropicália at the end of the 1960s, Gilberto Gil— who had been jailed in 1969 and then forced to leave the country—became Brazil's Minister of Culture.

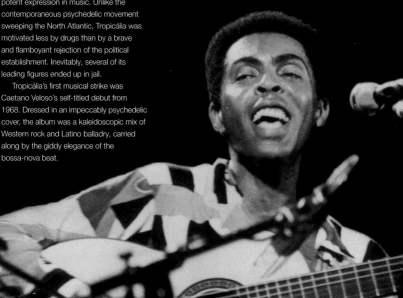

Janis Joplin

A HARD-DRINKING TOMBOY from Port Arthur, Texas, Janis Joplin got the blues early in life. After a couple of trips out to California, where she picked up a niggling drug habit, Joplin returned to San Francisco in summer 1966, just as the Bay Area's hippie movement was gathering pace. Hooking up with Big Brother & the Holding Company, a spirited psychedelic blues band, Joplin triumphed at the Monterey Festival the following June, thanks to a show-stealing version of Big Mama Thornton's "Ball and Chain" that defined her pained, breast-beating blues.

Despite the Top 20 success of "Piece of My Heart" in 1968, Big Brother's brilliant if ramshackle psychedelia was regarded as an impediment to Joplin's wider success, and the first woman of acid rock was encouraged to quit the band late that year. Now fronting her own Kozmic Blues band, a soul revue-style combo complete with horn section, Joplin toured incessantly, appearing at Woodstock and other rock festivals. In an attempt to avoid total burnout, she cleaned up her act, hired a bunch of straight musicians, the Full-Tilt Boogie Band, and had almost finished work on a fourth album, *Pearl*, when she was found dead of an accidental heroin overdose. Released posthumously, *Pearl* yielded two further classic Joplin songs, "Me and Bobby McGee" and the boozy a cappella "Mercedes Benz."

ABOVE *Janis Joplin sings with passion as she performs on a darkened stage at the Fillmore East, New York, in February 1969. Grateful Dead opened the concert for her.*

Janis Joplin

Born: *January 19, 1943, Port Arthur, Texas*
Died: *October 4, 1970*

Years active: *1962–70*
Genres: *acid rock, blues rock, blues, soul*

Key singles: *"Piece of My Heart"* (1968), *"Me and Bobby McGee"* (1971)

Key albums:
Cheap Thrills (1968), Pearl (1971)

Santana

NO ROCK BAND DID AS MUCH to advance the cause of Latin and African-derived beats as Santana. The surprise success of the Woodstock Festival, their combination of irresistible rhythms and virtuoso, often mellifluous, guitar playing, courtesy of Mexican Carlos Santana, introduced new dynamics and textures to psychedelic rock.

The result was instant success for their self-titled debut album, followed by international acclaim for its follow-up, 1970's *Abraxas*. Probably the band's most accomplished album, it also yielded two enduring favorites—a dynamic, cha-cha-cha-style reworking of Fleetwood Mac's "Black Magic Woman," and Santana's own virtuoso piece, the supremely lyrical "Samba Pa Ti." Both were significant steps in Santana's slow transformation from psych-inspired intensity toward a smoother, more commercially viable sound.

Prior to a dramatic late-1970s revamp, when the guitarist reemerged with an almost entirely different band and a tight, disco-friendly sound, Santana had released a number of impressive, still ambitious records, including the classy, spiritually driven *Caravanserai* (1972) and the funky fusion of *Welcome* (1973). The enormous sales of *Supernatural*, Santana's star-studded 1999 comeback album, confirmed that unlike most of the band's contemporaries, Santana's potential pulling power has grown rather than declined since the late 1960s. The guitarist is now regarded as a fusion pioneer.

RIGHT *In the late 1960s, Santana played wild, Latino-inflected acid rock. Since then Carlos Santana has explored styles ranging from jazz and disco to the blues.*

Santana

Formed: San Francisco, California

Years active: 1967 to present

Definitive lineup: Carlos Santana, Gregg Rolie, José "Chepito" Areas, David Brown, Mike Carabello, Mike Shrieve

Genres: rock, acid rock, Latin rock

Key singles: "Black Magic Woman" (1970), "She's Not There" (1977)

Key albums: Abraxas (1970), Caravanserai (1972)

Woodstock

THE POSTER PROMISED "Three days of peace and music." But thanks to a quirk of timing, the unprecedented scale of the venture, the talent on display, and the three-hour movie that followed, Woodstock has eclipsed even the Summer of Love as the key moment of 1960s optimism. In truth, cynicism and worse (the Manson murders had taken place the previous weekend) had already set in. But for a grand finale to a remarkable decade, Woodstock will do very nicely.

BELOW LEFT *Joe Cocker was one of the hits of Woodstock, thanks to his extraordinary reworking of the Beatles' "With a Little Help From my Friends."*

BELOW *Despite a shaky performance with his new enlarged band, Jimi Hendrix managed to pull out an era-defining rendition of "The Star-Spangled Banner" as the festival closed.*

Fast track to oblivion

LOSING ONE'S HEAD over love has always been a source of inspiration for songwriters. But, as the rock era took off, so did the matter of losing one's mind. The relationship between alcohol and the entertainment business has always been unquestioned. In the 1950s and early 1960s, hardly less prevalent but rather more secret was the ubiquity of "pep pills."

From keeping the Beatles alert in their Hamburg club days to fueling the early and mid-1960s Mod scene in London, prescription drugs—lampooned in the Rolling Stones' song, "Mother's Little Helper"—seemed to be a fact of modern life. Being more closely associated with the cultier jazz and beatnik scene, marijuana was regarded with far greater suspicion because it went hand in hand with less familiar sounds and, by association, new ways of thinking. By the mid-1960s, its use around the pop scene was an open secret.

The mass-produced arrival in 1966 and 1967 of the powerful hallucinogen LSD ("acid") changed everything. Almost overnight, music and fashions changed, and the specter of a generation of hairy hippies adrift in LSD-induced "trips" prompted a mass moral panic. A series of

busts—Donovan, the Rolling Stones, all the Bay Area acid-rock bands—duly followed, but the authorities needn't have worried. Instead of encouraging the overthrow of civilization, drug use turned out to be counterrevolutionary, acting as an aid to creativity, though more usually a fast track to oblivion—as evidenced by a series of drug-related deaths at the end of the 1960s: Brian Jones, Jimi Hendrix, Janis Joplin, and Jim Morrison. It's now, of course, accepted that tobacco and alcohol remain the biggest threat to the wellbeing of rock musicians.

ABOVE *Rolling Stone Brian Jones leaves West London Magistrates Court in Kensington, London, in May 1967, after being charged with drugs offences. Two years later, the gifted Stone was dead.*

Tommy & the concept album

THOUGH THE BEATLES' 1967 masterpiece *Sgt Pepper* alerted the wider world to the creative possibilities of the long-playing record, in truth everyone from crooners to jazzers had been releasing themed albums for years. Even *Pepper*'s conceptual unity was more imagined than real, a ruse enhanced by the spectacle of the Beatles in costume on the cover, and the clever device of reprising the title track.

Someone who firmly believed that pop was an art form every bit the equal of more respected fields, such as classical and opera, was Who songwriter Pete Townshend. Having explored the idea in miniature on the band's 1966 album, *A Quick One*, Townshend developed it across four sides for *Tommy*, the Who's 1969 "rock opera," which firmly ushered in the era of the concept album. With a narrative storyline, underlying themes and motifs, and drawing on various styles, from music hall to opera, *Tommy* did much to advance rock's cause.

The concept album—invariably dressed in a gatefold sleeve bearing "meaningful" artwork—quickly became a badge of honor among progressive rock groups, and soon everyone from Deep Purple to the Moody Blues sought to solve the world's problems, or at least find the spiritual path, in the space of one record. By 1975, when Rick Wakeman was mounting a huge, loss-making, conceptual work involving putting the myths and legends of King Arthur on ice, it was clear that the game was up. Rock's mock-classical aspirations were a chief plank in punk's desire to turn it all upside down.

ABOVE AND BELOW *After its initial appearance as a two-LP rock opera, the Who's Tommy became a movie and, in 1972, was performed on stage.*

"Three days of peace and music"

It was by no means the first hippie festival, the biggest, or even the best. It wasn't even held on the West Coast, where what Otis Redding dubbed "The Love Crowd" hung out. Woodstock took place on a dairy farm near Bethel in upstate New York. The Beatles, the Rolling Stones, Led Zeppelin, the Byrds, the Doors, even Bob Dylan who lived up the road, either had other commitments or else declined to perform. In fact, the only genuine superstars to grace the stage over the weekend of August 15–18, 1969, were Jimi Hendrix and Janis Joplin. Ironically, neither was at their best. But plenty others were, and Woodstock dramatically changed the fortunes of many acts who performed there.

The festival began with a pair of furious acoustic strummers, Richie Havens and Melanie, before Joan Baez ended the opening night with a reminder of the protest movement's folk origins. Country Joe McDonald's infamous "Fish Cheer" heralded a heavier Saturday fare, where Bay Area Latino-rockers Santana saw off several bigger names, including the Grateful Dead. The night ended with dramatic sets from Sly & the Family Stone and the Who.

Sunday witnessed a show-stopping display of idiot dancing from Joe Cocker, a coming of age set by Crosby, Stills, Nash & Young, and Jimi Hendrix closing the event on Monday morning. The several thousand stragglers who remained witnessed one of the most extraordinary feats in rock—the guitarist's dramatic reinterpretation of "The Star-Spangled Banner" as a powerful antiwar statement.

BELOW *Although Santana were one of the bands whose performance at Woodstock transformed their career, as this photo shows, the festival was as much about the unprecedented crowds.*

Frank Zappa

ALTHOUGH THE CUT-AND-PASTE effect has been widespread in rock since the early 1980s, thanks to the ubiquity of the sampler, two decades earlier Frank Zappa was mixing and matching styles in real time. Fronting a band named, aptly, the Mothers of Invention, Zappa was a musical prodigy, whose tastes ran the gamut from masters of the twentieth-century avant-garde (Varèse, Webern) to street-corner doo-wop (the Penguins, the 4 Deuces).

After serving a long apprenticeship writing and producing local artists in the environs of Los Angeles, Zappa and the Mothers emerged in 1966 with a pioneering two-LP set, *Freak Out!*, a mix of beat-group pastiche and lengthy, percussion-led improvisation. The group hit an inventive peak on *Absolutely Free* (1967) and *We're Only in It for the Money* (1968), two dazzlingly eclectic records that managed to lampoon the underground scene that was their constituent audience.

Disbanding the original Mothers in 1969, Zappa enjoyed great success with the jazz-rock solo album, *Hot Rats*, and managed to maintain his reputation as one of the most distinctive rock performers throughout the 1970s and 1980s. Risqué humor had always been a large part of Zappa's appeal, and in 1985 he took his fight against censorship in rock lyrics to the U.S. Senate. Just as he was being recognized as a composer in the classical sense of the word, rock's most prolific and musically literate modern master was struck down by prostate cancer.

Frank Zappa

Born:
December 21, 1940, Baltimore, Maryland

Died:
December 4, 1993

Years active:
1955–93

Genres: *rock, avant-garde rock, acid rock, jazz rock, progressive rock, doo-wop, contemporary classical*

Key singles:
"Trouble Every Day" (1966), "Peaches En Regalia" (1970)

Key albums:
We're Only in It for the Money *(1968),* Hot Rats *(1969)*

LEFT *Frank Zappa's Mothers of Invention made their debut in Britain in September 1967. Many London longhairs were confused by Zappa's repeated digs at hippies.*

FAR LEFT *A master satirist, and a sound sculptor who drew on a vast range of musical styles, Frank Zappa was also a hugely underrated guitarist.*

Captain Beefheart

NO ONE HAS TAKEN the classic rock combination of guitar/bass/drums as far out as Captain Beefheart. For several months between fall 1968 and spring 1969, Beefheart (actually Don Vliet from LA County, California) tapped out multiple instrumental fragments on a piano he couldn't play, each meticulously notated by his drummer Drumbo, who then taught the parts to the rest of Beefheart's Magic Band.

To many ears, the resulting two-disc set, *Trout Mask Replica* (1969), sounds like a formless cacophony, its rhythms syncopated to death, guitar lines veering off in multiple directions, and the singer barking nonsense verse with little regard for cues or timing. Others insist it's up there alongside Picasso's *Guernica* and James Joyce's *Ulysses* as rock's most awesome achievement. While the edgier acts of post-punk (the Fall, the Pop Group) have drawn inspiration from Beefheart, none comes close in terms of turning rock on its head so thoroughly.

Despite its ear-bending originality, *Trout Mask Replica* was built on a blend of the blues, R&B, psychedelia, and free jazz. A 1970 follow-up, *Lick My Decals Off, Baby*, was equally ambitious, though with *The Spotlight Kid* (1972) and *Clear Spot* (1973), Beefheart swam closer to the mainstream. Retiring in the mid-1970s, he returned for a trio of rapturously received punk-era albums, before abandoning music again in the 1980s. He painted primitive abstracts at his home in California until his death in 2010.

ABOVE *Beefheart (center) with his 1969-era Magic Band, the outfit responsible for rock's most impressive feat of musical daring, Trout Mask Replica.*

Captain Beefheart

Born: *January 15, 1941, Glendale, California*	**Years active:** *1964–83*	**Key singles:** *"Yellow Brick Road" (1967), "Ice Cream for Crow" (1982)*	**Key albums:** Trout Mask Replica *(1969),* Doc at the Radar Station *(1980)*
Died: *December 17, 2010*	**Genres:** *avant-garde rock, blues rock, acid rock*		

Featuring

Led Zeppelin • John Lennon • Paul McCartney • Marvin Gaye • Deep Purple • Black Sabbath •
Crosby, Stills, Nash & Young • Eagles • Miles Davis • Leonard Cohen • Yes • Genesis •
Marc Bolan & T. Rex • Roxy Music • David Bowie • Pink Floyd • Alice Cooper • The Stooges •
Kiss • Queen • Sly & the Family Stone • George Clinton & P-Funk • Fleetwood Mac • Elton John •
Eric Clapton • Rod Stewart • Bruce Springsteen • Bob Marley • Lee "Scratch" Perry • Patti Smith •
Ramones • Sex Pistols • Bee Gees • Elvis Costello • Blondie • AC/DC • The Clash •

1970s

1970s: Introduction

THE 1960S HAD BEEN A GIANT LEAP into the unknown. The decade that followed, which started with a hangover that cast a pall over much of the next ten years, felt like a retreat. The "We" decade had become the "Me" decade. Rock music, by now a vast and widely eclectic edifice, reflected the change, first by an extended period of loud, gaudy escape, then, later in the decade, with the last and perhaps most threatening of all the great rock subcultural movements—punk.

It didn't begin well. The demise of the Beatles in March 1970, followed by the deaths of three huge countercultural icons, Jimi Hendrix, Janis Joplin, and Jim Morrison, was a huge blow to rock's role as a key player in any wider social revolution. But as gigs began to move increasingly from concert halls into stadiums, and with album sales going through the roof, its power as an economic force continued to grow. It was taking itself more seriously, too, with progressive rock dominating the early part of the decade. That meant concept albums, further technical advances, greater emphasis on musicianship, and ever-more elaborate concert performances. Inevitably, glam rock's showy stars were treated with contempt.

ABOVE *After the gaudy excesses of glam and prog rock in the early 1970s, Bruce Springsteen brought a streetwise touch of sobriety and tradition to popular music.*

LEFT *The Sex Pistols' "God Save the Queen" briefly reacquainted rock with its insurrectionary potential.*

BELOW LEFT *Pink Floyd's The Dark Side of the Moon managed to transcend genre and became an international sales phenomenon.*

Sounds of the decade

"War":
Edwin Starr (1970)

"Maggie May":
Rod Stewart (1971)

"American Pie":
Don McLean (1972)

"Superstition":
Stevie Wonder (1972)

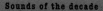

1970-1979

BELOW *Deep Purple's Ritchie Blackmore was one of a handful of guitarists whose virtuoso skills afforded them superstar status during the early 1970s. And it wasn't only guitarists...*

Hard rock, a tougher, more reined-in variant of psychedelic power trios, such as Cream and Hendrix, yielded hugely popular stadium acts, such as Led Zeppelin and Deep Purple, while the peculiarly British glam phenomenon aimed a much diluted version of rock at the preteen market. Less loud and showy were the (mainly American) singer-songwriters and country rockers, who tended to cater for a maturing audience of ex-hippies and baby boomers.

Cue punk rock. Antishowbiz, anti-indulgence, antihippie, and, in its purest form, even antirock, punk was a loud cry from the streets in a bid to reacquaint rock with its most primitive, rebellious urges.

Essentially British, though with some crossover with reggae, the rebel music coming out of Jamaica, punk represented a serious threat to the music industry and beyond. But as it faded, rap and hip hop, the punk rock of black urban America, emerged at the end of the decade to signal another radical sonic departure.

"Free Bird":
Lynyrd Skynyrd (1974)

"Fame":
David Bowie (1975)

"Bohemian Rhapsody":
Queen (1975)

"God Save the Queen":
Sex Pistols (1977)

"I Feel Love":
Donna Summer (1977)

"Night Fever":
Bee Gees (1978)

1970s: Time line

1970

January 1970

Simon & Garfunkel's *Bridge Over Troubled Water* is released. The album's enormous, chart-topping success confirms the arrival of the singer-songwriter era.

April 1970

Paul McCartney says he has no plans to work with the other three Beatles again. The "Paul is quitting the Beatles" headline confirms the arrival of a very different decade.

Paul quits

May 1970

Weeks after expressing his doubts about the trappings of stardom, guitarist Peter Green bows out of Fleetwood Mac, following an extraordinarily powerful farewell 45, "The Green Manalishi (with the Two-Prong Crown)."

March 1971

Coming just months after the controversial "Working Class Hero," Plastic Ono Band's "Power to the People" confirms the growing politicization of ex-Beatle John Lennon.

July 1971

Controversial Doors frontman Jim Morrison is found dead in his bath in Paris. He is buried in the city's famous Père Lachaise Cemetery.

November 1971

"Coz I Luv You" becomes the first in a run of six British No. 1 hits for Slade, whose penchant for garish costumes and soccer-crowd-style choruses intensify the growing phenomenon of glam rock.

August 1972

The rock 'n' roll revival, already under way in the United States with a Broadway production of *Grease*, is marked by an all-star festival at London's Wembley Stadium, featuring Chuck Berry, Jerry Lee Lewis, Little Richard, and, flogging retro clothes, future Sex Pistols manager Malcolm McLaren.

Jimmy Cliff

September 1972

Reggae music receives a further boost with the London premiere of *The Harder They Come*, starring singer Jimmy Cliff. Joining him on the soundtrack are the Maytals, the Melodians, and "Israelites" singer Desmond Dekker.

August 1970

The third and biggest Isle of Wight Festival features the Doors, the Who, Miles Davis, and Jimi Hendrix, but the event is interrupted when activists demand that it goes on for free.

Al Wilson

September 1970

The drug-related deaths of Jimi Hendrix and Canned Heat's sweet-voiced guitarist Al Wilson cast a further pall over rock's lifestyle revolution. The death of Janis Joplin, from a heroin overdose the following month, only adds to the feeling of failure.

1971

January 1971

Performance, starring Mick Jagger and Anita Pallenberg, girlfriend of Stones' guitarist Keith Richards, premieres in London. A dark, fragmentary study of pop decadence, it is later hailed as a British movie classic.

1972

February 1972

Weeks after the Bloody Sunday massacre in Northern Ireland, Paul McCartney releases "Give Ireland Back to the Irish." In June, John Lennon wades in with his own "Sunday Bloody Sunday."

March 1972

Ex-Beatle turned Apple moviemaker Ringo Starr shoots T. Rex at the Empire Pool, Wembley, London. Much of the footage ends up in *Born to Boogie*, released at the end of the year.

Ringo Starr and Marc Bolan

July 1972

After 1,279 performances, the hippie-inspired rock musical *Hair* closes on Broadway, further evidence that the Age of Aquarius has passed its expiry date.

October 1972

The arrest, for possession of marijuana, of Joe Cocker and six members of his entourage in Adelaide, Australia, sparks a national debate concerning drug use.

Elvis in Honolulu

1973

January 1973

A television audience reported to be in excess of one billion tunes in to watch Elvis Presley performing live by satellite at the International Convention Center in Honolulu, Hawaii.

March 1973

Having been performing it in concert since January 1972, Pink Floyd finally unveil *The Dark Side of the Moon* on vinyl.

1970s: Time line

Emerson, Lake & Palmer

March 1973

Progressive rock trio Emerson, Lake & Palmer embark on a world tour, taking with them 20 tons of equipment, a crew of 50 and a full, proscenium stage set.

May 1973

Hippie-style entrepreneur Richard Branson launches his Virgin record label with *Tubular Bells*, an extended instrumental work by multi-instrumentalist Mike Oldfield. The album will stay in the British charts for over five years.

July 1973

In terms of dramatic impact, David Bowie eclipses his glam-rock rivals by announcing his retirement from live performance at the climax of his show at London's Hammersmith Odeon.

April 1974

Swedish quartet ABBA win the Eurovision Song Contest with the distinctly contemporary sounding "Waterloo." Unusual for Eurovision winners, the group will go on to enjoy enormous mainstream success as a credible music act.

ABBA

June 1974

Initially touted as a Velvet Underground reunion, the "ACNE" (Ayers, Cale, Nico, and Eno) concert at the Rainbow, London, features four cult heroes performing solo sets.

Jefferson Starship

July 1974

The nucleus of acid-rock high-fliers Jefferson Airplane regroup as Jefferson Starship and record *Dragon Fly*, the first in a series of albums that will redefine the band along smoother 1970s lines.

1976

October 1975

Bruce Springsteen hype reaches fever pitch when both *Time* and *Newsweek* magazines feature him as cover star in the same week. The so-called "new Dylan" requests a dampening of publicity during his first visit to Britain in November.

April 1976

Ex-Humble Pie guitarist Peter Frampton tops the U.S. chart with a live album, *Frampton Comes Alive!* A tie-in 45, "Show Me the Way," features Frampton's notorious "talk box" voice effect.

September 1975

The chart-topping success of Rod Stewart's highly polished *Atlantic Crossing* signals the end of the Faces and the start of a new era in the singer's career.

1973-1976

August 1973

Despite numerous uncomplimentary reviews suggesting that the band had taken the concept album idea too far, Jethro Tull's *A Passion Play* hits No. 1 in the charts in the United States.

1974

January 1974

Bob Dylan and the Band embark on a widely acclaimed two-month U.S. tour, their first together since 1966. A two-LP live album, *Before the Flood*, duly follows.

March 1974

Embryonic new-wave act Television, featuring guitarist Tom Verlaine, debut at CBGB, a new rock club located on New York's Bowery. The venue quickly becomes the focal point for the city's burgeoning punk scene.

Television featuring Tom Verlaine

September 1974

The three-day Zaire 74 festival, starring James Brown, B. B. King, and Miriam Makeba, takes place in Kinshasa, Congo, in the buildup for the "Rumble in the Jungle" boxing match between Muhammad Ali and George Foreman.

1975

February 1975

Guitarist Ritchie Blackmore begins work on a solo project, *Ritchie Blackmore's Rainbow*, while still a member of Deep Purple. He later quits Deep Purple and fires all of Rainbow, before reemerging in the fall with a new lineup.

Ritchie Blackmore

June 1975

Troubled psychedelic troubadour Tim Buckley, who in recent years has restyled himself as the first man of "sex funk," dies of a heroin overdose at the end of a tour.

June 1976

15 Big Ones is the first Brian Wilson-produced Beach Boys album in a decade. The reclusive songwriter also joins the band for an NBC-TV

Brian Wilson (center)

broadcast in August, though there is little visual evidence that he's comfortable with the situation.

August 1976

Eric Clapton, a white British bluesman, baffles his audience in Birmingham, England, with an anti-immigration speech that concludes with the call to "Keep Britain white." The extraordinary outburst prompts the formation of Rock Against Racism.

September 1976

Boston's debut album charts in the United States, thanks in large part to the blossoming Album/Adult-Oriented Rock (AOR) FM radio stations. The growth of the AOR format means that America is largely unaware of the emergence of punk rock across the Atlantic.

1970s: Time line

October 1976
The Song Remains the Same, Led Zeppelin's concert-plus-fantasy-sequences movie, mostly shot during 1973, premieres in New York.

Sex Pistol Johnny Rotten

December 1976
A moral panic ensues after an expletives-filled television appearance by punk-rock antiheroes, the Sex Pistols, alerts Britain to the emergence of a new, nihilistic subculture.

1977

February 1977
A decade on from their formation in blues-obsessed London, an entirely different, California-based Fleetwood Mac top the U.S. charts with the era-defining and highly polished *Rumours*.

August 1977
King of Rock 'n' Roll Elvis Presley is found slumped on the floor of his en-suite bathroom at his Graceland mansion. An abundance of fatty foods, combined with misuse of prescription drugs, are said to have contributed to his death at 42.

1978

March 1978
Five months after the release of *Bat Out of Hell*, Meat Loaf appears on NBC-TV's *Saturday Night Live*, a key moment in transforming a little-known actor/singer into a national—and soon international—phenomenon.

Meat Loaf

April 1978
Bob Marley, who survived an assassination attempt on his life in 1976, headlines the One Love Peace Concert in Kingston, Jamaica. While performing "Jamming," he brings the country's two political opponents together on stage as an act of reconciliation.

October 1978
Keith Richards is given a suspended sentence in his heroin-trafficking case, which arose from a bust in Toronto, Canada, in February 1977. He is also asked to perform a charity concert.

1979

February 1979
Only just released on bail for the alleged murder of girlfriend Nancy Spungen the previous October, 21-year-old Sex Pistol Sid Vicious is found dead of a heroin overdose in New York.

May 1979
As a Mod revival gets under way in Britain, a movie adaptation of the Who's 1973 album *Quadrophenia* premieres in London. Up-and-coming new-wavers Sting and Toyah feature in the cast.

Toyah Willcox

1976–1979

May 1977
Punk neophytes the Clash, the Slits, Buzzcocks, and Subway Sect take off around Britain on the White Riot tour, which climaxes in a night of seat-shredding violence at London's Rainbow.

June 1977
After the Sex Pistols' "God Save the Queen" tops some British charts (though, suspiciously, not the official one), two of the group, including singer Johnny Rotten, are attacked in separate incidents.

July 1977
Pulsing electronica and hot disco vocals give Donna Summer a thrilling, if unlikely, summer chart-topper in Britain with "I Feel Love." Producer Giorgio Moroder's synthesized backing track will in time alter the sound of dance music forever.

April 1978
The *Saturday Night Fever* soundtrack, which has topped the U.S. chart since January, finally brings disco fever to Britain, when both the album and the Bee Gees' spin-off 45, "Night Fever," are installed at the top on both sides of the Atlantic.

Saturday Night Fever

June 1978
After an ignominious walkout by Johnny Rotten in January, the Sex Pistols limp on with a double A-sided 45, with bassist Sid Vicious and exiled British train robber Ronnie Biggs handling lead vocals.

September 1978
Despite the onslaught of punk, disco, and AOR, the Grateful Dead take their hippie-inspired jams to Egypt, where they perform three shows in the shadow of the Great Pyramid.

August 1979
Coming on the back of the success of Cheap Trick's "I Want You To Want Me," the Knack's "My Sharona" confirms the emergence of power pop, first mooted in 1977 after ex-Pistol Glen Matlock formed the Rich Kids.

September 1979
"Rapper's Delight" by the Sugarhill Gang is the latest and most convincing evidence that rap, the sound of subterranean New York, has the potential to go mainstream.

Sugarhill Gang

December 1979
Paul McCartney's Wings, the Who, and Queen join new-wave acts the Pretenders, Elvis Costello, and the Clash in a series of charity concerts at London's Hammersmith Odeon, to raise money for the people of Kampuchea.

Led Zeppelin

WITH AN ABUNDANCE of grandeur and heavyweight excess attached to their name, Led Zeppelin are the quintessential 1970s rock band, and the founding fathers of hard rock and the entire heavy-metal diaspora. No act did so much to create the cult of the "album band" as Led Zeppelin, who, while resisting television and the singles market, instead undertook long and lucrative stadium tours. Along the way, they released at least half a dozen of rock's most enduring big sellers, before a series of setbacks—climaxing in the booze-related death of drummer John Bonham—brought the band to a dramatic halt late in 1980.

The quartet, formed by ace London-based session guitarist Jimmy Page, had its origins in the Yardbirds. This, the most guitar-oriented of the British beat-boom groups, imploded in summer 1968, leaving Page—who had joined in 1966—to reassemble a new team to fulfill a prebooked tour of Scandinavia. By the end of the year, the New Yardbirds had become Led Zeppelin—a dynamic rock machine pitting Page's accomplished, hard-blues style against singer Robert Plant's white-blues wail and the most powerful engine room in the business. Over the course of four era-defining albums, between 1969's *Led Zeppelin* and 1971's *Led Zeppelin IV* (alias "Four Symbols"), the band banished any

residual psychedelia and created an all-conquering rock 'n' roll behemoth that combined virtuoso playing with a tough, riff-laden accessibility. On occasion, the superstar image—accentuated by countless tales of offstage debauchery—eclipsed Zepp's innate musicality, which, particularly on 1970's *Led Zeppelin III*, also drew on folk and Celtic sources.

A grandstanding mid-1970s, with their own label and a colossal concert movie (*The Song Remains the Same*), came to a sad finale in 1980. In later years the band's reputation was restored during the grunge era, prompting various box-set releases and one reunion in 2007, with Bonham's son Jason behind the kit.

LEFT *Led Zeppelin live at Madison Square Garden, New York, June 1977. The gong, the double-necked guitar, and the embroidered suit were all trappings of the 1970s rock superstar.*

RIGHT *Golden-maned and with a voice that soared like an instrument, Robert Plant was hard rock's quintessential frontman. But it was guitarist Jimmy Page who represented the soul of Led Zeppelin.*

Led Zeppelin

Formed: *London, England*
Years active: *1968–80*

Definitive lineup: *Robert Plant, Jimmy Page, John Paul Jones, John Bonham*

Genres: *hard rock, heavy metal*

Key singles: *"Whole Lotta Love" (1969), "Stairway to Heaven" (1971)*
Key albums: Led Zeppelin II *(1969),* Led Zeppelin IV *(1971)*

John Lennon

THE MOST OUTSPOKEN and controversial Beatle during the 1960s, John Lennon's keen antiestablishment inclinations came to a head between 1970 and 1972. He subsequently turned his back on politics following the landslide reelection of President Nixon. Instead, he embodied the decade's "the personal is political" philosophy, and infamously spent the last five years of his life rejecting fame and turning the old domestic order on its head by restyling himself "a house husband." During this up-and-down decade, he also recorded some of the finest work of his career.

John Lennon

Born: *October 9, 1940, Liverpool, England*

Died: *December 8, 1980*

Years active: *1957–75, 1980*

Genres: *rock, pop*

Key singles: *"Cold Turkey" (1969), "Imagine" (1971)*

Key albums: *John Lennon/ Plastic Ono Band (1970), Imagine (1971)*

Arguably, nothing Lennon did after the Beatles bettered his first solo album, *John Lennon/ Plastic Ono Band*, released in December 1970. A visceral meditation on love, pain, and loss, it remains one of the most deeply cathartic records ever made. Months later, Lennon gifted the world its most utopian anthem in "Imagine," which remains his best-known song. ("Gimme Some Truth," also from the *Imagine* album, was a reminder of his more caustic side.)

After the politically charged songwriting on *Some Time in New York City* (1972), Lennon hit a more sentimental streak for *Mind Games* (1973), which coincided with his break from wife Yoko Ono. He got honest again for *Walls and Bridges* (1974), summoned up his inner teenager for *Rock 'n' Roll* (1975), and returned home to his partner. He ended a spell out of the limelight by embracing an AOR sound for *Double Fantasy*, his 1980 comeback collaboration with Yoko. On December 8 that year, he died at the hands of a murderous fan.

BELOW *As Lennon entered the most political phase in his career, he appeared on the BBC's Top of the Pops, shorn of his long hair and sporting a prominent peace slogan. That's a blindfolded Yoko Ono behind him.*

Paul McCartney

AS THE MELODIOUS and most accommodating Beatle, who fought desperately to save the band, it is little surprise that Paul McCartney has been by far the most successful ex-member of the Beatles. After a long and sometimes erratic solo career, "Macca" has in recent years grown more comfortable with his "Fab" past, and has reemerged as the keeper of the Beatles flame. More than ever, his characteristically lengthy concerts draw on his work with the band, together with mainstays from his impressive solo catalog.

Between 1973's *Band on the Run* and the effervescent, dance-floor crossover hit, "Coming Up" (1980), McCartney neatly straddled the 1970s pop/rock divide with great success. But, creatively at least, his solo career got off to a slow, uncertain start with a couple of low-key albums that seemed almost in denial of his illustrious past. Forming Wings and striking up a writing partnership with ex-Moody Blues frontman Denny Laine changed all that. *Band on the Run* and *Venus and Mars* (1975) were highly successful, and by the late 1970s McCartney's knack of writing songs that the whole world wanted to sing

returned for the enormous seasonal hit, "Mull of Kintyre" (1977). Like many of his contemporaries, McCartney endured a difficult 1980s, though he reemerged revitalized after participating in the Beatles' 1995 *Anthology* project, with albums such as *Flaming Pie* (1997), while ventures into orchestral music and pseudonymous electronic projects (as the Fireman) confirm his continued desire to break from type.

ABOVE *By far the most successful ex-Beatle, Paul McCartney has kept remarkably active since 1970, with a variety of musical projects and regular gigging. Here he is performing in London in 1979, on another career high.*

Paul McCartney

Born: *June 18, 1942, Liverpool, England*

Years active: *1957 to present*

Genres: *pop, rock*

Key singles: *"Live and Let Die" (1973), "Coming Up" (1980)*

Key albums: Band on the Run *(1973),* Flaming Pie *(1997)*

Charity records

NOT ALWAYS ASSOCIATED with music of the highest quality, the charity record invariably relies on star power and an emotive cause instead of artistic greatness. Ever since the enormous mid-1980s success of "Do They Know It's Christmas?" and "We Are the World," which added to the money mountain created by the transatlantic Live Aid extravaganza, charity records have been racing up the charts, particularly at Christmas, with almost monotonous regularity.

The precedent for this large-scale, rock-to-the-rescue initiative was the Concert for Bangla Desh, organized by George Harrison and Ravi Shankar, who assembled an impressive cast, including Bob Dylan and Eric Clapton, for an August 1971 benefit concert at New York's Madison Square Garden. A subsequent triple-album box set sold well, though poor organization meant that millions of dollars failed to reach their intended destination until many years later. But lessons were learned, and greater transparency has since been demanded of the charitable rock initiative.

Charities and causes that have benefited in recent times include victims of the 9/11 disaster, the 2004 Asian tsunami, and Stand Up to Cancer. Arguably, in strictly creative terms, no one has managed to better Harrison's "Bangla Desh" single, which provided the initial spark for the subsequent live events.

BELOW *"Quiet Beatle" George Harrison eclipsed the success of 1970's* All Things Must Pass *and "My Sweet Lord" with the all-star Concert for Bangla Desh.*

Rock goes to the movies

WITH MOTION PICTURES STILL hugely powerful during the 1950s, the emergence of rock 'n' roll owed much of its initial popularity to the big screen. The movies *Blackboard Jungle* (1955) and *Rock Around the Clock* (1956) brought scenes of ecstatic, jiving, and even rioting teenagers to every major town in the Western world. Numerous star-studded movies, such as *Don't Knock the Rock* (1957), duly followed, including a run of increasingly flimsy Elvis Presley capers.

The Beatles' early success seemed to go hand in hand with the movies. *A Hard Day's Night* (1964) and *Help!* (1965) both reflected the new era's optimism, as well as the so-called Fab Four's life-affirming zaniness. A slew of similarly fun-packed pop capers followed (1965's *Catch Us If You Can*, starring the Dave Clark Five, was a rare exception), before Peter Watkins's magnificent *Privilege* (1967) revealed the more sinister potential of pop. Two movies from 1970, *Woodstock* and the Rolling Stones' *Gimme Shelter* (which climaxed in the murder of a fan in front of the stage at the Altamont Festival), revealed contrasting light and dark aspects of the new-fangled rock culture. By the end of the 1970s, both punk (*Jubilee*, *The Great Rock 'n' Roll Swindle*) and the revived Mod (*Quadrophenia*) subcultures were celebrated on celluloid.

THE MUSIC THAT THRILLED THE WORLD... AND THE KILLING THAT STUNNED IT!

The Rolling Stones Gimme Shelter

DIRECTED BY DAVID MAYSLES, ALBERT MAYSLES, CHARLOTTE ZWERIN · A MAYSLES FILMS, INC. PRODUCTION
DISTRIBUTED BY 20TH CENTURY-FOX FILM CORPORATION

A DAVID DEUTSCH PRODUCTION
THE DAVE CLARK FIVE
CATCH US IF YOU CAN GO!!
BARBARA FERRIS
Screenplay by PETER NICHOLS
Produced by DAVID DEUTSCH
Directed by JOHN BOORMAN

ABOVE *In contrast to the Beatles' warm and witty movie vehicles,* Catch Us If You Can *sent out a more complicated message, despite featuring the cheery Dave Clark Five.*

LEFT Gimme Shelter *documents the Rolling Stones' 1969 tour of the United States. More shockingly, it also depicts the murder of a fan at the Altamont Festival.*

In recent times, with rock having acquired a certain cachet, the star biopic has taken some imaginative turns with big-screen portrayals of Johnny Cash (*Walk the Line*, 2005), Bob Dylan (*I'm Not There*, 2007), and Ian Dury (*Sex & Drugs & Rock & Roll*, 2010).

Marvin Gaye

THE TRANSFORMATION of Marvin Gaye, from fully integrated member of Motown's inner circle (he was, after all, married to boss Berry Gordy's daughter) to a blissed-out maverick who dared to break the mold, was one of popular music's most remarkable feats of rock-inspired maturity. The golden boy of Hitsville USA becoming a socially conscious internationalist with his majestic, if initially misunderstood, epic *What's Going On* (1971) marked a watershed for Motown and for black music in general.

For the best part of the 1960s, Marvin Gaye played the game. Gifted with a sublimely sweet voice and picture-book looks, he was the Nat "King" Cole of the Motown Sound, a rare male vocal soloist on the label, who still liked to play drums on Motown sessions long after his breakthrough in 1963 with "Pride and Joy" and "Can I Get a Witness."

A blissed-out maverick

A string of mid-1960s hits with Tammi Terrell was cut short when Terrell was diagnosed in 1967 with a brain tumor. The news hit Gaye hard. Even the extraordinary artistic achievement of Gaye's "I Heard It Through the Grapevine," taped in 1967 and an international No. 1 in 1968 and 1969, failed to lift the singer's gloom. Berry Gordy's initial reluctance to back the record, Motown's biggest seller at the time, anticipated the problems Gaye encountered in getting Gordy to sanction the release of his masterwork, *What's Going On*. Once again, the singer's musical instinct was proved right. By now a stoned and bearded mystic, Gaye dreamt up a sonic tapestry unlike any other—a seemingly effortless blend of psychedelia, soul, and jazz, delivered with singer-songwriterly acumen.

Let's Get It On (1973) was even more successful, though by the mid-1970s, personal problems, followed by the advance of disco, left Gaye sidelined. In 1982 the utterly contemporary and erotically charged "Sexual Healing" witnessed a magnificent revival in Gaye's fortunes, which was cruelly curtailed on April 1, 1984, when the singer was shot dead by his fundamentalist father.

Marvin Gaye

Born: *April 2, 1939, Washington, DC*

Died: *April 1, 1984*

Years active: *1958–84*

Genres: *soul, pop, R&B, funk*

Key singles: *"I Heard It Through the Grapevine" (1968), "Sexual Healing" (1982)*

Key albums: What's Going On *(1971),* Let's Get It On *(1973)*

Hard rock

WHILE IT'S OFTEN said that the
Kinks' "You Really Got Me" (1964)
struck the first power chord for hard
rock, in terms of sheer metallic
attitude, Link Wray's 1957 single,
"Rumble"—an instrumental deemed
so menacing that it was subject to
a radio ban—is more likely the
elemental moment. The heavier,
darker aspects of psychedelia raised
the stakes during the late 1960s,
and in the years after 1969 hard
rock—soon interchangeable with
heavy metal and sometimes,
derogatorily, cock rock—began
to crystallize as a genre.

The emergence of Led Zeppelin, followed by
Deep Purple and Black Sabbath, located the
music's center of gravity in Britain, though
San Francisco's Hell's Angels-endorsed and
improbably loud power trio, Blue Cheer, had
anticipated the genre with January 1968's
Vincebus Eruptum.

TOP *Though more basic than rivals Led Zeppelin and Deep Purple, Black Sabbath, fronted by Ozzy Osbourne, had more influence on punk and thrash metal.*

ABOVE *Deep Purple's Ian Gillan performing in Copenhagen in 1972. The band, noted for their epic live performances, combined muscular riffs with musical flash.*

OPPOSITE *Gravel-voiced Paul Rodgers of Free was the quintessential cock-rock hero. The band's "All Right Now," a huge transatlantic hit in 1970, marked the arrival of hard rock in the singles charts.*

Two other psychedelic-era power trios, the Jimi Hendrix Experience and Cream, fed more readily into early 1970s hard rock. Hendrix's dandy sexuality was downshifted into something more robust and accessible by blue-jeaned frontmen, such as Robert Plant (Led Zeppelin), Ian Gillan (Deep Purple), and Paul Rodgers (Free). Tighter rein was kept on the rhythm section, too, with any acid-inspired flourishes brought into line with a more structured, sledgehammer riffery. This was most apparent in America, where bands such as Grand Funk Railroad, Mountain, and, later, Aerosmith clearly opted for ballsiness over postpsychedelic fancy.

If Led Zeppelin at times looked and sounded like the Who (or, perhaps, the Jeff Beck Group) writ large, Black Sabbath were something else again. Slower, more obviously au fait with pulp Satanism, and, crucially, devoid of almost every trace of the blues, Sabbath's chugga-chugga primitivism was embodied in the near catatonic stage presence of singer Ozzy Osbourne and became a template for 1980s thrash metal. At the other extreme were flamboyant mid-1970s crossover acts Queen and Kiss, whose visual excess fed into 1980s metal.

Ballsiness and sledgehammer riffery

5 Top hard-rock artists

Jimi Hendrix: *"Voodoo Child (Slight Return)"* (1970)

Led Zeppelin: *"Black Dog"* (1971)
Free: *"All Right Now"* (1970)

Black Sabbath: *"Paranoid"* (1970)
Deep Purple: *"Black Night"* (1970)

Deep Purple

EARLY 1970S BELTERS, such as "Speed King," "Strange Kind of Woman," and "Smoke on the Water" (the first port of call for every budding guitarist), inevitably define Deep Purple as a first-generation hard-rock band. December 1972's two-LP set *Made in Japan*, where songs were stretched from 7 to 20 minutes in length, remains the quintessential hard-rock live album. But like rivals Led Zeppelin, Deep Purple were always more than that.

A surprise Top 5 U.S. hit in 1968 with a strong, groovy version of Joe South's "Hush" threatened to make Deep Purple Britain's answer to Vanilla Fudge. But after poaching big-lunged vocalist Ian Gillan and bassist Roger Glover from Episode Six, organist Jon Lord steered the group in a classical rock direction with a concerto for band and orchestra released at the end of 1969. By summer 1970, though, the robust playing of guitarist Ritchie Blackmore had engineered a move toward a tougher sound with *In Rock*, Purple's breakthrough album, which was followed by two crossover 45s, "Black Night" and "Fireball" (1971), and even heavier albums, including concert set *Made in Japan*.

Gillan's departure late in 1973 was followed by Blackmore's two years later to form Rainbow. Though both enjoyed further success with their own projects, as well as Purple's return to action in 1984, it's the band's early 1970s work that still reverberates loudest.

Deep Purple

Formed: *Hertford, England*

Years active: *1968–76, 1984 to present*

Definitive lineup: *Ian Gillan, Ritchie Blackmore, Jon Lord, Roger Glover, Ian Paice*

Genres: *hard rock, heavy metal*

Key singles: *"Black Night" (1970), "Fireball" (1971)*

Key albums: Machine Head *(1972),* Made in Japan *(1972)*

LEFT *Ritchie Blackmore with his trademark Fender Stratocaster. It was the instrument he used to record "Smoke on the Water," one of the most famous riffs in rock and a rite of passage for aspiring guitarists.*

Black Sabbath

COMMONLY REGARDED as the founding fathers of heavy metal, Black Sabbath had an impact, especially in their earliest work, that was felt far beyond—from stoner rock ("Sweet Leaf") and punk ("Paranoid") to goth ("Black Sabbath"). Critical credibility was a long time coming, although the kind of accusations hurled at the band—that they were clichéd, repetitive, and relatively untutored—looked like assets after the arrival of punk.

Hailing from England's Midlands, Black Sabbath were a blue-collar response to the electrifying, virtuoso-driven, blues-rock bands, such as Cream. Just as Alice Cooper was doing in the United States, the Ozzy Osbourne-fronted quartet kept a tighter grip on the sound, dropped the guitar tunings, and hammed up the horror to meet the thrill-seeking demands of the new decade's antiflower children. The result was a pair of albums (*Black Sabbath* and *Paranoid*), both released in 1970, that met with instant success on both sides of the Atlantic.

As touring and the rock 'n' roll lifestyle took an inevitable toll, Sabbath's vision became increasingly blurred. After a brief resurrection in 1978 with the punkish "Never Say Die" hit single, frontman Ozzy Osbourne was replaced in 1979 by Ronnie James

Dio—the man responsible for popularizing the now ubiquitous two-finger "metal horns" gesture. Ozzy returned to the fold in 1996 and stayed for the best part of a decade, becoming a household name in the process thanks to his starring role in MTV's phenomenally successful *The Osbournes* reality television show.

ABOVE *Even during Sabbath's 1970s heyday, the headline-grabbing antics of Ozzy Osbourne tended to dominate the band. Since his starring role in the MTV drama based around his family, he has become a household name.*

Black Sabbath

Formed:
Birmingham, England

Years active:
1968–2006

Definitive lineup:
Ozzy Osbourne, Tony Iommi, Geezer Butler, Bill Ward

Genres: *hard rock, heavy metal*

Key singles:
"Paranoid" (1970), "Never Say Die" (1978)

Key albums: Black Sabbath *(1970),* Paranoid *(1970)*

Country rock

COUNTRY MUSIC had been a key element in the birth of rock 'n' roll and rockabilly during the 1950s, but that was soon forgotten during the R&B-prompted beat boom. Giving comic Beatle Ringo Starr Buck Owens' "Act Naturally" to sing speaks volumes about perceptions of a genre forged in the tough, honky-tonk barrooms of the white American South but later tamed by Nashville's desire for slickness. By the late 1960s, though, all that had changed, and by the mid-1970s, country rock was firmly established, highly respected, and arguably the prevailing musical force of its time.

OPPOSITE *Just as country rock acts looked toward tradition to find meaning after the rootlessness of psychedelia, so too did swamp bluesmen Creedence Clearwater Revival.*

BELOW *After a stint in the Byrds, Gram Parsons (right) formed the Flying Burrito Brothers to explore the country and rock interface.*

Bob Dylan had ventured to Nashville early in 1966 to finish off work on *Blonde on Blonde*, but it wasn't until 1969's *Nashville Skyline*—which included a wobbly duet with Johnny Cash on "Girl from the North Country"—that he plowed the form more extensively. By now, country rock had received a boost with the rootsy Americana of the Band's *Music from Big Pink*, the emergence of Crosby, Stills & Nash (with Neil Young joining later), and the Byrds' *Sweetheart of the Rodeo* (also 1968). The defining influence on the latter had been Gram Parsons, a rock 'n' roll enthusiast who had converted to country music in the mid-1960s.

Parsons, who soon left to pursue a purer form of country rock with the Flying Burrito Brothers and on two solo albums before his death in 1973, also had an impact across the Atlantic. Introducing Rolling Stones guitarist Keith Richards to country tunings, Parsons' influence is clearly heard on the band's 1972 masterpiece, *Exile on Main St.* Essentially, though, roots in Britain meant the folk tradition, most successfully explored by Fairport Convention.

While southern swamp rockers Creedence Clearwater Revival enjoyed great success at the end of the 1960s with their variant form, it was the more melodious country rock of the Eagles that eventually triumphed, becoming the defining sound of the mid-1970s. Post-punk, the style never quite recovered, and in recent years, America's search for musical roots has generally passed the influence of Nashville by in favor of earlier folk styles.

5 Top country-rock artists

The Band: Music from Big Pink *(1968)*
The Byrds: Sweetheart of the Rodeo *(1968)*

Creedence Clearwater Revival: Creedence Clearwater Revival *(1969)*

Gram Parsons: Grievous Angel *(1974)*
Eagles: Hotel California *(1976)*

Crosby, Stills, Nash & Young

THE FIRST SUPERGROUP based on songwriting skills and harmony singing instead of instrumental prowess, Crosby, Stills, Nash & Young— initially a trio before Young joined in summer 1969—enjoyed a remarkable 12 months in the wake of their Woodstock appearance. But within weeks of the chart-topping "Déjà Vu," released in March 1970, the quarrelsome quartet split after a summer tour of the United States, cutting short what many assumed would have been a decade-defining career.

Formed in summer 1968 by exiles from three successful mid-1960s bands, David Crosby (the Byrds), Stephen Stills (Buffalo Springfield), and Graham Nash (the Hollies), the original trio was perhaps conceived as the West Coast's answer to the Band. But with strong management and record company backing, and the instant success of their self-titled May 1969 debut, CSN's potential was far greater, as evidenced by the singles-chart success of the jaunty "Marrakesh Express."

The arrival of fiery guitarist Young—also ex-Buffalo Springfield and already pursuing a solo career—added a further shot of electricity to the band's sound, most notably on the extended version of Young's own "Southern Man," which featured on the postsplit two-LP concert set, 4 Way Street. A series of later reunions have never quite rekindled the magic, though the quartet's graying reputation has been largely restored by the 1990s interest in Americana and, more recently, freak folk.

Crosby, Stills, Nash & Young

Formed: Los Angeles, California

Years active: 1968–70, 1973–74, 1977 to present

Definitive lineup: David Crosby, Stephen Stills, Graham Nash, Neil Young

Genres: folk rock, rock

Key single: "Marrakesh Express" (1969)

Key albums: Déjà Vu (1970), 4 Way Street (1971)

BELOW CSN&Y joined by guest Joni Mitchell at London's Wembley Stadium in 1974.

Eagles

REACHING OUT beyond a rock audience with their multimillion-selling *Their Greatest Hits (1971–1975)* mid-1970s collection, the Eagles anticipated rock's transition from a faintly oppositional force to something virtually indistinguishable from family entertainment. Having picked up on the strain of country-tinged rock first ignited by the Band, the Eagles smoothed out the rough edges and became the defining sound of mid-1970s America.

ABOVE *By the mid-1970s, the soothing, soft-rock sounds of the Eagles dominated the rock music landscape, especially in the United States, which more readily appreciated the band's in-concert prairie imagery. The band's frontmen were Glen Frey (second left) and Don Henley (right).*

Like the Band, the Eagles started out as a backing group, accompanying aspiring country rocker Linda Ronstadt both on record and on tour. Signing to David Geffen's Asylum Records, home to Ronstadt as well as sometime collaborator Jackson Browne, the Eagles enjoyed almost instant U.S. success when their eponymous 1972 debut yielded three hit 45s. While all four members sang (fifth member Don Felder joined in 1974), Don Henley and Glenn Frey, who had emerged as the key songwriters, handled most of the leads.

Having toughened up their sound for 1974's *On the Border*, it was a ballad, "Best of My Love," that gave the band their first

No. 1 — a feat repeated the following year with the *One of These Nights* album and title track. After the career high of the *Hotel California* album and 45, the Eagles procrastinated over the follow-up, *The Long Run* (1980). Within months of its release, they'd split. Since 1994, Frey, Henley, and guitarist Joe Walsh have kept the band going, essentially as a concert draw.

Eagles

Formed:
Los Angeles, California

Years active:
1971–80, 1994 to present

Definitive lineup:
Glenn Frey, Don Henley, Don Felder, Randy Meisner, Bernie Leadon

Genres: *rock, country rock*

Key singles: *"Best of My Love"* (1974), *"Hotel California"* (1977)

Key albums: *On the Border* (1974), *Hotel California* (1976)

Jazz rock

WHEN BRITISH PSYCHEDELIC dadaists turned jazz-rock
instrumentalists the Soft Machine were invited to play the London
Proms in 1970, it was yet another mark of pop's progress from being
electrified folk music of the people to something even the classical
establishment could recognize as art. They weren't alone.

Frank Zappa and the Mothers of Invention, as well as the brassier Blood, Sweat & Tears and Chicago, had also clearly drawn from jazz during the late 1960s. Most significantly, it was trumpeter Miles Davis's increasingly loud embrace of the rock aesthetic that propelled fusion into the limelight during the early and mid-1970s. Invariably, it was Miles's sidemen who led the way. Tony Williams (Lifetime) and John McLaughlin (Mahavishnu Orchestra) formed loud and fast jazz-rock bands, while Herbie Hancock (Headhunters), Chick Corea (Return to Forever), and Joe Zawinul and Wayne Shorter (Weather Report) drew more from funk and world beat.

Postbop jazz's emphasis on improvisation and virtuoso playing had been LSD's secret partner in the development of acid rock. But the early 1970s emergence of jazz rock and fusion was more comfortable with the progressive ethos, which privileged a more studious, show-off tendency over the more haphazard approach of the hippie era. By the late 1970s, fusion had given way to a Muzak-driven smooth jazz style typified by Spyro Gyra and George Benson and favored by movie and TV music producers.

Fusion was comfortable with the progressive ethos...

5 Top jazz-rock artists

Miles Davis: Bitches Brew *(1970)*
The Tony Williams Lifetime: Turn It Over *(1970)*

Soft Machine: Third *(1970)*
Mahavishnu Orchestra:
The Inner Mounting Flame *(1971)*

Weather Report: Weather Report *(1971)*

Miles Davis

FROM PLAYING a supporting role in Charlie Parker's postwar be-bop quintet, Miles Davis emerged as a key figure in late-1950s cool jazz (*Kind of Blue*, 1959), his music growing ever more cryptic and sophisticated during the 1960s. By 1969, with his ear bent toward the dramatic new electric sounds of Jimi Hendrix and Sly & the Family Stone, Davis had again grown restless. Over the next five years, the jazz explorer embraced first electric rock, then funk, alienating huge swathes of his old audience while seeking to attract a new, younger crowd.

The launchpad for Davis's greatest musical adventure was *Bitches Brew* (1970). Awash in electricity and rock-inspired rhythms, this sprawling, pivotal double album, which at times ventured close to space rock, was the catalyst for a remarkable career turn. Davis broke out of the rarified concerthall circuit to perform at rock venues, such as the Fillmores in New York and Los Angeles, and made a notable appearance at the Isle of Wight festival in 1970. This renewed, revitalized activity resulted in a series of expansive, improvised live albums, each more supercharged, electronic, and daring, with Davis's wah-wah'd trumpet blowing gusts of inspiration over some astonishingly hyperactive avant-funk grooves.

ABOVE *When Davis—seen, here in 1969—started to take note of rock, especially the work of Jimi Hendrix, jazz purists deserted him in droves.*

LEFT *His embrace of funk, electronics, and rock guitar during the 1970s is perhaps Miles Davis's most fertile period.*

This phase reached some kind of zenith with the 1972 studio set, *On the Corner*, which had been intended to reach out to a black urban audience but ended up alienating both critics and crowds. In 1975, "electric Miles" withdrew for several years, reemerging in 1981 for a final decade that included a brief return to his interpretive past on 1985's *You're Under Arrest*.

During the 1980s, the rapturous rhythms and daredevil experimentation of the electric-Miles era found new expression via noisy post-punkers the Pop Group, Prince, and the fragmented beats of hip hop. Since his death, these once career-threatening explorations into the realm of electric jazz-funk are now regarded as perhaps the most significant in his illustrious career.

Miles Davis

Born: *May 26, 1926, Alton, Illinois*
Died: *September 28, 1991*

Years active: *1944–75, 1981–91*
Genres: *jazz, jazz rock*

Key albums: Bitches Brew *(1970),* On the Corner *(1972)*

Singer-songwriters

THOUGH HE FOUND FAME as a protest singer, Bob Dylan's perhaps
most enduring influence has been in heralding a wave of singer-
songwriters eager to stamp their own signature sound and style on
the world. In 1970, by which time Dylan was already lampooning the
trend on the neatly titled *Self Portrait*, the singer-songwriter boom
took hold, with the enormous success of Simon & Garfunkel's *Bridge
Over Troubled Water* paving the way for a new generation of earnest,
soul-baring troubadours.

BELOW *Though the singer-
songwriter genre became
big business during the early
1970s, many of its most
gifted musicians made
their best work during
the late 1960s. Few were
more impassioned and
experimental than Tim
Buckley, pictured here
in 1968.*

The most successful was pianist Carole
King, a veteran of the Brill Building school
of instant-pop songwriting, whose 1971 set
Tapestry remained a best seller for years.
James Taylor, too, enjoyed great success
early in the decade, though it was Neil
Young, whose penchant for low-slung guitar
workouts later recast him as a grunge
generation antihero, and future pop-jazz
venturer Joni Mitchell, who successfully
transcended genre cliché.

Perhaps the most highly regarded of
all singer-songwriters was and remains
Leonard Cohen, whose simple, somber
arpeggios and acutely poetic lyrics come
packaged in albums bearing titles such
as *Songs from a Room*. More adventurous,
at least musically, was Tim Buckley, who
led a phalanx of acoustic soloists from
the Elektra label. The era also saw the
emergence of numerous women, notably
Buffy Sainte-Marie and Melanie, both of
whom have enjoyed newfound status as
warble-voiced icons of freak folk.

Leonard Cohen

WHILE HE HAS OFTEN BEEN typecast as a bedsit miserablist, and the archetypal cult antihero, the warmth, humor, and universality of Leonard Cohen's work has in recent years been recognized to the point of virtual sainthood. That might not sit easily with Cohen as a practicing Buddhist, but for a gifted public entertainer who had his first book of poetry published in 1956, it's long overdue.

ABOVE *While the reputations of better-known contemporaries have dimmed, the onetime "bedsit bard," famous for his lugubrious voice and lyrical songs, has enjoyed a huge renaissance in recent years.*

With his limited guitar technique and a lugubrious voice that rarely breaks out of monotone, Cohen developed an instantly recognizable style, both intimate and personal without ever straying into mawkishness. His 1967 debut, *Songs of Leonard Cohen*, featuring mainstays of his career "So Long, Marianne" and "Suzanne," anticipated the singer-songwriter boom later that decade. *Songs from a Room* (1969), his most successful album, yielded another evergreen, "Bird on a Wire." Artists including Judy Collins and Fairport Convention lined up to cover his songs. Meanwhile, two of Cohen's finest, the mesmeric "Famous Blue Raincoat" and "Love Calls You by Your Name," graced his 1971 set, *Songs of Love and Hate*.

After a collaboration with Phil Spector on *Death of a Ladies' Man* (1977) yielded mixed results, it was interpreters such as postgoth balladeer Nick Cave who kept Cohen's work alive. *I'm Your Man* (1988) found the singer revitalized, his voice deeper than ever, and Cohen was on the road to a rehabilitation that climaxed in an extended world tour that began in 2008. Many new admirers have come to his work via the Christmas 2008 multiartist success of his 1984 song "Hallelujah."

Leonard Cohen

Born:
September 21, 1934, Montreal, Canada

Years active:
1956 to present

Genres: *folk, singer-songwriter*

Key singles:
"Suzanne" (1967), *"Hallelujah" (1984)*

Key albums: Songs of Leonard Cohen *(1967),* I'm Your Man *(1988)*

Progressive rock

PSYCHEDELIA HAD BLOWN the pop rulebook apart. Progressive rock attempted to put it back together again, but with scant regard for matters of melody, hooks, and brevity. Taking off in earnest at the end of the 1960s, after the improvisations and effects-laden overload of acid rock had exhausted itself, "prog" peaked during the early 1970s, when it was often held up as the antithesis of glam in the rock-versus-pop wars.

Back in the days of Beatlemania, when respected critics would fancifully compare aspects of the Beatles' work with that of the great composers, pop groups had few aspirations other than hoping that their next record would be "a hit." By the middle of the decade, orchestral versions of those hits of the day became a feature of the pop industry, but few could have imagined the eruption of pop operas, rock concertos, and classically minded aspirations and conceits at the end of the decade.

Although Procol Harum's enigmatic and Bach-inspired 1967 hit "A Whiter Shade of Pale," the Moody Blues, and the Nice (who wreaked instrumental havoc on Leonard Bernstein's "America") paved the way, it was the emergence in 1970 of the big three—

Yes, Genesis, and Emerson, Lake & Palmer (ELP)—that announced prog's arrival in earnest. King Crimson and Van der Graaf Generator represented pure prog at its most dynamic and extreme, though even blues-rock mavericks Jethro Tull found themselves toying with complex song structures, noodly virtuoso playing, fanciful lyrics, and a general aura of aloofness.

BELOW Jethro Tull's flute-playing songwriter and frontman Ian Anderson was one of the most distinctive faces of prog rock during the early 1970s.

Noodly virtuoso playing

ELP took prog's "classical rock" ambition to the limit with a live rendering of Mussorgsky's *Pictures at an Exhibition* (1971), but the biggest accolades were reserved for grand new works, such as Pink Floyd's *The Dark Side of the Moon* and Mike Oldfield's virtuoso achievement, *Tubular Bells* (both 1973).

Prog's lofty aspirations made it an object of ridicule for punk rockers, but with Pink Floyd, Genesis, and Canadian latecomers Rush flourishing well into the early 1980s, progressive rock never fully went away. Its best instincts have enjoyed something of a revival during the past two decades, with Radiohead studiously playing with tempos and textures, as well as ignoring the clock, and even the bombast of stadium rockers, such as Muse, owes something to prog's sense of the overblown.

ABOVE *Emerson, Lake & Palmer required several articulated lorries to carry their equipment and stage set as they took their extravagant live show around the world.*

5 Top progressive artists

Jethro Tull: *Aqualung* (1971)
Yes: *The Yes Album* (1971)
Genesis: *Foxtrot* (1972)

Emerson, Lake & Palmer: *Welcome Back My Friends to the Show That Never Ends…Ladies and Gentlemen…Emerson, Lake & Palmer* (1974)

Rush: *Permanent Waves* (1980)

Yes

A BAND THAT REMAINS virtually synonymous with progressive rock, Yes possessed the cosmic consciousness, the conceptual aspirations, and, of course, the virtuoso playing, all of which made them the genre's second most successful act after Pink Floyd. At their peak during 1972 and 1973, Yes released three albums—*Fragile*, *Close to the Edge*, and *Yessongs*—with their classic lineup before 1974's *Tales from Topographic Oceans* signaled the end of the public's unquestioned thirst for lengthy, intricate pieces and fanciful lyrics concerning space and spirituality.

Yes

Formed: *London, England*

Years active: *1968–81, 1983 to present*

Definitive lineup: *Jon Anderson, Steve Howe, Rick Wakeman, Chris Squire, Bill Bruford*

Genre: *progressive rock*

Key singles: *"Roundabout" (1971), "Owner of a Lonely Heart" (1980)*

Key albums: Fragile *(1971)*, Close to the Edge *(1972)*

Emerging in 1969, Yes took a while to hit their stride. The arrival, in 1970, of guitarist Steve Howe, followed by flamboyant keyboard wizard Rick Wakeman the following year, prompted a more focused art-rock direction. Building on 1971's *The Yes Album*, and notably that set's epic piece, "Starship Trooper," Yes came of age with *Fragile* (1971), the first to boast a distinctive Roger Dean sleeve as well as

a moderately popular single, "Roundabout." But, unlike Pink Floyd, who gritted their teeth and persevered, Yes allowed their personal differences to rip the band apart.

In 1980, bassist Chris Squire—the only surviving original member—invited novelty pop duo Buggles on board. Since 1988, various versions of the band have soldiered on, none ever hoping to recapture the band's glorious heyday.

LEFT *Keyboard players in particular seemed to come to the fore during the progressive rock era, none more so than Yes's silver-caped soloist Rick Wakeman.*

Genesis

THE MOST THEATRICAL of progressive rock's triumvirate—which also included Yes and Emerson, Lake & Palmer—Genesis underwent the most surprising career change. The departure, in 1975, of frontman Peter Gabriel robbed the group of their visually minded conceptualist, but won them a new lease of life, exploring their ever-present melodic tendencies within the context of a more pop-friendly sound. The result was a Genesis of two halves—and a hugely successful solo career for the band's drummer turned second vocalist, Phil Collins.

There was an almost classical perfection about five well-trained—both musically and socially—teenage boys from elite private school Charterhouse, fired up by the possibilities of post-*Sgt Pepper* pop, forming a group named after the first book of the Old Testament. Their 1969 debut, *From Genesis to Revelation*, was a callow venture into orchestral pop, but by 1970's *Trespass*, with guitarist Steve Hackett and Collins now on board, the compositions were becoming decidedly more complex.

Refining their style on *Nursery Cryme* (1971) and *Foxtrot* (1972), Genesis hit a peak in 1973 with *Selling England by the Pound*, and its spin-off minor hit single, "I Know What I Like (In Your Wardrobe)." Gabriel's surprise departure, after the two-disc concept album, *The Lamb Lies Down on Broadway*, virtually brought the band's prog-rock days to an end, though the more concise Collins-fronted recordings earned the group far more in terms of sales.

Genesis

Formed: *Surrey, England*

Years active: *1967–99*

Definitive lineup: *Peter Gabriel, Steve Hackett, Tony Banks, Mike Rutherford, Phil Collins*

Genres: *progressive rock, rock, pop*

Key singles: *"I Know What I Like (In Your Wardrobe)" (1973); "Follow You Follow Me" (1978)*

Key albums: Selling England by the Pound *(1973)*, And Then There Were Three *(1978)*

BELOW *Genesis, fronted by Peter Gabriel, were one of the first prog bands to take rock theater seriously.*

Glam rock

THE BEATLES WERE GONE. Rock was for students and grown-ups. Singer-songwriters sang to new parents. The singles chart was increasingly a playground for opportunist producers wanting to turn bubblegum into gold. In the United States, a new breed of preteen weenybopper acts emerged to fill the gap—from the effervescent Jackson 5 and the Osmonds to teenage heartthrob David Cassidy. In Britain, the response was more complicated—and bizarre.

BELOW *David Bowie's final appearance as alter ego Ziggy Stardust took place at London's Hammersmith Odeon in July 1973, amid hysterical scenes and rumours of imminent retirement. The theatrical gesture was paramount in glam rock.*

Glam rock, or glitter rock as it was known initially, came into being one Thursday night in March 1971. Festival circuit B-lister Marc Bolan, now fronting an electric four-piece T. Rex, appeared on weekly British TV chart show *Top of the Pops* wearing glitter under his eyes. Within days, a generation of newly awakened pop fans that had sent his "Hot Love" to the top of the chart for six weeks were following suit. Bolan was the first of the 1970s superstars, and in his wake came a number of fellow long-term strugglers—soul-blues shouter Rod Stewart, singer-songwriter Elton John, boot-boy rockers Slade, art-rock mavericks Roxy Music, renegade hard-rockers Mott the Hoople, Detroit-raised tomboy Suzi Quatro, bubblegum opportunists Sweet, Big Apple kitsch kings New York Dolls, and, of course, Bolan's pal and rival David Bowie.

RIGHT *While glam was a peculiarly British phenomenon, the New York Dolls added a dose of Lower East Side decadence and delir-___ into the.___*

"I could write
Number Ones
forever"

Marc Bolan

What united them was a hunger for fame, a penchant for dramatic song intros and air-punching, terrace-style hooks, and a willingness to look ridiculous in public. With Western economies in a severe downturn, glam rock—much as Busby Berkeley's elaborate musicals had done during the early 1930s Great Depression—provided loud, gaudy escapism. But it was inspirational, too, with Bolan and Bowie in particular instilling sartorial excess into the DNA of an incipient punk generation. And though derided, the music has outlasted much else from the era, thanks in large part to the signature production sound achieved by Tony Visconti (T. Rex), Nicky Chinn and Mike Chapman (Sweet, Suzi Quatro), and Mike Leander (Gary Glitter).

5 Top glam-rock artists

T. Rex: *"Metal Guru" (1972)*
David Bowie: *"Starman" (1972)*
Alice Cooper: *"School's Out" (1972)*

Roxy Music: *"Virginia Plain" (1972)*
New York Dolls: *"Jet Boy" (1973)*

ABOVE LEFT *Marc Bolan, the first glam-rock superstar, upset his underground fan base when he transformed hippie Tyrannosaurus Rex into rocker T. Rex.*

Marc Bolan & T. Rex

A POPULAR FIGURE of the late-1960s British underground, Marc Bolan (born Mark Feld in London on September 30, 1947) made a spectacular transformation during 1971, becoming the decade's first pop hero. Ushering in a glittering era of glam rock, Bolan's career turnaround prompted much debate. With his poster-boy looks, screaming fans, and instantly recognizable T. Rex signature sound, the reinvented Bolan was clearly a pop phenomenon—but one with a marked rock sensibility. He bragged like mid-1960s Dylan, swaggered like Chuck Berry, possessed a poetic sensibility, and harbored guitar-hero aspirations. In a reversal of late-1960s pop's artful pose, Bolan traded in his cult status for superstar acclaim.

Marc Bolan & T. Rex

Formed: *London, England*

Years active: *1967–77*

Definitive lineup: *Marc Bolan, Mickey Finn, Steve Currie, Bill Legend*

Genre: *glam rock, pop, rock, freak-folk*

Key singles: *"Hot Love" (1971), "Metal Guru" (1972)*

Key albums: Electric Warrior *(1971)*, The Slider *(1972)*

Bolan's unique vocal warble had been a perfect vehicle for Tyrannosaurus Rex, his pixified rock 'n' roll duo, but by 1970 the group's fantasy-driven vibe sounded distinctly passé. Expanding to an electrified four-piece, while abbreviating the band's name, Bolan hit on a sparkling streak of mystical teen anthems, including "Hot Love," "Telegram Sam," and "Metal Guru."

Having chronicled his fall from grace in 1974 with "Teenage Dream," Bolan's reinvention as an Americanized soul punk was greeted with incredulity. A renewal of fortunes as the self-styled "Godfather of Punk" in 1977 was cruelly cut short when he was killed in a car crash on September 16.

BELOW *A changeling of the highest order, Bolan—once an "Ace Face" Mod and a Dylan-inspired beatnik—found his own "voice" in the form of a distinctive, otherworldly vibrato.*

Roxy Music

VINTAGE HOLLYWOOD, 1960s art school, and neon-lit rock 'n' roll were just some of the influences that lay behind Roxy Music, perhaps the most extraordinary group to emerge in the early 1970s. Ostensibly glam rock, thanks to stylish frontman Bryan Ferry and feather-festooned, synth-playing maverick Eno, Roxy Music were in some ways a very British response to the Mothers of Invention, mixing and mismatching musical styles like colors from an artist's palette.

Roxy Music, it seemed, did things differently. Their debut album appeared in June 1972 before they had tested the water on stage or with a single. Its 1950s-style glamour-model cover suggested a band out of place and time, though the Top 5 success of "Virginia Plain" that fall confirmed Roxy as the year's most extraordinary new arrivals.

The release of 1973's *For Your Pleasure*, which included paeans to ersatz dance crazes ("Do the Strand"), blow-up dolls ("In Every Dream Home a Heartache"), and krautrock ("The Bogus Man"), was swiftly followed by Eno's departure. The band then became an increasingly varnished vehicle for Ferry's desire for mainstream recognition, prompting a split in 1976. Having enjoyed a renaissance at the end of the decade with a more dance-floor-friendly sound, Roxy's occasional revivals in the twenty-first century still prompt "Is Eno returning?" headlines, such is the esteem in which the band's earliest work is held.

Roxy Music

Formed: *London, England*

Years active: *1971–76, 1978–83, 2001 to present*

Definitive lineup: *Bryan Ferry, Eno, Andy Mackay, Phil Manzanera, Paul Thompson*

Genres: *glam rock, art rock, pop, rock*

Key singles: *"Virginia Plain" (1972), "Pyjamarama" (1973)*

Key albums: *Roxy Music (1972), For Your Pleasure (1973)*

David Bowie

IT IS NO EXAGGERATION to say that modern music probably begins with David Bowie. Treating sound as style, and career development as a succession of artfully conceived paradigmatic shifts, Bowie has provided the blueprint for enduring megastar success ever since, from Michael Jackson and Madonna to Prince and U2. Pioneer, pasticheur, and poseur in roughly equal amounts, Bowie's mastery of the essential elements of rock stardom is second to none. However, his triumph was hard won.

Having tried his hand as a beat-group frontman, and as an orchestral pop, Summer of Love maverick, Bowie's initial success with the topical novelty hit "Space Oddity" in 1969 had one-hit wonder written all over it. But during his apprenticeship days, the singer also ventured into theater and mime, both skills utilized to great effect when he reemerged in 1972 at the height of glam rock. Inspired by pop artist Andy Warhol, Bowie introduced a camp, ironic sensibility into rock by masquerading as Ziggy Stardust, an alter-ego device that enabled him to wrestle conceptually with the nature of stardom and deliver a stage show that took rock theater to new levels.

ABOVE *Even during the 1990s and beyond, Bowie has continued to create challenging new music and tailor his image to remain hotly contemporary.*

LEFT *Gaunt and gifted, the mid-1970s David Bowie pioneered electronic music and made a successful venture into movies in 1976 in* The Man Who Fell to Earth.

RIGHT *Bowie utilized his training in mime for his stage appearances as Ziggy Stardust.*

Rock's most mutable star, willfully style-hopping

After "retiring" Ziggy at London's Hammersmith Odeon in July 1973, Bowie emerged from the cloak of alter ego to become rock's most mutable star, willfully style-hopping from "Plastic Soul" (*Young Americans*) to electro-fixated cold wave (*Low*), worldly postdisco (*Let's Dance*), to the dark club rhythms of drum 'n' bass (*Earthling*). Bowie has also been a hugely influential tastemaker, his championing of the hitherto unloved Velvet Underground and Iggy Pop being crucial in planting seeds for punk rock. And his enthusiasm for stylistic excess, which was taken up by the Soho-based New Romantics in the early 1980s, has been a constant in popular music ever since. It's sometimes easy to forget that at the heart of Bowie's success is his remarkable gift as a songwriter. From "Space Oddity" and "Let's Dance" to his 1971 signature tune, "Changes," his work spans, documents, and defines several distinct eras.

David Bowie

Born: *January 8, 1947*
Years active: *1964 to present*

Genres: *rock, pop, dance, experimental*

Key singles: *"Space Oddity" (1969), "Sound and Vision" (1977)*

Key albums: The Rise and Fall of Ziggy Stardust and the Spiders from Mars *(1972),* Low *(1977)*

Rock theater

THEATER HAS ALWAYS been intrinsic to rock's appeal, from Presley's pelvic thrusts to Screamin' Jay Hawkins' "I Put a Spell on You" sorcery. The free expression of psychedelia saw a new era of guitar-trashing showmanship (Hendrix, the Who), as well as audience provocation courtesy of Doors' frontman Jim Morrison. But it was Frank Zappa protégé Alice Cooper who blew the idea right open.

Pronouncing the Love Generation dead, "shock-rocker" Cooper emerged in 1971 with a controversial *Killer* stage show, where the leather-clad protagonist Alice would mutilate baby dolls, then hang for his crimes at the climax of each performance. More Detroit-based deviancy came courtesy of Iggy Pop, routinely self-harming in gestures of bodily abuse that would be echoed later by the punks.

During the early 1970s, rock's encroaching giganticism saw ever-more grand onstage spectaculars, with progressive acts, such as Genesis, Jethro Tull, and even the Kinks, venturing into rock theater. The man who did most to advance the form, though, was David Bowie, who in 1972 masqueraded as alter ego Ziggy Stardust, before retiring the character and returning with a series of entirely different shows—and musical styles. Routinely dismissed as "inauthentic" at the time, Bowie showed that "faking it" was wildly misunderstood and a key element in rock 'n' roll. Time has proved him right.

BELOW *Although rock theatre is most often associated with glam acts such as David Bowie and Alice Cooper, Genesis's Peter Gabriel proved that prog rock was not immune to showmanship.*

IO downtime by Mike
itarist still in his late teens,
e new Virgin label, *Tubular*
 album-chart success of
sical motif that grows
ver, over 48 minutes,
Floyd's *The Dark Side of the*
ear—as the quintessential
When an extract was used
ught the work to an
horror-movie association
ecause *Tubular Bells* was
ic piece and a far cry
prog of bands such as

The album's style (and success), which Oldfield reprised on 1974's *Hergest Ridge*, marked the apotheosis of the rock virtuoso. But while Oldfield, like the era's great session men, such as pianist Nicky Hopkins, preferred to remain largely anonymous, others, like Yes's caped keyboardist Rick Wakeman, augmented their musical talents with a flamboyance to rival even the most ego-driven glam hero.

By the mid-1970s, with audiences tiring of 30-minute drum solos and interminable organ battles, only guitar heroes, such as Led Zeppelin's Jimmy Page, seemed to retain any respectability. Punk sounded the death knell, and the prog-era virtuoso was brilliantly lampooned by punk band Buzzcocks on "Boredom" (1977), with its monotonous two-note guitar solo.

Pink Floyd

THE ACID-HASTENED BREAKDOWN and departure of original frontman and songwriter Syd Barrett seemed to bring Pink Floyd's brief, psychedelic-era brush with fame to a close. Instead, the erstwhile darlings of the London underground scene turned pop pretenders survived a difficult transition period in the late 1960s to become, in the 1970s, the prime exponents of progressive rock. Vast mixed-media stage productions that brought a series of impeccably produced concept albums to life earned Pink Floyd their reputation as leading proponents of rock's Wagnerian tendency, shoehorning music, art, and a melancholic disposition into each and every masterpiece.

House band of London's hippie haunts UFO and the Roundhouse, the Cambridge-raised, art-school-educated Floyd hid behind light shows and a wall of sound as they stretched their R&B-inflected set into lengthy improvised "freak-outs." Barrett's striking looks and ability to knock out perfectly formed psychedelic pop singles ensured a brief spell of success ("See Emily Play" climbed to No. 6 in Britain in the summer of 1967), before the group—now with Barrett's replacement David Gilmour—returned to longer, often instrumental pieces aimed at the albums market.

Working the new college and concert hall circuit, Pink Floyd embarked on soundtrack work and a halfbaked, orchestral rock suite

ABOVE *Nick Mason, Dave Gilmour, Roger Waters, and Rick Wright look fame in the eye in 1973.*

LEFT *With the success of 1973's* The Dark Side of the Moon, Pink Floyd's *extravagant light shows would become more intricate still.*

Atom Heart Mother (1970). A signature sound of sorts was achieved on the side-long postpsych epic "Echoes" (on 1971's *Meddle*) and fully developed on *The Dark Side of the Moon* (1973). A suite of songs based around a pessimistic theme cooked up by bassist Roger Waters, *Dark Side* was both clever and commercial, and became the era's keynote album.

Themes of alienation and insanity were more fully developed on *Wish You Were Here* (1975) and *The Wall* (1979), the latter also adapted for a 1982 feature film. The acrimonious departure of Waters in 1985 barely affected the continued success of these shy superstars, whose inactivity since the mid-1990s was broken for a one-off reunion with Waters at Live 8 in 2005.

Pink Floyd

Formed: *London, England*
Years active: *1965–94*
Definitive lineup: *Syd Barrett/David Gilmour,* *Roger Waters, Rick Wright, Nick Mason*
Genres: *psychedelia, progressive rock*

Key singles: *"See Emily Play" (1967), "Another Brick in the Wall (Part II)" (1979)*

Key albums: The Piper at the Gates of Dawn *(1967)*, The Dark Side of the Moon *(1973)*

Krautrock

INITIALLY REGARDED as an esoteric, experimental
offshoot of early 1970s progressive rock, "krautrock"—
a catchall term coined by the British music press—
enjoyed a critical renaissance during the 1990s, and
in terms of influence at least, it has eclipsed its more
commercially successful relation. Unlike prog, where
rock musicians cast themselves in the manner of late-
nineteenth-century romantic composers, krautrock
was defiantly twentieth century. Less concerned with
the symphonic form and virtuoso ornamentalism than
with more linear rhythms forged from ethnic trance
music and the New York avant-garde, krautrock also
drew heavily on the wayward psychedelia of the early
Pink Floyd and the brutal repetition of the Velvet
Underground's more outré moments.

The quintessential and most
consistently thrilling krautrock
act were Can. Based in Cologne,
Germany, where they formed in
1968, Can included two ex-
students of radical contemporary
composer Karlheinz Stockhausen.
They approached their work both
intellectually and on an instinctive
level, and wedded their ideas to
rhythms as syncopated and
hypnotic as the tightest James
Brown or most electrifying Miles
Davis groove.

At the distant psychedelic end of the krautrock spectrum were Amon Düül II who, like many on the German rock scene, emerged from the politically charged, commune-dwelling era of student revolt. However, the first band to make an impact, in Britain at least, were the defiantly experimental Faust. An album-length collage of fragments known as *The Faust Tapes*, issued with some fanfare by new label Virgin at the price of a single, seemed to confirm the impression that krautrock was disjointed and difficult. But the "motorik" 4/4 rhythms of Neu!, the prototrance soundscapes of Tangerine Dream, and above all the accessibility of the synthesizer-wielding Kraftwerk—who enjoyed a British No. 1 hit in 1975 with "Autobahn," a shortened version of the title track on their album—proved otherwise. Since then, post-punk, hip hop, trance music, and early 1990s indie have all drawn heavily from krautrock.

ABOVE *Kraftwerk's irresistibly metronomic "Autobahn," a surprise hit single in 1975, opened up the possibilities of electronic dance music.*

LEFT *Emerging from the Munich commune scene, Amon Düül II began as an acid-rock improvisation band before instilling some kind of structure for their masterwork, Yeti.*

5 Top krautrock artists

Amon Düül II: Yeti *(1970)*
Can: Tago Mago *(1971)*
Neu!: Neu! *(1972)*
Faust: The Faust Tapes *(1973)*
Kraftwerk: Autobahn *(1974)*

Alice Cooper

FIRED UP ON HOLLYWOOD kitsch and vaudevillian horror, Alice Cooper turned rock on its head by emphasizing theater over any quasi-classical aspirations. Not everyone was amused. Taking an axe to dolls and having "Alice" killed off at the end of each show prompted accusations that rock had grown sick and debauched. Insisting that society got the entertainment it deserved, Cooper's infamy increased with every outrage—fabricated fun that anticipated rock's future as a naughty but essentially harmless pursuit.

As evidenced on their 1969 debut album, *Pretties for You*, the original Alice Cooper group delivered skits as much as songs, unfairly earning them a "Worst Band in the World" reputation. After tightening up the sound for themed albums/stage shows, such as *Killer* (1971) and *Billion Dollar Babies* (1973), as well as the playground rebellion holiday hit, "School's Out" (1972), Cooper instead became the era's most visible—and influential—showman, prompting the entire rock-theater boom.

Increasingly detached from his band, Cooper went solo in 1975. He endured a much-publicized personal collapse before a long recovery—hastened by the Top 10 success of "Poison" in 1989—and his subsequent reemergence confirmed him as one of rock's most potent caricatures. Let that not obscure the fact that the group's breakthrough set, *Love It to Death* (1971), gave birth to a robust, FM-friendly rock sound that remains more or less the standard today.

Alice Cooper

Formed: *Phoenix, Arizona*

Years active:
1963 to present

Definitive lineup:
Alice Cooper, Dennis Dunaway, Glen Buxton, Michael Bruce, Neal Smith

Genres:
psychedelia, rock

Key singles: *"I'm Eighteen" (1970), "School's Out" (1972)*

Key albums: *Killer (1971), Billion Dollar Babies (1973)*

LEFT *Onetime Frank Zappa protégés and self-styled "Worst Band in the World," the Alice Cooper band moved to Detroit, upped the horror quotient, and virtually created rock theater single-handedly during 1970 and 1971.*

The Stooges

INITIALLY KNOWN as the Psychedelic Stooges, this Detroit-based band soon came to embody everything that was counter to Love Generation ideals. A decade on, the often-ridiculed Stooges were being praised as a key inspiration for the new wave, with the Damned and the Sex Pistols covering their songs, and frontman Iggy Pop hailed as the "Godfather of Punk."

In common with the early Alice Cooper band, the Stooges reveled in a musical primitivism and onstage theatricality that offended many and was often interpreted as antirock. But in light of punk, the magnificent trio of albums released between 1969 and 1973 sound more like definitive testaments to rock 'n' roll than almost everything else released during these years.

The Stooges (1969), produced by ex-Velvet Underground man John Cale, took the gnarly alienation of garage rock to the extreme, with songs such as "I Wanna Be Your Dog" reveling in narcissism and nihilism. *Fun House* (1970) was even louder and more visceral. Arguably, both were eclipsed by 1973's *Raw Power*, featuring new guitar ace James Williamson and produced by superfan David Bowie. The band disbanded shortly afterward. Iggy enjoyed a late-1970s solo renaissance, and has shown remarkable resilience as a live performer, even revisiting the Stooges' original albums on stage in recent years.

ABOVE *Detroit's Stooges powered garage rock minimalism to earsplitting, industrial strength capacity. Meanwhile, frontman Iggy Pop, pictured at an infamous 1970 show in Cincinnati, acted out the era's tendency toward self-destruction.*

The Stooges

Formed: *Ann Arbor, Michigan*

Years active:
1967–71, 1972–74, 2003 to present

Definitive lineup:
Iggy Pop, Ron Asheton, Scott Asheton, Dave Alexander

Genres: *garage rock, punk rock*

Key singles:
"I Wanna Be Your Dog" *(1969)*, "Down on the Street" *(1970)*

Key albums:
Fun House *(1970)*, Raw Power *(1973)*

Kiss

AMERICA TENDED TO DISMISS British glam rock as effeminate and lightweight. So it invented Kiss, a ballsy quartet in comic-grotesque face paint, who delivered loud, gaudy entertainment that, by the late 1970s, had captured the North American heartlands. The band were a lot harder to love in punk-fixated Britain, which scorned any hint of hoary rock spectacle, though after their infamous unmasking in 1983, Kiss found belated favor as part of the glam-metal boom. When the original band reunited in 1996, they were able to take their place as one of the key influences on rock in the post-punk era.

That there was nothing particularly original about Kiss made them an attractive proposition in 1973 for music industry executive Neil Bogart, who needed a surefire bet for his newly launched Casablanca label. Drawing their robust riffs from early arena rockers, such as Grand Funk Railroad and Mountain, throwing in glam-inspired, unison-voiced choruses and a little Alice Cooper-style razzmatazz, Kiss emerged amid a neon-lit, smoke-filled stage to become, as declared on their best-selling 1975 *Alive!* concert album, "the hottest band in the land."

Though Alice Cooper's producer Bob Ezrin sought to broaden the sound for *Destroyer* (1976), the first in a run of four U.S. platinum albums, it was in concert that the band were at their best. And, despite numerous successful records since, that's the way it has stayed.

BELOW *In complete contrast to earnest country rock and singer-songwriters were Kiss, who refashioned glam rock for domestic consumption, brightening up U.S. rock in the mid- and late 1970s. Founder member Gene Simmons is pictured left.*

Kiss

Formed:
New York

Years active:
1973 to present

Genres: *hard rock, glam metal*

Definitive lineup:
Paul Stanley, Gene Simmons, Ace Frehley, Peter Criss

Key singles:
"Rock and Roll all Nite" (1975), "I Was Made for Lovin' You" (1979)

Key albums:
Alive! (1975), Destroyer (1976)

Queen

RIDING ON THE COATTAILS of glam rock, though too musically sophisticated for a young teen audience, Queen possessed a hard-rock appeal that served them well for their first two albums. After 1974's *Sheer Heart Attack*, the band began to confound easy categorization, virtually defining their own genre. The record that did it, the 1975 super-hit "Bohemian Rhapsody," was more than a song: it was a mini-opera, complete with stunning visuals that hastened the growth of the pop video.

Though idiosyncratic and wildly theatrical, the single nevertheless gave little hint of what was in store. An eclectic string of hits continued well into the new decade, which in many ways mirrored Queen's extravagant and playful flamboyance. By now firmly recast as a singles act, the band mixed and matched styles, from rockabilly ("Crazy Little Thing Called Love," 1979) to disco-funk ("Another One Bites the Dust," 1980) and raised-hands stadium rock ("Radio Ga Ga")—which by 1985 and Live Aid had become Queen's natural home.

This musical eclecticism, which had strayed far from Queen's mid-1970s rock/pop forte, saw a dip in interest in the United States. However, the death of frontman Freddie Mercury in 1991, coupled with a long-running stage show (*We Will Rock You*) and a return to touring with ex-Free vocalist Paul Rodgers, has kept Queen's profile high

ABOVE *The enigmatic and elusive Freddie Mercury (top and above right) and gifted guitarist Brian May were the driving force behind Queen and became one of rock's great double acts.*

Queen

Formed:
London, England

Years active:
1971 to present

Definitive lineup:
*Freddie Mercury,
Brian May,
John Deacon,
Roger Taylor*

Genres: *rock,
hard rock, pop*

Key singles:
*"Bohemian
Rhapsody" (1975),
"Crazy Little Thing
Called Love" (1979)*

Key albums: Sheer
Heart Attack *(1974),*
A Night at the
Opera *(1975)*

Funk

BETWEEN THE MID-1960s and mid-1970s, funk was the predominant, cutting-edge, black music form. With the emphasis firmly on rhythm at the expense of chord sequences or the well-worn 12-bar style, funk was syncopated and propulsive, with the accent firmly on the (first) downbeat—"the one," according to James Brown. While Brown cited Little Richard as the first man of funk, it was Brown who merited the accolade of godfather of funk, thanks to a series of sides from the mid-1960s onward that single-handedly launched the radical, "more black" style. On genre-defining 45s, such as "Out of Sight" (1964) and "Cold Sweat" (1967), guitars, brass, and voices were all utilized primarily to enhance the groove.

ABOVE *Curtis Mayfield released a string of legendary blaxploitation soundtracks, including 1972's Super Fly.*

BELOW *After several hits during the early 1960s, the Isley Brothers got funky, notably on the 1973 hit "That Lady."*

Brown's influence was felt as far as Germany, where krautrock acts such as Can cooked up a psychedelicized take on Brown-style syncopation. Closer to home, jazz pioneer Miles Davis took Brown's template and exaggerated it wildly across a series of early 1970s albums awash with chattering wah-wah sounds and wildly fragmented funk grooves.

Having split from Brown in 1970, his backing band the J.B.s helped develop funk in the new decade, with Bootsy Collins among those who joined forces with George Clinton's P-Funk project. Similarly disposed to psychedelic influence were Sly & the Family Stone, whose 1971 album *There's a Riot Goin' On* both enthralled and mystified

ABOVE *Isaac Hayes performing at London's Rainbow in 1978. The poster promised a night of "full-bodied soul-stirring music," his trademark since his breakthrough, "Theme from Shaft." From Stax producer to the voice of Chef in South Park, Hayes was a man of many talents.*

with its dark funk groove. Stax session musician, songwriter, and producer Isaac Hayes enjoyed massive international success with "Theme from *Shaft*" (1971), the most prominent of a series of early 1970s blaxploitation soundtrack songs.

Other established artists, such as Curtis Mayfield ("Super Fly," 1972), Motown's Stevie Wonder ("Higher Ground," 1973), and Herbie Hancock (*Head Hunters*, 1973),

found their inner funk and broadened its appeal. So did white acts, such as David Bowie ("Fame," 1975), but by this time disco was emerging as a serious dance-floor competitor. Elements of funk lived on through disco acts, such as Chic, and of course Prince, though more pervasive was the incessant sampling of James Brown records (notably "Funky Drummer") on which so much of 1980s hip hop was built.

5 Top funk artists

Isley Brothers: It's Our Thing *(1969)*

Funkadelic: Free Your Mind…And Your Ass Will Follow *(1970)*

Sly & the Family Stone: There's a Riot Goin' On *(1971)*

Curtis Mayfield: Super Fly *(1972)*

James Brown: The Payback *(1973)*

Sly & the Family Stone

HE MAY BE ONE OF ROCK'S most extraordinary characters, but the mythology that surrounds Sly Stone can overshadow the magic of the Family Stone's music, a heady groove of psychedelicized funk that, between 1968 and 1972, enjoyed enormous success in the United States. Sealing the group's fame at Woodstock in 1969, where "I Want to Take You Higher" became the festival's anthem, Sly—like the era—soon experienced a drug-prompted meltdown.

After more than a year in the making, *There's a Riot Goin' On* (1971) was on first inspection a classic burnout record, though its brooding, less-is-more groove and ruined idealism has since been rightly acclaimed as hugely influential. By the mid-1970s, though, Sly Stone, like fellow traveler Miles Davis, had seriously unraveled.

It had been a roller-coaster decade for the man who, in the mid-1960s, had been producing records for upcoming San Francisco psychedelic bands, such as

Grace Slick & the Great Society. Suspecting he could do better, Sly assembled a mixed-race, mixed-gender musical "family" that sprang onto the national stage with the irresistible "Dance to the Music" (1968). Further unity-aspiring hits, such as "Everyday People" (1968) and "Stand!" (1969), followed, before Stone's gradual retreat as the 1970s moved on. Though he has since cleaned up, and even makes the occasional public appearance, the eccentric persona has been a hard one to shake off.

Sly & the Family Stone

Formed: *San Francisco, California*

Years active: *1966–75*

Definitive lineup: *Sly Stone, Larry Graham, Cynthia Robinson, Freddie Stone, Gregg Errico, Rose Stone, Jerry Martini*

Genres: *psychedelic soul, funk*

Key singles: *"Dance to the Music" (1968), "Family Affair" (1971)*

Key albums: *Stand! (1969), There's a Riot Goin' On (1971)*

LEFT *Sly & the Family Stone pictured during their late 1960s heyday. The band epitomized the hopes of social integrationists, and a series of thrilling, clever, and hugely successful records only seemed to further the cause.*

George Clinton & P-Funk

FLAMBOYANT FREAK-FUNK innovator George Clinton was the barmy brains behind P-Funk, quite possibly the most outlandish musical venture undertaken during the 1970s, and the missing link between James Brown and Prince. Clinton fronted two bands—Parliament and Funkadelic—simultaneously: the former aimed at the dance floor, the latter at the mind-fried end of the aesthetic spectrum.

By mid-decade, with slap-bassist Bootsy Collins driving the groove, Parliament were in the ascendant, though P-Funk albums continued to appear under both names until the decade's end. Since then, the enduring influence of Clinton's extraordinary acid-dance-floor hybrid has seen his reputation soar from niche maverick to global pioneer.

Clinton's original intention had been to hitch a ride on the Motown gravy train, though his move to Detroit in the mid-1960s resulted in a deal with a far less significant label. Nevertheless, the Parliaments notched up one U.S. hit single before a legal dispute lost Clinton the right to use the band name. So he formed Funkadelic, a mashed-up psychedelic-funk combo like no other, as evidenced on a head-spinning trio of albums released during 1970 and 1971. By 1976, Clinton had assumed tighter control of both bands, with the focus more readily trained on the tighter, up-tempo grooves of Parliament. It was Funkadelic that earned Clinton his best-known single, though, in 1978's "One Nation Under a Groove."

George Clinton & P-Funk

Formed:
Detroit, Michigan

Years active:
1967 to present

Genres: *funk, soul, psychedelic funk*

Key singles: *"Give Up the Funk (Tear the Roof off the Sucker)" (1976, Parliament), "One Nation Under a Groove" (1978, Funkadelic)*

Key albums: *Free Your Mind…and Your Ass Will Follow (1970, Funkadelic), Mothership Connection (1975, Parliament)*

Fleetwood Mac

THE 1970S RENAISSANCE of Fleetwood Mac was one of the most dramatic turnarounds in rock. With only the rhythm section of bassist John McVie and drummer Mick Fleetwood surviving from the late-1960s blues-boom lineup, it's probably more accurate to talk of two Fleetwood Macs. Mac I were hailed during 1969 and the early months of 1970 as potential rivals to the Beatles, though Mac II are the better remembered of the two lineups.

The blues-fixated original Fleetwood Mac didn't stay purists for long. Guitarist and songwriter Peter Green wrote several of the era's most notable hits, including the delicate "Man of the World" (1969), the Latin-flavored "Black Magic Woman" (1968), and two rock crossover hits, "Oh Well" (1969) and "The Green Manalishi" (1970). After Green's sudden, drug-prompted departure in spring 1970, Mac floundered, eventually winding up in California, where they met soft-rock duo Lindsey Buckingham and Stevie Nicks. A best-selling, self-titled set in 1975 was followed two years later by *Rumours*, an FM-radio phenomenon and

one of the most successful rock albums ever. Fleetwood Mac's convoluted intrapersonal affairs, from which much of the material derived, exploded during the making of the two-disc follow-up, *Tusk* (1979), and has blighted the band's erratic, on-off course ever since.

BELOW LEFT *Mac II, fronted by Stevie Nicks, is perhaps the better remembered of the two groups, thanks in large part to the success of Rumours.*

BELOW *The soul of the original Fleetwood Mac evaporated after guitarist Peter Green (right) quit in 1970. John McVie (left) and Mick Fleetwood (second left) rebuilt the band from scratch.*

Fleetwood Mac

Formed: *London, England*

Years active: *1967 to present*

Definitive lineup: *(Mac I) Peter Green, Mick Fleetwood, John McVie, Jeremy Spencer, Danny Kirwan (Mac II) Lindsey Buckingham, Stevie Nicks, Christine McVie, Mick Fleetwood, John McVie*

Genres: *blues, blues rock, pop, rock*

Key singles: "Oh Well" (1969), "Dreams" (1977)

Key albums: Then Play On (1969), Rumours (1977)

Elton John

THE TRANSFORMATION of an anonymous and struggling singer-songwriter into pop's most ostentatious showman owes much to the liberating force that was glam rock. Having scored a surprise hit in the United States with "Your Song" in 1970, the pianist had looked set to become a sensitive "albums-market" artist, before the joyous abandon of glam soon had him knocking out nostalgia-tinged hits, such as "Crocodile Rock" (1972) and "Saturday Night's Alright for Fighting" (1973).

Pop's ostentatious showman

Despite releasing six albums between 1970 and 1972, the sheer range of hits like 1972's "Honky Cat" (funky charm), "Daniel" (1973) (an unlikely antiwar song), and 1974's "Candle in the Wind" (mawkish sentimentality) confirmed that Elton John—along with long-term lyricist Bernie Taupin—was foremost a singles artist.

By mid-decade, he was breaking records as a stadium act in the United States, though it took a duet ("Don't Go Breaking My Heart" with Kiki Dee) to give

him his first American No. 1 in 1976. After a commercial decline during the late 1970s, followed by battles with the tabloids over his sexuality, and his own struggles with various addictions, Elton reemerged stronger than ever at the end of the 1980s, enjoying No. 1 hits with "Sacrifice" (1989), "Don't Let the Sun Go Down on Me" (a 1991 duet with George Michael) and, most memorably, a revamped "Candle in the Wind" in 1997 to commemorate Diana, Princess of Wales.

ABOVE *Elton John had been merely a bit player in late-1960s pop. By 1975, with his song-writing talents and inner showman gleefully unleashed, he was packing out arenas such as the Dodger Stadium in Los Angeles.*

Elton John

Born: *March 25, 1947, Pinner, Middlesex, England*
Years active: *1964 to present*

Genres: *pop, rock, glam rock, MOR*

Key singles: *"Your Song" (1970), "Rocket Man" (1972)*

Key albums: Elton John *(1970),* Goodbye Yellow Brick Road *(1973)*

Eric Clapton

A BLUES PURIST turned acid-rock virtuoso with 1960s power trio Cream, Eric Clapton made an extraordinary career reinvention during the 1980s by forsaking his guitar-guru past and following Phil Collins into the lucrative realm of the mature, Armani-suited pop balladeer. So successful were hits such as the best-selling albums *August* (1986) and *Unplugged* (1992), as well as that year's "Tears in Heaven" (inspired by the death of his four-year-old son), that Clapton's previous life as a heroin- and booze-addicted guitar hero was virtually invisible to his new audience.

Clapton won his reputation with west London R&B combo the Yardbirds, before—with the group drifting toward the more lucrative pop market—joining the highly esteemed John Mayall's Blues Breakers in April 1965. This year-long association, cemented with the 1966 *Blues Breakers with Eric Clapton* LP, earned him a "Clapton is God" reputation. After two explosive years with Cream, Clapton's overnight conversion to the Band while touring the United States in 1968 prompted him to abandon hell-for-leather blues-rock in favor of a more temperate, soulful blues sound, with his 1970 *Layla* album (as Derek and the Dominos) a career best.

A 1974 cover of Bob Marley's "I Shot the Sheriff" earned Clapton a surprise U.S. No. 1 and did much to popularize reggae, especially in the United States. Almost as surprising has been his blues-playing renaissance, kicked off by the 1994 covers set, *From the Cradle.*

Eric Clapton

Born: *March 30, 1945, Ripley, Surrey, England*
Years active: *1962 to present*

Genres: *blues, R&B, psychedelia, rock*
Key singles: *"Layla" (1971), "I Shot the Sheriff" (1974)*

Key albums: Layla and Other Assorted Love Songs *(1970)*, 461 Ocean Boulevard *(1974)*

ABOVE *Eric Clapton's renaissance began with a hit cover of Bob Marley's "I Shot the Sheriff," followed by further spiritually charged songs, such as Dylan's "Knockin' on Heaven's Door."*

Rod Stewart

AN AMBITIOUS, Mod-styled peacock on London's mid-1960s R&B scene, Rod Stewart emerged during 1970 as frontman with the new-look Faces, formed from the remnants of the Small Faces. By late 1971, both band and Stewart as a soloist had broken internationally, with the singer enjoying the unprecedented accolade of topping both single and album charts on both sides of the Atlantic (with "Maggie May" and *Every Picture Tells a Story*).

It was Stewart's laddish Cockney persona, coupled with a rasping, soulful voice that could melt hearts, that enabled him to pursue two simultaneous careers during the early 1970s. But the growing and increasingly lucrative AOR market opening up in the United States prompted a marked change in direction with the slick and helpfully titled *Atlantic Crossing* (1975), a huge success that spelt the end for the Faces and the emergence of Stewart the jet-setting superstar. It marked a remarkably fertile period for the singer, with a series of chart-topping singles ("Tonight's the Night,"

1976, and "Do Ya Think I'm Sexy?," 1978)— and albums (*A Night on the Town*, 1976, and *Foot Loose & Fancy Free*, 1977).

While, like many of his contemporaries, Rod Stewart has had little new to offer since his late-1970s heyday, in recent years a hugely popular series of *Songbook* albums, featuring Great American standards from the 1930s and 1940s, has confirmed him as a masterful interpreter.

Rod Stewart

Born: *January 10, 1945, London, England*

Years active: *1964 to present*

Genres: *R&B, pop, rock*

Key singles: *"Maggie May" (1971), "Sailing" (1975)*

Key albums: *Every Picture Tells a Story (1971), Atlantic Crossing (1975)*

ABOVE *In 1975 Rod Stewart quit the Faces and took off on a transatlantic trip into the pop mainstream—and into superstardom.*

Bruce Springsteen

IN DIRE NEED OF NEW heroes, the mid-1970s—with a little help from his record label—duly anointed Bruce Springsteen the glum decade's Dylan and hoped he would survive the hype. He did. Almost four decades later, it's clear that the heartland rocker known as "The Boss" more than fulfilled all the "great white hope" publicity he was initially burdened with.

An international folk hero whose lengthy concerts are greeted as near-spiritual affirmations of rock 'n' roll, Springsteen embodies various strands of postwar popular music. He remains a pivotal figure in its continued development, straddling both old values of authenticity and the market-led inclinations of post-1970s mainstream rock.

Before becoming an icon—a T-shirt and denim-clad figure wrapped in the U.S. flag—Springsteen was a New Jersey-raised rocker turned aspiring songwriter. Emerging at roughly the same time as New York poet Patti Smith, he was similarly steeped in and passionate about rock 'n' roll, though he eschewed the more disobedient traditions mined by Smith in favor of character-filled R&B (*The Wild, the Innocent & the E Street Shuffle*, 1973); bold, classic production (*Born to Run*, 1975); and radio-friendly recession rock (*The River*, 1980).

BELOW AND OPPOSITE *After the visual excesses of the glam and progressive era, Springsteen rose to prominence on the back of a "common man" image. It worked especially well in the United States.*

LEFT *Springsteen spars with E. Street Band luminary Clarence Clemons at the Civic Center, Santa Monica, in September 1976. He was still promoting his breakthrough set,* Born to Run, *at the time.*

Born in the U.S.A...

By this time, Springsteen had already become something of an American institution, a rock of ages who demonstrated that, in contrast to punk's nihilistic rage, his humane, homespun response to the plight of the common man would win out. In 1984, he released the album that confirmed it, the iconic, hope-filled *Born in the U.S.A.* Despite its occasional excavation of darker themes, this hoary-voiced and fist-raisingly positive set rocked the arenas and was loudly embraced by the Reagan generation, who greeted the record as a celebration of the nation, and his numerous tours with a lighter-flame reverence more befitting a prophet.

Creatively, Springsteen has been more subdued since *Tunnel of Love* (1987), admitting to losing his way during the 1990s, and more recently has spent time becoming involved in causes and charity work.

Bruce Springsteen

Born: *September 23, 1949, Long Branch, New Jersey*

Years active: *1972 to present*
Genre: *rock*

Key singles: *"Born to Run" (1975), "Dancing in the Dark" (1984)*

Key albums: Born to Run *(1975),* The River *(1980)*

Reggae

THE GROWTH OF A STYLE of music forged on the impoverished streets of southeast Jamaica into a global phenomenon is one of the most remarkable in late-twentieth-century popular music. Reggae served up a distinctive sound, reawakened the world to the spirituality of music, raised awareness of the postcolonial struggle among developing nations, and prompted a revolution in recording techniques. It also produced the most prominent non-Western music superstar—Bob Marley.

At its most potent in the mid-1970s, when Marley was on the rise and the remarkable sound of "dub" lurked in the undergrowth, reggae had its origins in the ska music of the early 1960s. Though its influence has since waned, it can still clearly be heard in dance hall and ragga, as well as rap-inspired vocalizing that had its origins in the braggadocio of the early Jamaican sound-system DJ talkers, or "toasters."

The slowing of ska's hyperactive tempo to a rocksteady beat in 1967 paved the way for the even slower rhythms of reggae, characterized by a brooding, heavily foregrounded drum-and-bass beat. During 1969, Desmond Dekker ("Israelites"), the Upsetters ("Return of Django"), and the Harry J. Allstars ("The Liquidator") all made inroads into the British singles charts. But it was the gradual transformation of the Wailers, fronted by the obviously iconic Bob Marley, into a serious album act that opened up the reggae market. (Marley, like many reggae artists, converted to Rastafarianism in the wake of the visit of spiritual leader Haile Selassie to Jamaica in 1966.)

BELOW LEFT *One of the key albums during reggae's mid-1970s surge in popularity was Burning Spear's Marcus Garvey, which was dense with Rastafari and political messages.*

BELOW *Aside from working with Bob Marley, Lee Perry is best known as a dub pioneer whose best work emanated from his legendary Black Ark studio during the 1970s.*

A genre with a mission

By the mid-1970s, the spacious dub sound, pioneered by King Tubby and Lee "Scratch" Perry, found an eager audience among a generation of British-born Jamaicans in London. Homegrown acts, such as Steel Pulse and dub poet Linton Kwesi Johnson, shared Rock Against Racism bills with punk bands. The Clash covered Junior Murvin and Lee "Scratch" Perry's "Police and Thieves," while the Slits and PiL explored the style more thoroughly.

After Marley's tragic, premature death in 1981, reggae's popularity continued to soar, though as a genre with a mission it seemed to lose its way. Subsequent, controversy-blighted developments, such as dance hall and ragga, have since kept urban Jamaican developments newsworthy.

5 Top reggae artists

Jimmy Cliff/various: The Harder They Come (soundtrack) (1972)
The Wailers: Catch a Fire (1973)

Burning Spear: Marcus Garvey (1975)
Lee "Scratch" Perry: Super Ape (1976)
King Tubby: King Tubby Meets Rockers Uptown (1976)

ABOVE Until Island Records promoted Bob Marley in the manner of a rock star, chartbound reggae had been dominated by instrumentalists such as the Upsetters and the Harry J. Allstars.

Bob Marley

UNTIL 1974, BOB MARLEY was lead singer with the Wailers, a singing group based in Kingston, Jamaica, formed in 1963 around the nucleus of its teenage vocal frontline of Marley, Peter Tosh, and Bunny Wailer. Then, at the prompting of Island Records, Marley was marketed as a rock star, while his ex-colleagues were replaced by a new band, including the rhythm section of Carlton and Ashton Barrett and a female backing trio. Within three years, the charismatic, mellow-voiced Marley had become a superstar.

BELOW *Bob Marley and the Wailers checking in at the Odeon in Birmingham, England, in July 1975, during their acclaimed Natty Dread tour.*

Marley, together with his "wailing Wailers," initially worked with producer Clement "Sir Coxsone" Dodd, with whom they recorded a mix of band-penned ska tunes (including "Simmer Down," a No. 1 hit in Jamaica in 1964) and covers of popular songs, such as the movie theme "What's New, Pussycat?"

After spending several months in 1966 working in a factory in the United States, Marley returned to Jamaica, converted to Rastafarianism, and briefly teamed up with "the Upsetter," producer Lee Perry. Johnny Nash's 1972 success with Marley's "Stir It Up" raised the Wailers' profile, though it was 1973's *Catch a Fire*, closely followed by *Burnin'* (both on Island), that gave the band a foothold in rock-obsessed Britain. Eric Clapton's huge success with Marley's "I Shot the Sheriff" the following year paved the way for Marley's breakthrough in 1975 with the plaintive "No Woman, No Cry."

With 1977's *Exodus*, and its tie-in hit "Waiting in Vain," Marley's international stature was assured. His personal safety, however, was not, and after an attempt on his life in December 1976 he remained in exile in Britain for two years. Returning to Jamaica in 1978 for the One Love peace concert, Marley reasserted his political agenda with 1979's *Survival*, but after a European tour early in 1980, the melanoma that had first been diagnosed in 1977 grew critical. In May 1981, Bob Marley died in Miami en route to his home, Jamaica.

ABOVE LEFT *The dynamic Marley on stage at London's Rainbow in June 1977. Days earlier, he had received the toe injury that led to a diagnosis of cancer, which would cause his death four years later.*

ABOVE RIGHT *Marley in the United States in June 1978, promoting his latest album,* Kaya. *Behind him looms an image of Haile Selassie, onetime emperor of Ethiopia and a revered figure in the Rastafari faith.*

Bob Marley

Born: *February 6, 1945, St. Ann, Jamaica*
Died: *May 11, 1981*

Years active: *1962–81*
Genres: *reggae, ska, rocksteady*

Key singles: *"Get Up, Stand Up" (1973), "Waiting in Vain" (1977)*

Key albums: Catch a Fire *(1973)*, Exodus *(1977)*

Lee "Scratch" Perry

NO PERSON IS MORE synonymous with dub reggae at its deepest and darkest than Lee Perry. While his onetime protégé Bob Marley was enjoying crossover pop-chart fame in the late 1970s, Perry's *Super Ape* albums became the hip alternative, the Clash were covering his "Police and Thieves" (and inviting him to produce their "Complete Control" in return), and Perry's four-track Black Ark studio—sited in his family's home in Kingston, Jamaica—became the stuff of legend.

Lee "Scratch" Perry

Born: *March 20, 1936, Kendal, Jamaica*

Years active: *late 1950s to present*

Genres: *reggae, dub, ska, rocksteady*

Key singles: *"Return of Django" (1969), Junior Murvin's "Police and Thieves" (cowriter/producer, 1976)*

Key albums: *Blackboard Jungle Dub (1973), Super Ape (1976)*

The king of dub, though not necessarily the man who invented the style (King Tubby has an equally good claim on that), Perry remains a prolific producer with a career that stretches back to the late 1950s, when he cut his teeth working at Clement Dodd's legendary Studio One facility in Kingston. After a spell with Joe Gibbs, another noted ska producer, Perry created his own Upsetter label and persona, debuting in typically arresting fashion with "People Funny Boy," which boasted a sample of a crying baby.

After enjoying pop crossover success in Britain in 1969 with "Return of Django," Perry's studio band the Upsetters concocted dubwise takes on spaghetti western and kung-fu soundtrack music, with Perry taking time out to record some of the Wailers' finest material during the early 1970s. Marley moved on, but after the pioneering *Blackboard Jungle Dub* (1973), a collaboration with King Tubby, Perry embarked on a rich decade of productions from his backyard studio.

When Black Art burned down in mysterious circumstances, Perry relocated to Britain, where he gave up smoking—but never music. He now works out of a more sedate studio/home in Switzerland.

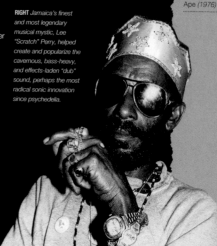

RIGHT *Jamaica's finest and most legendary musical mystic, Lee "Scratch" Perry, helped create and popularize the cavernous, bass-heavy, and effects-laden "dub" sound, perhaps the most radical sonic innovation since psychedelia.*

Fela Kuti and afrobeat

WITH A DYNAMIC, James Brown groove underpinning the big, brassy, and joy-filled energy of Ghanaian highlife, Fela Kuti's afrobeat carried a powerful healing message ("Music is the weapon!") that made him the bane of Nigeria's ruling military elite. Though he was a developing world icon and a consciousness-raiser of the stature of Bob Marley, Fela Kuti's music has taken longer to reverberate around the world than Marley's.

BELOW *Kuti with ex-Cream percussion virtuoso Ginger Baker. During the 1970s, the pair worked together on various projects, including Kuti's* Live! *album, recorded with his band Africa '70.*

BELOW *Kuti at London's Brixton Academy in 1983. Appreciation of his work has grown in recent years, partly through the success of the theatrical production* Fela!

Its emphasis on the groove, overlaid with hypnotic call-and-response voices and a huge, two-of-everything sound, was never suited to fit the Western playlist format. But Kuti's insistent, richly textured beat has proved remarkably resilent, as the success of the recent *Fela!* musical has proved.

After a spell in the cultural hotbed of America during the late 1960s, Kuti returned to Lagos in 1970 and formed Africa '70, an ensemble complete with multiple horns, guitars, and dancers. The infusion of politics and wildly popular music proved too potent for the authorities, who in 1977 crushed his Kalakuta Republic commune. Reemerging to form his Movement of the People political party, Kuti—who married 27 wives in an onstage ceremony in 1978—was back in jail in 1984 on trumped-up charges.

Finding an international audience with a new outfit, Egypt '80, Kuti's activism continued to land him in trouble. But it was AIDS that finally floored him, and in 1997 the 58-year-old "King of Afrobeat" was dead.

Punk rock

WRAPPED IN THE RHETORIC of revolution, punk emerged in 1976 and 1977 as a threat not only to social order but to rock itself. When the Sex Pistols declared, "We're not into music, we're into chaos," a generation of have-a-go antiheroes, disenfranchised by progressive rock flash and the cerebral concerns of singer-songwriters, answered the call with a DIY movement that took rock back to the clubs and put a fabulous fire in its belly. An iconoclastic mix of indignation and invention, the grassroots amateurism of punk sent shock waves though the music industry.

It wasn't entirely without precedent. Punk had been a term of mild abuse aimed at the garage-rock combos of mid-1960s America, a proudly numbskull tradition taken to noisier, more destructive extremes by the Velvet Underground and the Stooges. The Sex Pistols' Svengali-like manager Malcolm McLaren, who briefly managed the New York Dolls in the mid-1970s, understood this. Throwing in his own predilection for outré rock 'n' rollers from the 1950s, and for the subversive, politically charged slogans of the Situationist International, popular on the riot-torn streets of Paris in 1968, McLaren's mischievous ideology created an aura that was remarkably different to that of previous subcultures.

TOP *The Clash, fronted by singer Joe Strummer, brought a political dimension to punk rock during the late 1970s.*

ABOVE *Patti Smith was a crucial figure in the transition from art rock to punk.*

"We're not into music, we're into chaos..."

Although the immediate roots of punk rock could be found at CBGB in New York (a regular haunt of the Ramones and Patti Smith), and on London's pub-rock circuit, it was the Sex Pistols who changed everything. When the Pistols headlined the two-day, 100 Club Punk Rock Festival in London, in September 1976, no more than a dozen bands were affiliated to the new antirock style. Within a year, the Pistols were the hottest band in the world, and had spawned thousands of imitators. By 1978, punk's initial thrust had fragmented, essentially into the pop-friendly New Wave or more challenging post-punk.

RIGHT *Sex Pistols' frontman Johnny Rotten snarled and swore his way to become the disobedient voice of the Blank Generation.*

5 Top punk artists

Sex Pistols: *"God Save the Queen"* (1977)

The Clash: *"White Riot"* (1977)

The Damned: *"New Rose"* (1976)

X-Ray Spex: *"Oh Bondage, Up Yours!"* (1977)

The Adverts: *"One Chord Wonders"* (1977)

Patti Smith

A TEENAGE OUTCAST from New Jersey, Smith was turned on to the inspirational power of music after catching the Rolling Stones on television, an experience that liberated her both spiritually and sexually. It was an epiphany that never left her, for a constant feature in Smith's career has been her evangelical belief in rock 'n' roll as a force for personal, even political transformation.

Patti Smith

Born: *December 30, 1946, Chicago, Illinois*

Years active: *1971 to present*

Genres: *punk, rock*

Key singles: *"Hey Joe" (1974), "Because the Night" (1978)*

Key albums: *Horses (1975), Radio Ethiopia (1976)*

The power of Patti Smith's message was never greater than during the mid-1970s when, after several years as a beat-inspired, Rimbaud-fixated poet in New York, she began fronting a bona fide rock band and emerged with the groundbreaking *Horses* (1975). An iconoclastic mix of forgotten garage-rock riffs and sprawling, stream-of-consciousness improvisation, *Horses*—draped in a sexually ambiguous Robert Mapplethorpe cover—was streetwise and radical. A new wave had arrived.

While associated both with the burgeoning new-wave scene centered on New York's CBGB and with fellow New Jersey antistar Bruce Springsteen, Smith—a poet, a woman, an artist—preferred to stand alone. Her untamed energy and monochrome image anticipated punk, though that relationship was complicated by the more polished direction of her 1976 follow-up, *Radio Ethiopia*. Another epiphany, in 1980, found Smith forsaking rock 'n' roll for motherhood and family, but when she reemerged in the mid-1990s, her belief in rock as a force for what she often calls "illumination" remained intact.

LEFT *No one did more to reacquaint rock with its rebel soul than Patti Smith. Her early performances, such as the one depicted here in Copenhagen in 1976, were raw and explosive.*

Ramones

THE RAMONES—four leather and denim-clad clones from Queens, New York, who rattled out two-minute, speed-driven paeans to glue-sniffing and pinheads—were the original comic-book punk rockers. Leading lights of New York's blossoming, mid-1970s punk scene, the defiantly rudimentary Ramones had as much in common with classic 1960s pop as they did with their more iconoclastic brethren in London's Kings Road.

ABOVE *The Ramones flaunt what is still regarded as the quintessential rock 'n' roll look. That's Johnny (foreground) seeking to upstage frontman Joey.*

Returning pop to its original outcast status, the Ramones' rebellion was symbolic, their lightning pace wall of sound akin to back-alley Phil Spector. Above all, the glorious, grainy simplicity of songs such as "Now I Wanna Sniff Some Glue" and "Blitzkrieg Bop" on their 1976 debut album roused a new, so-called Blank Generation into action.

Despite their seminal and lasting influence, the Ramones never found much mainstream success. After the short, sharp shock of their first two albums, it was a third, 1977's *Rocket to Russia*, that contained their catchiest melodies. But it was only when Spector was coaxed into producing *End of the Century* (1980) that they landed a Top 10 hit single—a cover of the old Spector hit, "Baby, I Love You."

The Ramones changed drummers over the years, though their musical template remained consistent right through to 1996, when "da brudders" (they weren't) packed it in. In the title of their 1984 album *Too Tough to Die* proved not to be prophetic: by 2004, Joey (aged 49), Dee Dee (50), and Johnny (55) were dead.

The original comic-book punk rock outcasts

Ramones

Formed:
New York

Years active:
1974–96

Definitive lineup:
Dee Dee Ramone, Johnny Ramone, Joey Ramone, Tommy Ramone

Genre: *punk rock*

Key singles:
"Blitzkrieg Bop" (1976), "Baby, I Love You" (1980)

Key albums:
Ramones (1976), Rocket to Russia (1977)

Sex Pistols

IT'S DIFFICULT TO IMAGINE how polite and acquiescent rock and pop had become by the mid-1970s. Four *Clockwork Orange*-inspired ruffians from inner London, who went by the unlikely name of the Sex Pistols, changed all that. Playing roughly hewn Small Faces, Stooges, and Monkees covers in and around the London club and college circuit, the band quickly earned themselves a reputation as noisome numbskulls bent on dragging rock into the gutter.

That was exactly the kind of thing that muckraking manager Malcolm McLaren—who still equated rock with glinting flick knives and filthy fantasies—wanted to hear. Throughout 1976, a provocative new punk subculture grew up around SEX, the outré London fashion hangout McLaren ran with partner Vivienne Westwood at 310 Kings Road. The hip haberdashery did a fine line in inflammatory T-shirts bearing slogans such as "Never Trust a Hippie" and "Anarchy in the UK"—sentiments soon echoed in the Pistols' own songs. When the new iconoclasts were branded "unmusical," guitarist Steve Jones retorted: "We're not into music, we're into chaos."

"Never Trust a Hippie"

TOP *"Johnny Rotten" brought a new sense of attack to performance during 1976, fronting the outrageously dynamic Sex Pistols.*

ABOVE *Manager Malcolm McLaren doesn't look too perturbed by his arrest during the Sex Pistols' infamous boat trip in May 1977.*

ABOVE *After Sid Vicious (left) joined, the Sex Pistols' infamy grew greater still, though what looked good in publicity photographs turned out to be fatal for the band—and for Sid, who was dead by February 1979.*

After the Pistols outraged Britain with a string of four-letter words on live television in December 1976, they were hastily dropped by EMI, and their first national tour was derailed by a series of bans. Two months later, bassist and key songwriter Glen Matlock was sacked; he was a closet Beatles fan, claimed McLaren. Matlock's replacement was Sid Vicious, the genuinely nonmusical and chain-swinging sidekick of frontman Johnny Rotten.

From this moment on, what the press had initially dubbed "the nightmare of British culture" quickly descended into farce, with drug busts, beatings, and establishment-baiting boat trips climaxing in January 1978 with an acrimonious split at the end of the band's battle-scarred U.S. tour. But the Pistols' impact, both musically and culturally, was immense. They had single-handedly invented punk. "God Save the Queen" topping the British singles chart in the week of Elizabeth II's Silver Jubilee celebrations felt genuinely insurrectionary. And *Never Mind the Bollocks, Here's the Sex Pistols* remains one of the classic rock records.

Sex Pistols

Formed: *London, England*
Years active: *1975–78*

Definitive lineup: *Johnny Rotten, Steve Jones, Glen Matlock, Paul Cook*

Genre: *punk rock*
Key singles: *"Anarchy in the UK" (1976), "God Save the Queen" (1977)*

Key albums: Never Mind the Bollocks, Here's the Sex Pistols *(1977),* The Great Rock 'n' Roll Swindle *(1979)*

Disco fever

THE MID-1960S VOGUE for discotheques, both fashionably French sounding and impossibly groovy, was eclipsed during the rock era by the proliferation of festivals and the expansion of pop into seated concert halls and, by the early 1970s, stadiums. Around this time, a new club scene underground, mainly catering to black and gay audiences, emerged in New York. Boasting hi-tech sound systems, which sent the new, "four-to-the-floor" post-Philadelphia soul beats resounding around sweaty, glitterball-flecked rooms, the emerging disco music soundtracked a new era of hedonism that centered on sex and the dance floor.

The first superstar of disco was Donna Summer, whose early Giorgio Moroder-produced work reached a head-spinning, metronomic climax in 1977 with "I Feel Love." Rockers such as Frank Zappa, who lampooned "the dancing fool" in song, were roused into a "Disco Sucks" frenzy in 1977 after the enormous success of *Saturday Night Fever*, with its Bee Gees-penned soundtrack and John Travolta moves, sent disco culture global.

Ironically, as the war between rock and disco peaked, so too did the style, with Chic's Nile Rodgers and Bernard Edwards creating a bass line that was sampled to death during the 1980s ("Good Times") and penning the ultimate paean to dance-floor delirium ("Lost in Music"). Hi-NRG, techno, house—and everyone from Prince to Grace Jones—all emerged as variants of the form.

BELOW With her outlandish costumes and retinue of assistants, Donna Summer was the first diva of dance. Her 1977 hit, "I Feel Love," remains a pop landmark.

Bee Gees

AFTER AN ABJECT EARLY 1970s, which saw them plunge from international stardom to the supper-club circuit, the Bee Gees' reemergence as the first family of disco later in the decade was a reinvention as remarkable as it was unexpected. But while the soaraway success of the *Saturday Night Fever* movie soundtrack (1977) virtually reduced the Gibb brothers' earlier career to something akin to prehistory, the binding factor that lay behind all elements of the trio's extraordinary career has been an unswerving belief in the power of harmony and melody.

That, together with a crowd-pleasing professionalism, was fostered in the young trio of English expatriates, who sang their way around Australia during the early 1960s, before deciding to try their luck in Swinging London. Between 1967 and 1969, the group scored a series of hits with melancholy, ballad-style material (such as "Massachusetts," "World," "I've Gotta Get a Message to You"), and released an ambitious concept album, *Odessa* (1969), before fraternal rivalries between frontmen Barry and Robin caused the latter to quit. Though it briefly looked as if Robin's solo success would eclipse that of the band's, neither party was happy with the rupture.

Regrouping in 1970, the Bee Gees briefly conquered the U.S. market with "Lonely Hearts" and the chart-topping "How Can You Mend a Broken Heart?" before again falling into disrepair. A management-prompted exploration into soul-influenced disco saved them, and after the chart-topping success of "Jive Talkin'" (1975), the Bee Gees were permanently associated with a peculiarly falsetto-driven dance-floor nirvana.

ABOVE *Pretenders to the Beatles' crown in the late 1960s, the Bee Gees enjoyed a career-defining rebirth during the late 1970s as silver-clad disco deities. Their* Saturday Night Fever *soundtrack provided an escapist alternative to punk.*

Bee Gees

Formed: *Brisbane, Australia*

Years active: *1958–2003*

Definitive lineup: *Barry Gibb, Robin Gibb, Maurice Gibb*

Genres: *pop, disco*

Key singles: *"Jive Talkin'" (1975), "Night Fever" (1978)*

Key albums: Saturday Night Fever *(1977)*, Spirits Having Flown *(1979)*

New wave

INITIALLY VIRTUALLY indistinguishable from punk, new wave—a category inspired by a radical generation of artful, adventurous, French moviemakers from the 1960s—quickly became associated with all manner of new, upbeat, fresh-sounding bands that smashed a little added sophistication through punk's three-chord barrier.

During 1977, the term certainly signified something a little off-kilter to the tide of Sex Pistols imitators who rushed to cash in on punk. As numerous bands, small-time idealists, and entrepreneurs formed their own, often one-man-band, record labels, the new wave threatened to engulf and perhaps destroy the industry by offering a new economic model, as well as promising a clear break with the music of the past.

Then the terminology got hijacked. With punk rock beginning to look and sound distinctly passé, new wave was popularly regarded as the radio-friendly end of the post-punk diaspora. Linked by their desire to attain full commercial potential, a wide range of so-called new-wave artists became pop-chart regulars—from pub rockers (Ian Dury, Dr. Feelgood) and rock hopefuls (Boomtown Rats, the Motors) to erudite

From power pop to art punk

songwriters (Elvis Costello, Graham Parker), distinctly adult opportunists (the Police, Mink DeVille), and retro-inspired combos (the Jam, Blondie).

In the United States, the new-wave tag was even more wide ranging, comprising both Beatles-inspired power-pop combos (Cheap Trick, the Shoes) and art-punk mavericks (Television, Talking Heads, Pere Ubu). A popular 1977 compilation, titled *New Wave* and showcasing the best of the new American breed, managed to feature both prototype punk quartet the Ramones and the Runaways, a hyped-up all-girl combo from pre-punk times. More reasonably "new wave" were vigorous new acts, such as Talking Heads and the B-52's, neither of whom sounded much like punk rock but nevertheless owed their existence to the new punk-inspired aesthetic.

If defining the style was always slippery, nailing the fashion was not: skinny tie, granddad shirt, and tight black trousers.

5 Top new-wave artists

Elvis Costello: *"Watching the Detectives" (1977)*

Talking Heads: *"Psycho Killer" (1977)*
Television: *"Marquee Moon" (1977)*

Blondie: *"Picture This" (1978)*
B-52's: *"Rock Lobster" (1979)*

Elvis Costello

EVIDENCE THAT THE new wave was creating space for fresh voices came in summer 1977, when Elvis Costello broke through with the up-tempo bop of *My Aim Is True*. Initially regarded as a novelty act—and after Presley's death in August 1977 a tasteless one—thanks to the name and Buddy Holly-style specs, Costello's sophistication as a songwriter enabled him to flourish and endure without being hampered by genre rigidity.

Born Declan MacManus, the son of a singer and musician with the Joe Loss Orchestra, this onetime failed mid-1970s country rocker became the first star of celebrated British independent label Stiff Records. His debut album was soon followed by a unique-sounding hit single, the clipped, reggae-influenced "Watching the Detectives." From that moment, Costello was in the ascendant, following the most robust *This Year's Model* (1978) with the transatlantic success, *Armed Forces* (1979).

Costello's eclecticism became more apparent in the new decade, with a series of albums that drew on soul (*Get Happy!!*, 1980), country (*Almost Blue*, 1981), pure pop (*Punch the Clock*, 1983), and rootsy Americana (*King of America*, 1986). He has undertaken many collaborations (including those with Burt Bacharach, Paul McCartney, and the Brodsky Quartet), which have tended to eclipse his erratically paced solo career.

Elvis Costello

Born: *August 25, 1954, London, England*

Years active: *1974 to present*

Genres: *new wave, rock, singer-songwriter*

Key singles: *"Watching the Detectives" (1977), "Veronica" (1989)*

Key albums: This Year's Model *(1978)*, Armed Forces *(1979)*

RIGHT *Calling himself Elvis and coming on like a stroppy Buddy Holly marked Costello out from the pack in 1977.*

Blondie

LIKE ALICE COOPER a decade earlier, Blondie were a band from impeccably cultish origins and eventually became consumed by the persona of their singer. Unlike Cooper, Debbie Harry became a pop-culture pinup of the media age, the first in a long roll call from Madonna to Lady Gaga. Being fronted by a peroxide and punky lip-gloss icon seemed to do Blondie little harm in their unstoppable rise to fame as the acceptable face of the new wave.

Despite their origins in the club scene of downtown New York, Blondie emerged with a self-titled debut (1976) that knowingly harked back to the girl group sound of pre-Beatles America. With the departure of bassist Gary Valentine, and a lucrative new record deal, the early whiff of nostalgia was soon eclipsed by a more dynamic, power-pop sound better suited to new wave-obsessed Britain, where the group broke in 1978.

Over the next three years, Blondie hit a commercial high in 1979 with "Heart Of Glass," an irrepressible slice of new-wave disco that topped charts on both sides of the Atlantic, following it with a string of increasingly glossy hits. Harry's perceived dominance of the band, coupled with musical uncertainties, brought this extraordinarily successful pop machine to a close in 1982, though since 1997 they have been active on the comeback circuit.

Blondie

Formed:
New York

Years active:
1974–82, 1997 to present

Genres: *new wave, pop, disco*

Definitive lineup:
Debbie Harry, Chris Stein, Clem Burke, Frank Infante, Jimmy Destri

Key singles:
"Denis" (1978), "Heart of Glass" (1979)

Key albums: Plastic Letters *(1978),* Parallel Lines *(1978)*

ABOVE AND LEFT *One of a clutch of CBGB bands that went overground in the late 1970s, Blondie brought a remarkably well-tuned pop sensibility to their punk-lite sound.*

AC/DC

BY THE LATE 1970s, hard rock and heavy metal (as it was still known) had largely fallen out of critical favor. Uprooting in 1976 from Australia to Britain, AC/DC sneaked between the genres, thanks to their striking name and tough, accelerated sound. They were an electrifying enough proposition to find themselves briefly feted in punkish circles, though by the time of their 1979 breakthrough set, *Highway to Hell*, it was fairly obvious in which camp the dynamic live act belonged.

In February 1980, with AC/DC at a major crossroads in their career, their big-boozing frontman Bon Scott was found dead after a binge. Although formed in 1973 in Sydney by brothers Malcolm and Angus Young (whose onstage schoolboy persona was the band's visual calling card), Scott's gravelly voice had been a key element in the band's sound. That made the success of the Mutt Lange-produced *Back in Black* later that year, with ex-Geordie singer Brian Johnson in tow, all the more impressive, earning the band their first real success in the United States. AC/DC never quite hit such highs again, though unlike so many contemporaries, their reputation has never plummeted. Still touring the world to packed-out arenas, AC/DC have become one of the highest-grossing bands of all time.

RIGHT *Original frontman Bon Scott carries the band's guitar prodigy, Angus Young, on his shoulders, as AC/DC take their uncompromising sound to Hollywood in 1977.*

AC/DC

Formed: *Sydney, Australia*
Years active: *1973 to present*
Genres: *hard rock, rock, heavy metal*

Definitive lineup: *Bon Scott, Angus Young, Malcolm Young, Cliff Williams, Phil Rudd*

Key singles: *"Let There Be Rock" (1977), "Highway to Hell" (1979)*

Key albums: Highway to Hell *(1979)*, Back in Black *(1980)*

The Clash

FOR A BRIEF MOMENT during 1977, the Clash eclipsed the Sex Pistols as the authentic voice of punk. Early singles, such as "White Riot" and "Complete Control," and the social critique that ran throughout their 1977 debut album, gave vent to punk's political rage. Within a year, all that had changed with a second album, *Give 'Em Enough Rope*, aimed at a more mainstream American rock audience. That legacy—the Clash of taut, committed anthems and a confident swagger— has been the model for two generations of imitators.

Given their enormous cultural impact during 1977 and 1978, it's a testament to the band's achievements that they overcame their loud and messy punk origins to become one of a small handful of classic, quintessential rock 'n' roll bands. Nevertheless, while almost entirely lacking in gloss and finesse, 1977's *The Clash* remains the most evocative and indispensible document of dole-line rock.

By the decade's end, the wide-ranging and accomplished *London's Calling* (1979) briefly returned the Clash's cultural center of gravity to Britain, while nudging the group a little farther up the U.S. charts. A potentially career-busting triple set, *Sandinista!* (1980),

was followed by the frills-free sound of *Combat Rock* (1982), and with it, two of the band's biggest hits, "Should I Stay or Should I Go" and "Rock the Casbah."

ABOVE *The Clash post-London Calling. The frontline of Paul Simonon, Mick Jones, and Joe Strummer was one of the most iconic of its time.*

TOP *The Clash of their rage-filled 1977 debut album were almost unrecognizable once they hit America and shed their "punk" tag.*

The Clash

Formed:
London, England

Years active:
1976–86

Definitive lineup:
Joe Strummer, Mick Jones, Paul Simonon, Topper Headon

Genres:
punk rock, rock

Key singles:
"Complete Control" (1977), "London Calling" (1979)

Key albums: The Clash *(1977),* London Calling *(1979)*

Post-punk

PUNK IGNITED an explosion of tribes and terminology, stirred into action by its anything-goes aesthetic and rabid desire for change. At the populist end were the new-wave acts, essentially rock and pop played at a more accelerated pace. Lurking in the undergrowth, and far more in tune with punk's original message of rule-breaking, was a vast patchwork of lesser-known acts who thrilled the newly energized rock audience with hitherto unimagined sounds.

Early dissenters from punk's three-chord orthodoxy were Subway Sect (with their slogan: "No more rock 'n' roll for you"), shock 'n' awe noise terrorists Throbbing Gristle, and Siouxsie & the Banshees. The latter, originally Sex Pistols superfans, debuted at the 100 Club Punk Rock Festival in September 1976 with a free-for-all based around "The Lord's Prayer." By 1978, the Banshees had instigated a dissonant, austere sound (on *The Scream*) that owed far more to the Velvet Underground than the familiar rock 'n' roll swagger being peddled by contemporaries such as the Clash.

Around them clustered all manner of miscreants. John Lydon's post-Sex Pistols project, PiL (Public Image Ltd), owed more to krautrock and dub than numbskull punk. All-girl punk originals the Slits thrillingly dismantled orthodox boy rhythms. Wire, the Fall, the Pop Group, Pere Ubu (expats from Cleveland, Ohio, who relocated to London), Joy Division, Gang of Four, and electronics-based combos, such as Cabaret Voltaire and 23 Skidoo, extended punk's remit into fields variously dubbed avant-funk, industrial music, and neo-psychedelia.

After the death of Joy Division's Ian Curtis in May 1980, post-punk waned, though its influence was clearly heard in mid-1980s alternative rock, namely Sonic Youth, Big Black, and Butthole Surfers. In recent years, the genre name and a more streamlined, Gang of Four version of post-punk has been hijacked by bands such as Franz Ferdinand and the Killers.

OPPOSITE TOP *Siouxsie & the Banshees, rabid Pistols' fans who later became flag bearers of the post-punk boom.*

OPPOSITE BOTTOM *The Cure—led by Robert Smith, left—combined post-punk atmospherics with a melodic sensibility.*

OPPOSITE CENTER *The Slits made some remarkable recordings for John Peel before their reggae-influenced debut,* Cut.

RIGHT *Joy Division's Ian Curtis. Against all odds, the band—renamed New Order—survived and thrived after his death.*

5 Top post-punk artists

Siouxsie and the Banshees: The Scream *(1978)*

Wire: Chairs Missing *(1978)*
Gang of Four: Entertainment! *(1979)*

Joy Division: Unknown Pleasures *(1979)*
The Cure: Seventeen Seconds *(1980)*

Featuring

Michael Jackson • Duran Duran • The Police • Kate Bush • Depeche Mode • Prince • U2 •
The Smiths • Madonna • Def Leppard • Guns N' Roses • Sonic Youth • R.E.M. • Public Enemy •
Beastie Boys • Metallica • New Order

1980s

1980s: Introduction

THE DEFINING SOUND of the 1980s was digital technology. Whether it was hair-raising metal guitars, acid-house bleeps, or the rhymes, rhythms, and head-spinning samples of hip hop, it was technology that dominated.

The decade began with rock and pop occupying a privileged place in contemporary culture, thanks to the raucous, headline-hugging impact of punk and the energizing dance-floor revolution prompted by disco. Technology quickly moved center stage, though. In Britain the fashion elite New Romantics provided a vanguard audience for a new generation of cold wave-induced synth-pop acts (Depeche Mode, Soft Cell, Human League), who created catchy pop from clinical electro beats with varying degrees of emotion. But when urban black American DJs augmented their turntable talents with sampling machines, a sonic revolution every bit as powerful as punk took hold. Loud, abrasive, and defiantly subcultural, hip hop brought hitherto subversive notions of repetition, a collaged, mashed-up version of rock and pop's past, and a new, forceful "rap" vocal style into the mainstream, changing popular music forever.

BELOW A South Bronx pioneer, Grandmaster Flash is forever associated with 1982's "The Message," which unveiled hip hop as an ideal medium for social comment.

Sounds of the decade

"Ashes to Ashes":
David Bowie (1980)

"Tainted Love":
Soft Cell (1981)

"Sexual Healing":
Marvin Gaye (1982)

"The Message":
*Grandmaster Flash &
the Furious Five (1982)*

"Blue Monday":
New Order (1983)

"Walk This Way":
Run-DMC (1986)

The decade's other great musical initiative was the emergence of a more rudimentary form of dance music via Detroit-inspired techno, house, and the British acid-house boom. Almost entirely electronic, and coinciding with a new era of faux-psychedelic drugs (ecstasy) and open-air "raves," the style prompted the so-called Second Summer of Love during 1988 and 1989. Dance culture remained a dominant musical and social force for the next decade and a half.

Despite this, the 1980s were oddly conservative in many respects. The old guard, such as the Rolling Stones and David Bowie, sacrificed themselves to the new technologies and ended up hitting career lows. Banished to the sidelines by punk, metal reemerged stronger than ever, both in its extreme (thrash) and mainstream (soft metal) varieties. And the success of Live Aid in 1985 confirmed that rock was no longer the preserve of students and alternative culture habitués—but of the masses.

ABOVE *On July 13, 1985, Live Aid harnessed the power of pop and rock to help relieve the ongoing famine in Ethiopia. An estimated 1.5 billion people watched the dual concert broadcast live from London's Wembley Stadium—where acts included U2 (above left) and Status Quo (above)—and Philadelphia's JFK Stadium.*

"Push It":
Salt-N-Pepa (1987)

"Sweet Child o' Mine":
Guns N' Roses (1988)

"Voodoo Ray":
A Guy Called Gerald (1988)

"Fight the Power":
Public Enemy (1989)

1980s: Time line

1980

January 1980
Cliff Richard is awarded an OBE in the Queen's New Year's Honours list (he will become a "Sir" in 1995). Later rock-related recipients of royal patronage will include Bono, Ian Anderson, John Cale, David Gilmour, and Elton John.

February 1980
The hard-rock fightback begins in earnest with the release of *Metal for Muthas*, the first of two compilations showcasing the "New Wave of British Heavy Metal" movement.

April 1980
As the new national flag is raised, Bob Marley & the Wailers play a set at the independence ceremony in Harare, Zimbabwe—a key moment in African liberation.

May 1980
The television premier of Paul McCartney's latest 45, the infectious and lighthearted "Coming Up," is seen by John Lennon. Days later, he makes preparations for his comeback after a five-year silence.

August 1980
David Bowie launches "Ashes to Ashes," his epitaph for the 1970s, with a stunning video promo that includes a grown-up Major Tom wandering through a solarized landscape with assorted Blitz Club habitués.

December 1980
After John Lennon is shot dead by deluded fan Mark Chapman outside his Dakota residence in New York City, many celebrities quietly tighten up their security arrangements.

Mourners in New York City

September 1981
Adam & the Ants' transformation from punk-rock has-beens to wardrobe-obsessed pop heroes is complete when "Prince Charming" tops the British singles chart. Only when Adam goes solo next year will U.S. success follow.

Adam Ant

December 1981
An old Kraftwerk song from 1978, "The Model," is revived with chart-topping results. The group's influence on hip hop and on electropop manifests itself in the months ahead.

1982

January 1982
Electro duo Soft Cell land an old Northern soul club hit, "Tainted Love," on the U.S. chart. Though it stays there for a then-unprecedented 43 weeks, the duo prove too risqué for U.S. tastes and are eclipsed by fluffier contemporaries.

1980-1982

June 1980

A movie offshoot from a popular *Saturday Night Live* TV sketch featuring John Belushi and Dan Ackroyd, *The Blues Brothers* makes its debut. In the process, the movie revives interest in vintage soul and R&B.

The Blues Brothers

July 1980

Two months after the death of singer Ian Curtis on May 18, Joy Division release their swansong album, *Closer*. The austere cover art, featuring a photo of a tomb, had been chosen prior to Curtis's death.

Ian Curtis

1981

March 1981

With post-punk stalling at the checkout, rowdy metal trio Motörhead—fronted by biker's favorite Lemmy—record shows on their spring tour. The resulting *No Sleep 'til Hammersmith* tops the British albums chart in the summer.

May 1981

Ex-Sex Pistol John Lydon cowers behind a hail of bottles after a riot breaks out at New York club the Ritz when his latest band PiL "perform" provocatively from behind a screen.

June 1981

With Britain in the grip of race and poverty riots, ska revivalists the Specials change their style for a stunning swansong, "Ghost Town," which captures the prevailing mood.

August 1981

MTV, the world's first around-the-clock music television station, goes on air with a novelty song by British-based one-hit-wonders Buggles. The title? "Video Killed the Radio Star."

February 1982

Weeks after biting the head off a live bat at a gig in Texas, Ozzy Osbourne is arrested for a misdemeanor at the Alamo in San Antonio, Texas. In an eventful year, Ozzy marries his manager Sharon Arden in July.

March 1982

Ex-Runaways guitarist Joan Jett emerges as a million-selling artist in her own right with "I Love Rock 'n' Roll," a rousing cover of a little-known hit by mid-1970s British pop combo the Arrows.

Joan Jett

May 1982

With hip-hop culture—graffiti, break dancing—increasingly newsworthy, the phenomenon goes global with Grandmaster Flash and the Furious Five's "The Message," an irresistible and hugely successful slice of conscious rap.

1980s: Time line

Michael Jackson and Quincy Jones

1982

July 1982
Specially commissioned for the soundtrack of *Rocky III*, Survivor's "Eye of the Tiger" tops the U.S. chart for six weeks. Three decades on, it remains the favorite of fitness trainers the world over.

October 1982
The digital revolution gets firmly under way when the first commercially available compact discs appear in stores in Japan. Billy Joel's *52nd Street* is an early favorite.

1983

February 1983
Michael Jackson's *Thriller* tops the U.S. albums chart. An extraordinary success, it goes on to spend 37 weeks at the pop summit, sealing the singer's reputation as the King of Pop, in its journey to becoming the biggest-selling album of all time.

November 1983
Another original punk-rock face, ex-Generation X frontman Billy Idol, reaps the rewards of a glossy makeover when his solo album *Rebel Yell* goes into the Top 20 in the United States.

Quiet Riot

November 1983
Glam metal becomes a significant force when, eight months after its release, Quiet Riot's *Metal Health* tops the U.S. chart. Success for W.A.S.P. and Mötley Crüe duly follows.

1984

January 1984
Despite a ban by the BBC, Frankie Goes to Hollywood hit No. 1 in the British chart with their innuendo-flavored debut single, "Relax." The band will repeat the chart-topping feat with their next two singles.

Madonna

September 1984
The star of the first MTV Awards ceremony is jazz-fusion legend Herbie Hancock, who walks off with five prizes. It's newcomer Madonna who grabs the headlines, though, after an erotically charged performance of her forthcoming hit, "Like a Virgin."

1985

February 1985
Widely acknowledged as the founding fathers of punk and alternative rock, the Velvet Underground sanction the release of *VU*, a rapturously received collection of late-1960s outtakes that confirms the boom in retro releases.

1982–1985

New Order

March 1983
Refashioning themselves as an electro-dance act in the wake of Ian Curtis's death, ex-Joy Division miserablists New Order capture a new audience with the dolefully up-tempo "Blue Monday."

May 1983
Motown celebrates its first quarter century with the NBC-TV spectacular, *The Motown 25 Special*. Man of the moment is Michael Jackson, who moonwalks his way through his latest hit, "Billie Jean."

July 1983
The rock and metal renaissance receives a real boost when the San Francisco-based Metallica emerge with *Kill 'Em All*. Fast and hard, it fires a loud warning shot for the advance of trash metal.

March 1984
For decades a refuge for all manner of aspiring poets and pop professors, rock is never quite the same again after Rob Reiner's *This Is Spinal Tap* sends up its worst excesses.

April 1984
Heartened by the wider metal revival, the original Deep Purple reform after almost a decade of near devout unfashionability. The reunion LP, *Perfect Strangers*, does well, and the band stay together for the long haul.

May 1984
Tina Turner resuscitates her career with her fifth solo album, *Private Dancer*. "What's Love Got to Do with It," a quintessentially 1980s power ballad, is the biggest of several hit singles lifted from the album.

Tina Turner

Live Aid

July 1985
Simultaneous concerts in London and Philadelphia create history when Live Aid brings together the cream of rock and pop royalty in a bid to alleviate suffering in Africa in the wake of the famine in Ethiopia.

September 1985
As a mark of how pop's pendulum of power has shifted, music-publishing rights for much of the Beatles' catalog end up in the control of Michael Jackson, who outbids his ex-Beatle buddy Paul McCartney with a $47 million offer.

December 1985
After two decades that have seen Pink Floyd transform from a humdrum R&B covers band into prog-rock royalty, bassist and ideas man Roger Waters quits after a lengthy standoff with guitarist David Gilmour.

1980s: Time line

1986

February 1986
Swedish rock act Europe enjoy massive international success with "The Final Countdown," ushering in a golden age of soft metal. The song becomes an evergreen at numerous sporting occasions.

July 1986
The rock-rap crossover hit "Walk This Way," the brainchild of Def Jam producer Rick Rubin, unites Run-DMC with Aerosmith and paves the way for an extensive fusion of the two musical forms.

August 1986
Eager to showcase the lilting rhythms of South Africa's townships, Paul Simon utilizes the talents of Ladysmith Black Mambazo on his *Graceland* album. Controversy ensues, because his well-intended actions break the economic and cultural boycott of the apartheid-blighted country.

1987

March 1987
Buoyed by the reaction to their appearance at Live Aid, U2 capitalize with *The Joshua Tree*, a hugely successful anthem-packed set that consolidates the band's middle-ground appeal.

December 1987
The Pixies record *Surfer Rosa* with ex-Big Black main man Steve Albini engineering. The result provides a template for the characteristic loud/quiet style of grunge.

1988

February 1988
"Push It," by hip-hop duo Salt-N-Pepa, hits the U.S. Top 20. It does even better in Britain, where it narrowly misses the top spot.

Salt-N-Pepa

March 1988
Mick Jagger takes off on his first tour as a solo artist, further proof that the breakdown in relations at the heart of the Rolling Stones has reached tipping point. The band eventually make up, reemerging in 1989 with the back-to-form *Steel Wheels* album.

November 1988
The Seattle-based Sub Pop label launches its subscription-only mail-order record club with "Love Buzz" by little-known Washington State band Nirvana.

1989

January 1989
A month after Coca-Cola signed up George Michael to promote its products, Pepsi Cola unveils Madonna as its pop face for the next 12 months—at a reported fee of U.S.$5 million.

January 1989
Nirvana finish sessions for their debut album, *Bleach*, released in June to an enthusiastic, if limited reception. Two years on, and with a different drummer in tow, the band will break through, and grunge will take alternative rock into the mainstream.

Nirvana's Kurt Cobain

1986-1989

July 1987

Grindcore pioneers Napalm Death take metal to new extremes with their debut album, *Scum*. One song, "You Suffer," clocks in at 1.316 seconds—the world's shortest.

Eric Clapton, Chuck Berry, and Keith Richards

October 1987

In a further indication of rock's "living museum" tendencies, Chuck Berry is celebrated in a feature-length documentary movie, *Hail! Hail! Rock 'n' Roll*. Musical director is Rolling Stones' guitarist and Berry soundalike, Keith Richards.

November 1987

The atmospheric black-and-white footage for U2's 1988 documentary movie, *Rattle and Hum*, is shot at two shows in Denver, Colorado.

June 1988

Sting, Peter Gabriel, Simple Minds, and "Free Nelson Mandela" songwriter Jerry Dammers lead the tributes at a concert to celebrate Nelson Mandela's 70th birthday at London's Wembley Stadium. The veteran antiapartheid activist will finally be released from prison in February 1990.

August 1988

Two rock fans are trampled to death during Guns N' Roses' set at the Monsters of Rock Festival in Castle Donington, England.

October 1988

CHOBA B CCCP, otherwise known as *Back in the USSR*, becomes the first official Paul McCartney solo release exclusive to the Soviet Union. It's an album of rock 'n' roll cover versions.

March 1989

Warm, witty, and crammed with an abundance of wide-ranging samples, De La Soul's *3 Feet High and Rising* brings a new sensibility and manifold textures to hip hop.

Public Enemy

June 1989

Public Enemy's radical rap style reaches a wider audience when Spike Lee includes their incendiary "Fight the Power" in his latest movie, *Do the Right Thing*.

August 1989

Courtney Love forms Hole. Weeks earlier, she placed an advert in LA punk fanzine *Flip Side* that read: "I want to start a band. My influences are Big Black, Sonic Youth, and Fleetwood Mac."

Michael Jackson

AT THE SINGER'S memorial service on July 7, 2009, Motown Records founder Berry Gordy proclaimed Michael Jackson "the greatest entertainer that ever lived." Certainly, he was the most successful and, in terms of heralding a new era of all-singing, all-dancing MTV-sanctioned pop performers, one of the most influential too.

Michael was always the Jackson brother most likely to succeed in his own right, briefly emerging as a solo artist at the height of weenybop in 1972–73, ostensibly as a balladeer ("Got to Be There," "Ain't No Sunshine," "Ben"). By the end of the decade, that had all changed, thanks in large part to meeting producer Quincy Jones while shooting *The Wiz*. Jones was crucial to the making of Jackson's holy trinity of huge-selling albums (1979's *Off the Wall*, 1982's *Thriller*, and *Bad* from 1987), but the singer's falsetto-spattered, floor-shaking dance grooves had already been tested on "Shake Your Body (Down to the Ground)," a cowrite and a huge hit for the Jacksons at the end of 1978.

As evidenced on Jackson's own "Don't Stop 'til You Get Enough" the following year, Jones pared back the clutter, foregrounded the beat, and garnished it with crusty handclaps and sparkling percussion timbres. At the center of it all was Jackson's irresistible voice, as flamboyant as James Brown's, as sweet as a Stax siren's.

Thriller made great use of Michael Jackson's extraordinary physicality, which won him the belated backing of MTV, eventually paving the way for song-and-dance stars such as Madonna and Britney Spears to dominate. And 1983's "Beat It," featuring a squalling guitar break from Eddie Van Halen, helped heal the antipathy between rock and disco.

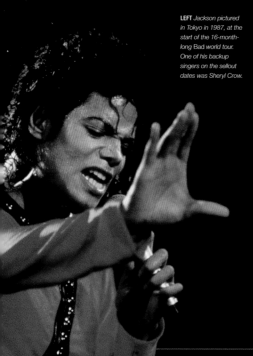

LEFT *Jackson pictured in Tokyo in 1987, at the start of the 16-month-long* Bad *world tour. One of his backup singers on the sellout dates was Sheryl Crow.*

TOP AND BOTTOM RIGHT *After touring with his brothers (top), Jackson worked on* Thriller *with producer Quincy Jones, seen here (bottom) with the King of Pop at the 1984 Grammys.*

FAR RIGHT *By the time Jackson began the U.S. leg of his* Bad *tour, in February 1988, "Man in the Mirror" was on its way to becoming the fourth consecutive No. 1 single from* Bad.

By the end of the 1980s, the multimillion-selling King of Pop seemed invincible, but a series of child-abuse allegations, coupled with seemingly bizarre revelations about life on his Neverland ranch in California, threatened to eclipse his talents as an entertainer. His death at 50 robbed the pop world of its most enigmatic star.

Michael Jackson

Born: *August 29, 1958, Gary, Indiana*
Died: *June 25, 2009*

Years active: *1964–2009*
Genres: *pop, soul, disco, funk, dance, rock*

Key singles: *"Don't Stop 'til You Get Enough" (1979), "Billie Jean" (1982)*

Key albums: Off the Wall *(1979),* Thriller *(1982)*

2 Tone

IF THE SEX PISTOLS had come to destroy rock 'n' roll (or at least that's what they claimed), they failed miserably. After punk, the rock landscape had altered dramatically, with even long-forgotten musical traditions, such as garage rock and mod, being rehabilitated. Most successful of all was the ska revival, a purely British phenomenon that revolved around the 2 Tone record label, based in Coventry in the English Midlands. Between 1979 and 1981 it enjoyed great success.

One record ignited the movement. With an upbeat rhythm heavily indebted to original Jamaican ska acts, such as the Skatalites and Pioneers (both of whom the Specials covered), "Gangsters" brought dancing back to the clubs. Only Terry Hall's downcast delivery betrayed the band's recent past as a support act for the Clash.

It was a stroke of ambition on the part of the group's key songwriter Jerry Dammers that enabled the now renamed Specials (formerly the Special AKA) to avoid the perils of one-hit-wonderment. The 2 Tone label,

5 Top 2 Tone artists

The Special AKA: "Gangsters" (1979)
Madness: "The Prince" (1979)
The Selecter: "On My Radio" (1979)

The Beat: "Tears of a Clown" (1979)
The Specials: "Ghost Town" (1981)

ABOVE The Specials in December 1979, weeks before scoring their first No. 1 hit. Keyboard player Jerry Dammers (right) was the force behind the 2 Tone label.

An upbeat rhythm... that brought dancing back to the clubs

with its stylish black-and-white logo and overt message of racial integration (the Specials, like most 2 Tone acts, were mixed race), was iconic and a beacon for new talent. It was respectful of its heritage too, as covers of Dandy Livingstone's "A Message to You, Rudy," and the incorporation of ska veteran Rico Rodriguez into the band attest.

Among the small stable of 2 Tone acts were Madness (who launched their career with "The Prince," a tribute to ska legend Prince Buster), the Selecter ("On My Radio" was the label's quirkiest 45), and the Beat (who debuted with a ska version of Smokey Robinson's "Tears of a Clown"). By 1981, as acts moved on and the Specials split in two, 2 Tone's label identity dissipated. It had enjoyed an extraordinary run of ten consecutive hit singles, and had a dramatic impact on street style. It phased out with one of the era's defining songs, the Specials' chart-topping social critique, "Ghost Town."

America eventually developed a taste for ska during the 1980s, with Fishbone and the Mighty Mighty Bosstones emerging with their own superintense, alternative rock take on the style.

TOP *The Selecter, fronted by Pauline Black, released one of the ska revival's quirkier, if less celebrated, singles in 1979's "On My Radio."*

ABOVE *Self-styled "Nutty Boys" from London, Madness were a 2 Tone signing, eclipsing the Specials with their cheeky Cockney ska.*

The launch of MTV

BEFORE THE ADVENT OF MTV, rock on television had been a scattershot affair, comprising chart shows (Britain's *Top of the Pops*), live broadcasts (*Don Kirshner's Rock Concert*), and snatched appearances on variety programs. On August 1, 1981, all that changed as the world's first round-the-clock music TV station hastened the development of the promotional pop video.

BELOW *The Trevor Horn-fronted Buggles's "Video Killed the Radio Star" (a one-hit wonder from 1979) proved the perfect curtain-raiser when MTV began broadcasting in 1981.*

"You'll never look at music the same way again," claimed the channel, though even MTV's original developers (which included, appropriately, ex-Monkees man Mike Nesmith) couldn't have envisaged the later supremacy of "video musicians" such as Michael Jackson, Madonna, and Lady Gaga.

MTV took its bow with a well-chosen novelty hit, Buggles's "Video Killed the Radio Star," though it was the second video broadcast that set the agenda. Pat Benatar's "You Better Run" was mainstream AOR rock, and the station soon got behind the metal revival (Van Halen, Def Leppard). The biggest early beneficiaries were photogenic British imports Duran Duran.

Eddie Van Halen's guitar break on Michael Jackson's "Beat It" (1983) earned the song rotation play, while countering criticisms concerning the relative absence of black music on the station. By the end of the decade, both hip hop and alternative rock enjoyed exposure, the latter becoming a huge force in the wake of Nirvana's 1991 breakthrough. Since what was arguably the channel's heyday, a combination of reality shows and routine pop and R&B acts has tended to diminish the MTV effect.

Duran Duran

FROM VAGUELY FUTURISTIC, faux-Bowie beginnings, Duran Duran became poster boys for synth-pop during the early and mid-1980s, thanks to their highly manufactured sound, neatly manicured pose, and heavy rotation on the newly influential MTV. Spearheading what was briefly hyped as a Second British Invasion of the United States in 1983, the Duranies took pop to a new, high-gloss level, their devil-may-care playboy image mirroring the hard-edged aspirational times through a series of no-expense-spared promo videos. Though deadly serious at the time, Duran Duran live on as a guilty pleasure for today's young ironists.

Duran Duran are forever associated with their filmic series of promo videos, which usually involved the impeccably coiffeured foursome on the high seas with bikini-wearing lovelies ("Rio") or living out some weird pseudocolonial scenario ("Hungry Like the Wolf," both 1982). Yet their infectious electropop, akin to a brittle update of Bowie's "plastic soul," was already proving to be a winning formula as early as 1981, when "Girls on Film" hit the British Top 5. *Rio* became a phenomenon in the United States, charting for over two years, but despite the involvement of Chic's Nile Rodgers for 1984's "The Wild Boys" and kudos-winning solo projects, Duran Duran lost their luster.

Their well-chosen, if poorly executed collection of cover versions, *Thank You* (1995), has been followed by several indifferently received albums that nevertheless still manage to chart, testimony to the loyalty of their core audience.

BELOW *Looking every inch the cross between 1970s glam rockers and the boy bands of the 1990s, Duran Duran transcended their synth-pop origins during the early 1980s with a string of huge, MTV-endorsed hits.*

Duran Duran

Formed:
Birmingham, England

Years active:
1978 to present

Definitive lineup:
Simon Le Bon, Nick Rhodes, John Taylor, Roger Taylor

Genres:
new romanticism, synth-pop

Key singles: *"Rio" (1982), "A View to a Kill" (1985)*

Key albums: Rio *(1982)*, Arena *(1984)*

The Police

AMID THE CONFUSION PROMPTED by the emergence of punk during 1977, two veterans of the music business and one jazz-playing art teacher bleached their hair uniform blond and landed on the London club scene. A decade older than most punk bands, and noticeably nimble with their instruments, the Police quietly signed to a major label and sneaked out an impressive 45. That song was "Can't Stand Losing You," an anguished, insistent slice of fired-up new-wave rock that introduced the world to the distinctive soprano tones of frontman Sting.

The talents of his colleagues, prog-rock renegades Stewart Copeland (Curved Air) and guitarist Andy Summers (Soft Machine), were also showcased on the 1978 debut, *Outlandos d'Amour*, which included two other 45s, "Roxanne" and "So Lonely." Eschewing faux-punk for a more elegant, reggae-inspired sound (as exemplified in the "white reggae" title of the chart-topping 1979 LP, *Regatta de Blanc*), the Police captured the mainstream market with "Walking on the Moon," noted as much for its smooth, off-the-beat flanged guitar motif as for its warm Caribbean-style rhythms.

By 1983, with the global success of the stalker anthem "Every Breath You Take" and its tie-in album *Synchronicity*, the three blonds had become a showpiece for the singer. Tellingly, since their split, only Sting has enjoyed a successful solo career.

The Police

Formed:
London, England

Years active:
1977–84, 1986, 2003, 2007–08

Definitive lineup:
Sting, Andy Summers, Stewart Copeland

Genres: *new wave, rock*

Key singles:
"Can't Stand Losing You" (1978), "Message in a Bottle" (1979)

Key albums:
Outlandos d'Amour *(1978),* Synchronicity *(1983)*

BELOW *Three gifted artists (including Sting, far left) who thrived during the 1970s.*

Kate Bush

LIKE DAVID "Space Oddity" Bowie before her, Kate Bush came to prominence on the back of a song so extraordinary and unlike anything else that she seemed destined for one-hit wonderland. And like Bowie, Bush trained with mime artist Lindsay Kemp, and later branched into movie projects and collaborated with numerous artists. But unlike her persona-shifting forebear, the flamboyantly voiced wunderkind behind the once heard, never forgotten 1978 British No. 1 hit "Wuthering Heights" has never quite managed to shake off that "madwoman in the attic" tag.

That's a shame because, after an initial flurry of records between 1978 and 1982 (peaking with the experimental set, *The Dreaming*), Bush has worked at a pace more in accord with her perfectionism, sustaining a commercially viable career without compromising her integrity. The result has been eight consistently unique and personalized albums that harness an almost progressive rock attitude to songs that possess all the emotional depth of a classic singer-songwriter. At the same time, Bush never sounds remotely dusty—the mark of a true original.

It was Pink Floyd's guitarist David Gilmour who initially alerted EMI to the young, prolific pianist-singer, whose earliest work (especially on 1978's *The Kick Inside*) possessed all the unrestrained, deeply felt romanticism of a sensitive, wildly gifted teenager. By 1982's *The Dreaming*, Bush's inner mystic was maturing fast, though it was the rich textures of the chart-topping *Hounds of Love* (1985) that assured her auteurist reputation. Motherhood, middle age, and an encroaching melancholy have marked her sporadic output since that time, but while her early work rate has long gone, her muse—last evident on 2005's impressive *Aerial*—has not.

ABOVE *Like David Bowie a decade earlier, Kate Bush announced her arrival with a single so outlandish and extraordinary that few imagined she'd build a career on it.*

Kate Bush

Born: *July 30, 1958, Bexleyheath, Kent, England*

Years active: *1975 to present*

Genres: *rock, pop, art rock*

Key singles: *"Wuthering Heights" (1978), "Running Up That Hill" (1985)*

Key albums: The Dreaming *(1982),* Hounds of Love *(1985)*

The rise of synth-pop

THE MASS PRODUCTION of digital equipment, not least the Yamaha DX7, prompted a flood of synthesizer-wielding acts during the early 1980s. Ostensibly British in origin, synth-poppers such as Duran Duran, Soft Cell, and later Depeche Mode and Pet Shop Boys, enjoyed surprise success in the United States, initially as part of the so-called Second British Invasion.

BELOW No one was more outrageous in early 1980s pop than Soft Cell's Marc Almond, but the "Tainted Love" man has since enjoyed a distinguished career.

BOTTOM After the surprise success of "Are 'Friends' Electric?," Gary Numan took rock theater to some bizarre places during the 1980s.

Most synth-pop bands had grown out of the new wave, where abrasive use of the synth and electronic sound had been pioneered by Throbbing Gristle and Cabaret Voltaire. But it was Kraftwerk, David Bowie's 1970s Berlin recordings, and Giorgio Moroder's electro-disco work for Donna Summer that inspired the 1980s variety acts.

Once the province of the avant-garde, the synthesizer underwent a dramatic transformation as musicians harnessed it to conventional, melodic songwriting. Initially, its most successful exponent was Gary Numan, who mesmerized the British public in 1979 with "Are 'Friends' Electric?," a neat slice of faux-Bowie fancy. Numan was not alone in replicating Bowie's austere, cold-wave vocal style, though an exception to this was Soft Cell's Marc Almond, who brought a warm theatricality to a sometimes po-faced genre. The Human League, too, undermined their own austerity by adding two young female backing singers and going for pop broke.

From Daft Punk to Goldfrapp and Kylie Minogue, synth-pop has never really gone away, and a revival of depression-era kitsch has given it yet another new lease of life.

Depeche Mode

FROM SHAKY, synth-pop beginnings, floppy-haired Depeche Mode defied their apparent disposability to become one of the world's most popular and enduring electro-rock outfits. They have weathered the potentially calamitous departure of chief songwriter Vince Clarke in 1981 and, in 1995, the attempted suicide of frontman Dave Gahan.

Less worthy of headlines has been a remarkable feat of sonic surgery, whereby the digital-pop despair of early singles, such as "New Life," "Just Can't Get Enough" (1981), and "Everything Counts" (1983), was eclipsed by a more robust and mystery-laden sound that has since won them a huge international audience, ranging from teenage pop fans to black-clad goths and industrial-metal fiends.

With Martin Gore emerging as the group's main songwriter, Depeche Mode upped the angst and the sophistication: 1984's *Some Great Reward* prompted an international breakthrough. But it was the introduction of guitars on 1987's *Music for the Masses* that marked the most authoritative break from their early innocence. In 1990, *Violator* hit the U.S. Top 10 as well as yielding their most perfectly formed moment of pop melancholia, "Enjoy the Silence."

After 1997's comeback set *Ultra*, presaged by the grainy "Barrel of a Gun," the new century has seen a mildly less hyperactive Mode (*Exciter*, 2001). The Top 3 U.S. success of 2009's *Sounds of the Universe* confirms that there's still more to Depeche Mode than spectacular merchandizing sales.

Depeche Mode

Formed:
Basildon, Essex

Years active:
1980 to present

Definitive lineup:
Dave Gahan, Martin Gore, Alan Wilder, Andrew Fletcher

Genres: *synth-pop, electropop, alternative dance*

Key singles:
"Enjoy the Silence" (1990), "Barrel of a Gun" (1997)

Key albums: *Music for the Masses (1987), Violator (1990)*

LEFT *Depeche Mode's Martin Gore and Dave Gahan. During the mid-1980s, the band began to shed their synth-pop image for a more robust, guitar-oriented sound. It worked—in recent decades, Depeche Mode have become a huge international draw.*

Hip hop

THE WORLD HAD BARELY recovered from the shock of punk when, in August 1979, the first stirrings of a rap revolution tumbled from the grooves of a 12-inch single by a bunch of studio musicians known as the Sugarhill Gang. Recycling a bass line from Chic's recent hit, "Good Times," the song was a vehicle for some virtuoso monologues from Master Gee and two other Sugarhill colleagues. A big hit in Britain, and a Top 40 success in the United States, "Rapper's Delight" sounded like a classic novelty hit. Instead, it introduced the world to perhaps the last genuinely monumental development in popular music.

RIGHT *Hip hop developed from South Bronx street parties, where rival MCs would outperform each other with beats and raps. Grandmaster Flash was one of the first to break out.*

BELOW *New York trio Run-DMC emerged in 1983 with "It's Like That," signaling a new era of tougher, more minimalist hip hop.*

Hip hop provided a mouthpiece for the dispossessed. It was, said Public Enemy's Chuck D, the CNN of black America. While "Rapper's Delight" had been aimed firmly at the dance floor, 1982's "The Message," by Grandmaster Flash and the Furious Five, was positively Dylan-like in its energizing effect. Hip hop's origins in the South Bronx housing projects, in the rapid-fire speeches of Malcolm X and Muhammad Ali, and in the black-consciousness raps of the Last Poets and Gil Scott-Heron, were soon transcended as the style detonated across music and other cultural boundaries.

Armed with twin decks and Roland drum machines, Bronx activist Afrika Bambaataa drew on krautrock, Run-DMC collaborated with Aerosmith, and the Beastie Boys further helped the music across the racial divide. Public Enemy, whose intimidating sound was accompanied by a keen political consciousness, further progressed the form. More militant still were NWA from Los Angeles, gangsta rappers whose taunting of the police piled on the controversy that continued to envelop hip hop.

Despite the music's growing sophistication, with De La Soul's seamless sampling and Wu-Tang Clan's agitated chaos at opposite ends of the spectrum, it was the murderous "Rap Wars" of the mid-1990s that dominated the headlines. After the huge success of white rap superstar Eminem, hip hop has grown further still, both at the center of pop and as an influence on numerous global musics.

5 Top hip-hop artists

Eric B. & Rakim: Paid in Full (1987)
Public Enemy: It Takes a Nation of Millions to Hold Us Back (1988)

NWA: Straight Outta Compton (1988)
Dr Dre: The Chronic (1992)

The Notorious B.I.G.: Ready to Die (1994)

Prince

LIKE HIS SPIRITUAL ancestors James Brown (the funk) and Frank Zappa (the eclecticism), Prince wants to do it all himself. Entrepreneur, compulsive showman, talent scout, label boss, movie star, and, above all, a prolific studio habitué, the diminutive music obsessive from Minneapolis emerged rainbow-like during the still deeply tribal early 1980s. Strong willed from the off, the teenage prodigy exacted a serious advance from Warner Brothers, who perhaps envisaged him as a more erotically charged, rock-friendly version of Michael Jackson.

Both the label and the world at large got more than it bargained for. A series of increasingly confident and personalized records climaxed in 1984 with the vast *Purple Rain* project—the power ballad, the album that, in the United States at least, refused to budge from the No. 1 spot for months, and the megalomaniacal movie. Prince went into overload with his own label (Paisley Park) and band (the Revolution), releasing the subtle *Parade* (1986) and vast *Sign o' the Times* (1987), and was writing the best songs of his career, including "Kiss" and "Nothing Compares to You."

Then, in true misunderstood genius fashion, he canceled a finished album, warred with his label, and changed his name (to an unpronounceable squiggle). "The Most Beautiful Girl in the World" (1994) may have been his last hit, but the onetime future of pop hasn't entirely slipped out of the headlines, as 2010's European newspaper giveaway of his album *20Ten* confirms.

Power ballads, Purple Rain, megalomania...

Prince

Born:
*June 7, 1958,
Minneapolis,
Minnesota*

Years active:
1976 to present

Genres: *funk,
pop, rock,
psychedelic
rock, R&B*

Key singles:
*"1999" (1982),
"Purple Rain"
(1984)*

Key albums:
*Purple Rain
(1984),
Parade (1986)*

OPPOSITE TOP
*Performing live in
1985 on the back of
his album and movie
project, Purple Rain.*

OPPOSITE BOTTOM
*Prince now favors
suits over the
flamboyance of his
heyday, though his
enigmatic qualities
remain undimmed.*

LEFT *Once tipped
as a rival to Michael
Jackson, Prince
revealed a wider
range of influences,
with some critics
hailing him as the
phantom progeny
of Jimi Hendrix.*

U2

FROM TENTATIVE beginnings at the quiet end of post-punk, U2 roared throughout the 1980s, attaining a level of success so extraordinary that, now into the twenty-first century, their commercial and iconic supremacy remains unchallenged. Despite the fact that the band have delivered some of their most sophisticated and compelling work in recent years, U2's glory days remain rooted in the period between Live Aid in 1985 and the Zoo TV world tour of 1992 and 1993.

It was *The Joshua Tree* (1987) that did it. Part cold-wave gloom, part rockist glory, the album benefited from Eno's artfully sculpted production, creating a vast sonic landscape over which Bono's magnified Jim Morrison meets Jesus Christ persona declaimed with fist-clenching righteousness. At last, America fully succumbed, and by the time of the *Rattle and Hum* concert set (1988) U2 had virtually become the equals of those rock giants whose songs they covered (the Beatles, Dylan).

It had been a remarkable transition for the callow quartet from Dublin, whose early work seemed far too polite and middle ground to convince either post-punk or synth-pop audiences. The Edge's spacious guitar sound owed much to Magazine/Banshees' John McGeoch, Bono's style was fashionably melodramatic, and the bass lines weren't too far off Joy Division's, as 1983's "New Year's Day" confirmed. But like all hugely successful bands, U2 possessed an acute instinct for taking the right creative—and commercial—decisions, which witnessed an incredible transformation during the mid-1980s.

Since 1991's *Achtung Baby*, a beatsier, trashier, and altogether more satisfying thing of beauty, U2 have mixed and matched in the manner of Prince and Madonna. After a decade in thrall to the American rock tradition, they began to ape Marc Bolan (1995's "Hold Me, Thrill Me, Kiss Me, Kill Me" from the *Batman Forever* soundtrack) and even Radiohead ("Vertigo" from 2004's *How to Dismantle an Atomic Bomb*). But the enormous success of "It's a Beautiful Day" (from 2000's *All That You Can't Leave Behind*) confirms that the impressive maturing of U2 hasn't come at the expense of jettisoning their core songwriting nous.

U2

Formed: *Dublin, Ireland*
Years active: *1976 to present*

Definitive lineup: *Bono, The Edge, Adam Clayton, Larry Mullen*

Genres: *rock, pop, alternative rock*

Key singles: *"The Fly" (1991), "Hold Me, Thrill Me, Kiss Me, Kill Me" (1995)*

Key albums: The Joshua Tree *(1987),* Achtung Baby *(1991)*

The Smiths

AN ASPIRING LAUREATE of ruined idealism, Manchester-born Morrissey was perfectly poised to lead the lament for a fallen punk project that had promised so much. Trading off guitarist Johnny Marr's light, near effervescent, Afrobeat touches, the Smiths' frontman's stylized singing and iconic peculiarities did much to redraw the lines of "indie" music—away from difficult to merely different.

During their four-year existence, the Smiths enjoyed huge influence and vast cult appeal, with their split in 1987 coming at a time when mainstream success seemed a formality. The upbeat feyness that characterized early 45s, such as 1983's "This Charming Man," was augmented by a more foreboding tone on songs such as "How Soon Is Now?" (1985), "Panic" (1986), and "Death of a Disco Dancer" (1987).

This deepening of the sound has continued during Morrissey's solo career, where, liberated from unflattering 1980s production, his beautifully observed—if sometimes controversial—lyricism has a far more satisfying musical dance partner. Like fellow Mancunian Mark E. Smith of the Fall, Morrissey refuses to pay lip service to any orthodoxies other than his own. And while that might result in uncomfortable swipes at, for example, multiculturalism, it can also result in a song such as "Munich Air Disaster 1958" (2004), which no one else could have handled with such mysterious beauty.

The Smiths

Formed:
Manchester, England

Years active:
1982–87

Definitive lineup:
Morrissey, Johnny Marr, Andy Rourke, Mike Joyce

Genres: *alternative rock, pop, rock*

Key singles: *"How Soon Is Now?" (1985), "Panic" (1986)*

Key albums: *The Smiths (1984), The Queen Is Dead (1986)*

LEFT *The Smiths performing on British TV show The Tube in March 1984. The band's return to the pop-song format helped broaden the appeal of alternative rock.*

Alternative rock

THOUGH INDEPENDENT labels had always coexisted alongside the majors, it was the punk-inspired "indie" boom of the late 1970s that introduced the idea of a unified and viable "alternative" market. Musically, though, it was far from homogenous, comprising everything from provocative antirock (the Industrial label) and politically charged sound (Rough Trade) to 1960s pop pastiche (Postcard Records). In the early 1980s the majors cottoned on and formed their own fake "indie" labels, and the music changed.

The Smiths (in Britain) and R.E.M. (in America) spearheaded an almost exclusively guitar-based "indie" scene built on "classic" rock values, from beat-boom craftsmanship to elements culled from psych, punk, and—by the mid-1980s—hard rock. While the British scene became increasingly fey (the jangly "C86" movement), America cranked up the power with Black Flag, Hüsker Dü, Sonic Youth, and the Pixies creating the backdrop for the emergence of Nirvana and the Seattle-based grunge scene at the end of the decade.

Since then the line between alternative and the mainstream has blurred further to become virtually meaningless. Britpop, the British response to grunge, was hailed as alternative in the mid-1990s, but was largely classic pop pastiche. Radiohead had far more in common with the independent pioneers— yet they sold out stadiums. The twenty-first century post-punk revival, fronted by the Strokes and Franz Ferdinand, has brought alternative music full circle.

ABOVE *Having establishing their name on alternative rock label SST during the early 1980s, Minneapolis-based Hüsker Dü signed to Warner Brothers in 1986, released one album, then split.*

LEFT *Sonic Youth's Lee Ranaldo and Kim Gordon in the mid-1980s, just prior to their crossover from the avant-garde fringe to being the most influential American alternative rock act of the decade.*

Madonna

LIKE MICHAEL JACKSON, Madonna owes much of her success to bottom-line populism combined with a highly marketable persona, though she has always been more willing to draw on ideas that lie just beyond the mainstream. Unlike Jackson, she has cleverly played out her darker side in public, with the result that her private life remains relatively unexciting by comparison. And as Courtney Love and Lady Gaga (among others) have repeatedly confirmed, a little onstage scandal can certainly go a long way.

If her self-styled blonde ambition stems from an early admiration for Marilyn Monroe, Madonna's risqué emergence—a picture of defiance in distressed lace—owed much to punk femmes, the Slits. Playing the part of the newly confident thrill-seeking teenage girl suited Madonna's postdisco sound and helium-voiced early hits. Two years after her 1982 debut, she had her first No. 1 hit with "Like a Virgin."

Mid-decade, Madonna was winning plaudits for her vigorous performance at Live Aid, had moved into movies, married actor Sean Penn, and introduced a touch of sophistication to her music. It wasn't without controversy, as the furore that surrounded 1990's "Like a Prayer" (actually a song for a Pepsi ad) proved.

ABOVE Madonna took the aggressive, distressed-lace sexuality of punk bands, such as the Slits, and reconfigured it for mainstream audiences.

ABOVE RIGHT When Madonna took to the transatlantic stage for Live Aid in July 1985, she delivered a thrillingly upbeat set.

A little scandal, a whiff of danger ...

But a whiff of danger, extended by the publication of her book *Sex*, banned videos, and further accusations of sacrilege that dogged her 1990 world tour, served Madonna well as the blithe 1980s gave way to a new, grittier decade.

After a fine movie portrayal of Eva Peron in 1996, a new, more artful Madonna emerged. She collaborated with electronic dance DJ William Orbit on 1998's *Ray of Light*, before releasing "Beautiful Stranger," perhaps the most delicious single of her career, the following year. Since then, while records such as *American Life* (2003) and *Hard Candy* (2008) have failed to maintain Madonna's previous chart unassailability, her tie-in tours remain as lucrative as ever.

RIGHT *Madonna has conceived her career as a series of set pieces. In the 1980s, she kept returning to a Marilyn Monroe-inspired exploration of fame.*

Madonna

Born: *August 16, 1958, Bay City, Michigan*
Years active: *1979-present*

Genres: *pop, dance*
Key singles: *"Into the Groove" (1985), "Beautiful Stranger" (1999)*

Key albums: Like a Virgin *(1984)*, Ray of Light *(1998)*

Metal

IF 1970S HEAVY METAL had been dominated by Led Zeppelin, Deep Purple, and Black Sabbath, the 1980s saw the genre flourish while drawing upon a wider set of earlier influences. Out went any last traces of the blues, and in came a more dynamic sound inspired by punk, with an attention to showmanship more worthy of a glam rocker. "Heavy metal" was trimmed down to the more instant "metal," though as the decade progressed the style generated an increasingly baffling number of subgenres.

The catalyst for the change in metal's fortunes was the New Wave of British Heavy Metal (NWOBHM), which emerged alongside punk during the late 1970s. At the forefront were young, new bands from the north of England, such as Iron Maiden, Saxon, and Def Leppard, who fed off the energies of punk, released a string of independent records, and caught the attentions of *Sounds* magazine. Equally important were AC/DC, whose high-octane rock fed into early 1980s metal, and above all, the headbanging, dirgelike attack of Motörhead, fronted by gruff-voiced Lemmy.

Lemmy's thunderous bass-playing inspired metal's "How low can you go?" approach to deep frequencies. At the other end, Eddie Van Halen's distinctive "tapping" guitar technique, which encouraged soloists to sound flashier than ever, inspired a generation of squall-happy lead guitarists.

As post-punk faded, metal made a two-pronged bid for glory, with Def Leppard crossing the Atlantic and taking the MTV route to success, and Metallica spearheading the more outré speed or thrash metal style. Most extreme of all was grindcore, a short-lived mid-1980s phenomenon popularized by Napalm Death and characterized by growling, indecipherable vocals, ferocious tempos, and songs that sometimes lasted no longer than a few seconds.

But it was the mainstream success of Bon Jovi, the emergence of Guns N' Roses, and the continued rise of Metallica that established the wider world of metal as the premier rock force of the decade. That began to change in the early 1990s, when grunge-affiliated acts, such as Soundgarden and Pearl Jam, prompted a closer alliance between metal and alternative rock.

ABOVE LEFT *From the haunts of the NWOBHM, Def Leppard—fronted by Joe Elliott—had become a huge stadium act by the mid-1980s.*

ABOVE *Jon Bon Jovi, whose poster-boy looks helped his band enter the pop mainstream.*

Flashy, squall-happy lead guitarists...

5 Top metal artists

Motörhead: Ace of Spades *(1980)*
Iron Maiden: The Number of the Beast *(1982)*

Def Leppard: Pyromania *(1983)*
Bon Jovi: Slippery When Wet *(1986)*

Guns N' Roses: Appetite for Destruction *(1987)*

Def Leppard

DEF LEPPARD WERE INSTRUMENTAL in shaping the sound of 1980s metal by infusing their melodic, twin-guitar attack with anthemic choruses and a high-gloss, insistent backbeat. When 1983's *Pyromania* earned them a career-defining, multimillion-selling album in the United States, it was just as the five-piece from Sheffield, Yorkshire, had intended: the fulfillment of a fantasy first mapped out on "Hello America," a track from their 1980 debut album.

Prime movers in the New Wave of British Heavy Metal, Def Leppard's global ambition was fulfilled after recruiting producer/cowriter Mutt Lange for 1981's *High 'n' Dry*. With a pop-friendly style as close in spirit to glam-rockers Sweet as it was to vintage hard rock, the band crossed over when "Photograph"—the first single from 1983's *Pyromania*—became an MTV staple and a huge U.S. hit. Fallings out with Lange and replacement producer Jim Steinman were followed by tragedy

when drummer Rick Allen lost an arm in a car accident. The band rallied, Lange returned, Allen relearned how to play his (electronic) kit using his feet, and 1987's *Hysteria* (1987) topped charts on both sides of the Atlantic, eclipsing sales of *Pyromania* and yielding seven hit singles.

Despite the death of guitarist Steve Clark in 1991, and the toughened-up sound of grunge, Def Leppard soldier on, their live shows now more wildly received than more recent recordings.

Def Leppard

Formed:
Sheffield, England

Years active:
1977 to present

Definitive lineup:
Joe Elliott, Steve Clark, Phil Collen, Rick Savage, Rick Allen

Genres: *metal, hard rock*

Key single:
"Photograph" (1983), "Love Bites" (1987)

Key albums:
Pyromania (1983), Hysteria (1987)

BELOW *Def Leppard's all-firing guitar frontline in characteristic axe-metal pose.*

Guns N' Roses

DESPITE THE THUNDERING success of the movie *Spinal Tap* (1984), a mockumentary that lampooned the gaudy excesses of the traditional guitar-wielding rock band, the late-1980s triumphs of Guns N' Roses proved that old habits—and old-style bad-boy antiheroes—die hard.

Fittingly, Guns N' Roses emerged from feted Hollywood nightclub, the Troubadour. Dressed in leather, bathed in red light, and performing covers of vintage Aerosmith and Rose Tattoo material, they initially appeared destined to become little more than an American answer to British goth-metal combo the Cult. Noting the 1980s' still unfulfilled desire for rock 'n' roll that was neither hardcore nor bubble-haired, label boss David Geffen personally intervened on the band's behalf, enlisting MTV's backing for the band's "Welcome to the Jungle" (1987). It became Guns N' Roses' first U.S. Top 10 single, after which the slow-burn *Appetite for Destruction* (1987) hit No. 1, as did another spin-off single, "Sweet Child o' Mine."

Fan deaths at festivals, intraband strife, and protracted sessions for their epic 1991 set *Use Your Illusion* (issued as two double-disc albums) were followed by a two-year world tour blighted by tantrums, walkouts, and frontman Axl Rose sporting a Charles

ABOVE AND TOP *Axl Rose (seen, top, with Guns N' Roses' British-born guitarist Slash) has for over two decades rejoiced in the role of the willfully disobedient rock 'n' roll frontman. The band's infamous antics and robust rock sound have proved remarkably resilient.*

Manson T-shirt. The departure of guitarist Slash in 1996 effectively ended the band, though Rose was back fronting a new lineup in 2001, with the decade-in-the-making album, *Chinese Democracy*, eventually appearing in 2008.

Guns N' Roses

Formed: *Los Angeles*

Years active: *1985 to present*

Definitive lineup: *Axl Rose, Slash, Izzy Stradlin, Duff McKagan, Steven Adler*

Genres: *rock, metal*

Key singles: *"Sweet Child o' Mine" (1988), "November Rain" (1992)*

Key albums: Appetite for Destruction *(1987),* Use Your Illusion *(1991)*

Hardcore

DESPITE HOSTING SUCH disparate new wave souls as the Ramones, Pere Ubu, and Blondie, America was too vast, too entrenched in blue-jean rock culture for the Sex Pistols-inspired cultural makeover that took place in Britain. Slowly, though, as the new decade progressed, punk's gnarly aesthetic—already tested to its limits in the late 1970s by New York's Teenage Jesus and the Jerks—started to permeate American rock.

A key motivating force was the impact of the U.S. hardcore scene, largely based around Washington, DC (home of the Minor Threat-run Dischord label) and the suburbs of California. Between 1979 and the mid-1980s, SST Records, based outside Los Angeles and the vehicle for the Henry Rollins-fronted Black Flag, was hardcore central. Echoing and intensifying the tough-nut punk of San Francisco controversialists Dead Kennedys, Black Flag—seemingly simultaneously in thrall to British outfits the Fall and UK Subs as well as industrial noise acts—inspired an underground rock revolution before splitting in 1986.

By that time, a new generation of SST signings had emerged, including the melodically astute Hüsker Dü, the powerfully eclectic Dinosaur Jr., and the willfully angular Minutemen. Above all were Sonic Youth, who formed the bridge between left-field post punk and the metallic overdrive that would underpin grunge. But if any one individual was midwife to rock's rediscovery of its primal hardcore grit and graininess, it was Steve Albini. Erstwhile guitarist with ferocious Chicago-based trio Big Black,

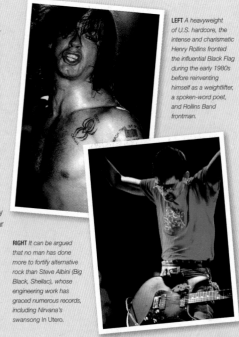

LEFT *A heavyweight of U.S. hardcore, the intense and charismatic Henry Rollins fronted the influential Black Flag during the early 1980s before reinventing himself as a weightlifter, a spoken-word poet, and Rollins Band frontman.*

RIGHT *It can be argued that no man has done more to fortify alternative rock than Steve Albini (Big Black, Shellac), whose engineering work has graced numerous records, including Nirvana's swansong In Utero.*

Intense, tough-nut grit and graininess...

Albini has since gone on to engineer hundreds of acts, from the Pixies and Nirvana to PJ Harvey and contemporary hardcore acts, such as Trash Talk.

In hitting new levels of noise and abrasion, hardcore also impacted on thrash metal, while the late-1980s emergence of industrial metal also owed much to its earsplitting pushing of boundaries. The political dimension of early hardcore (notably in the provocations of Dead Kennedys' frontman Jello Biafra) inspired the "straight-edge" movement of hardcore bands that, in essence, advocated a clean-living, vegetarian lifestyle.

ABOVE *The Dead Kennedys' original stage-diving frontman and provocateur, Jello Biafra.*

LEFT *Bad Brains' singer H.R. and guitarist Dr. Know in 1987, shortly before a rift over musical direction prompted H.R.'s temporary departure.*

5 Top hardcore artists

Dead Kennedys: Fresh Fruit for Rotting Vegetables *(1980)*

Black Flag: Damaged *(1981)*

Bad Brains: I Against I *(1986)*

Big Black: Songs About Fucking *(1987)*

Napalm Death: Scum *(1987)*

Sonic Youth

IT'S NO EXAGGERATION to say that Sonic Youth—ably assisted by Big Black and Butthole Surfers—spearheaded the return of rock's disobedient tradition during the late 1980s. Emerging from New York's experimental loft scene early in the decade, their guitars suitably detuned, Sonic Youth channeled their wayward inclinations into a new sensibility that melded post-punk angularity with a thirst for exploration more commonly associated with psychedelia.

Sonic Youth

Formed: *New York City*

Years active: *1981 to present*

Definitive lineup: *Thurston Moore, Lee Ranaldo, Kim Gordon, Steve Shelley*

Genre: *alternative rock, experimental rock*

Key singles: *"Teen Age Riot" (1988), "Silver Rocket" (1989)*

Key albums: *Sister (1987), Daydream Nation (1988)*

Sonic Youth hit their stride with 1987's *Sister*, an unrelentingly intense and claustrophobic set that included early favorite "Schizophrenia," followed by the ferociously confident double-disc set *Daydream Nation* (1988). The extra space suited Sonic Youth's style, with songs such as "Silver Rocket" and "Total Trash" vehicles for mass midsong breakouts as guitarists Thurston Moore and Lee Ranaldo stripped away a decade of guitar clichés.

Inspiring a new transatlantic generation of aspiring alternative-rock musicians, from London-based shoegazers (My Bloody Valentine) to Seattle's burgeoning grunge acts (Nirvana), Sonic Youth bagged themselves a deal with Geffen at the end of the decade, but even major-label budgets failed to rein in their wild side. Unlike many of those who followed in their wake, Sonic Youth are still out there, still twisting their music into fascinating shapes.

LEFT *Midwives to grunge, Sonic Youth were crucial in the late-1980s drift away from sanitized production sounds and clichéd rock riffs, preferring to draw their inspiration from the Velvet Underground, psychedelia, and post-punk.*

R.E.M.

LIKE A MORE CULTISH, American version of U2, R.E.M. enjoyed a long, slow journey from faintly retro post-punk darlings of the Paisley Underground to stadium rockers of the early 1990s praised even by the emerging grunge iconoclasts.

Sounding every bit as if the Byrds had been time-machined into the post-punk era, R.E.M. possessed a classic elegance that was noticeably missing in the work of their contemporaries. The band's calling card—ringing guitar arpeggios, driving new-wave bass lines, and Michael Stipe's wearied delivery—has rarely deviated, though as the 1980s progressed, starting with the 1987 crossover set *Document*, R.E.M.'s sound grew more muscular.

Yielding the U.S. Top 10 hit, "The One I Love," *Document* paved the way for a string of major-label successes throughout the 1990s. *Out of Time* (1991), featuring the folksy and infectious "Losing My Religion," was followed by the significantly bleaker *Automatic for the People* (1992) and its aching anthem "Everybody Hurts."

Tempos were upped and timbres roughed up for 1994's *Monster*, which was followed by a rare tour and the departure of drummer Bill Berry. Since then, R.E.M. seem to devote as much time to causes as they do to maintaining their status as the aristocrats of college rock groups.

R.E.M.

Formed: *Athens, Georgia*

Years active: *1980 to present*

Definitive lineup: *Michael Stipe, Peter Buck, Mike Mills, Bill Berry*

Genres: *alternative rock*

Key singles: *"Losing my Religion" (1991), "Everybody Hurts" (1993)*

Key albums: Document *(1987),* Automatic for the People *(1992)*

LEFT *The melodic, yearning style of R.E.M. singer Michael Stipe has been one of the defining sounds of alternative rock since the band's mid-1980s breakthrough.*

RIGHT *R.E.M. pictured in June 1984 shortly after the release of their second album,* Reckoning, *which was quickly picked up by college radio.*

Live Aid

THERE HAD BEEN charity concerts before, most notably George Harrison's Concert for Bangla Desh in 1971, but never ever on this scale: one 16-hour extravaganza held across two transatlantic venues, featuring 69 acts and watched by a global audience of some 1.5 billion people. Organizer Bob Geldof, erstwhile frontman of second-tier new-wave combo the Boomtown Rats, demanded in no uncertain terms that viewers "give us your money." And they did. A target figure of £1 million (U.S.$1.9 million) was set. The eventual amount pledged to relieve the famine in Africa was U.S.$140 million. No wonder the event has since been dubbed "The Greatest Show on Earth."

BELOW *In the absence of an appearance by the Rolling Stones, Mick Jagger duetted with Tina Turner for a short set.*

According to folk-protest veteran Joan Baez, Live Aid was the 1980s' answer to Woodstock. Both events certainly caught the zeitgeist, with Live Aid far better organized, more obviously philanthropic, and a more mainstream event than its forebear. It also saved lives—between one and two million by most estimates.

The catalyst for the event was an October 1984 BBC News report by Michael Buerk from Korem in Ethiopia. Echoing events in Biafra in the late 1960s, its images of starving and dying children prompted Geldof into action. Within weeks, he had assembled Band Aid, an all-star cast of UK-based musicians for a fund-raising single, "Do They Know It's Christmas?" Its enormous success encouraged Geldof to

BELOW *Though his microphone didn't work for his version of "Let it Be," Paul McCartney later enjoyed the opportunity to sing alongside Bono.*

The greatest show on earth...the day that music changed the world

think bigger. Securing the cooperation of many of the world's major recording artists—some such as Led Zeppelin reforming specially for the event, others like Mick Jagger and Tina Turner making unprecedented joint appearances—Live Aid was set to go on July 13, 1985.

Veteran boogie rockers Status Quo got the event under way with "Rockin' All Over the World," establishing the tone for the next 16 hours of overwhelmingly crowd-pleasing rock and pop. Among the big winners were

Madonna, U2, and Queen. Losers were Bob Dylan (whose set with Rolling Stones Keith Richards and Ronnie Wood was woefully under-rehearsed), Adam Ant (the only artist whose sales failed to prosper after the event), Paul McCartney (whose microphone didn't work), and all those acts that either declined (Bruce Springsteen) or weren't invited to share in what is now regarded as perhaps *the* major event in rock history.

LEFT *Onetime singer with new-wave act Boomtown Rats, a determined Bob Geldof wrote himself into history with Live Aid.*

BELOW *Crowds gather in Wembley Stadium for the British element of the dual-continent Live Aid extravaganza.*

Public Enemy

POLITICALLY CONSCIOUS, musically sophisticated, and with a controversial stage show that drew heavily on the iconography of Black Power, Public Enemy radicalized hip hop while at the same time taking it to the wider rock market.

LEFT The contrasting styles of Chuck D (left) and Flavor Flav (right) created a thrilling mix of entertainment and activism.

ABOVE Public Enemy were the most explosive, innovative, and political of the hip-hop acts to emerge during the 1980s.

Public Enemy

Years active:
1982 to present

Definitive lineup:
Chuck D, Flavor Flav, Professor Griff, Terminator X, The Bomb Squad

Genre: hip hop

Key singles:
"Rebel Without a Pause" (1987), "Fight the Power" (1989)

Key albums: It Takes a Nation of Millions to Hold Us Back (1988), Fear of a Black Planet (1990)

This hip hop/rock crossover reached its peak in 1991, when the Long Islanders teamed up with thrash-metallers Anthrax for a guitar-enriched reworking of PE's 1987 single "Bring the Noise." Earlier, the group had incorporated metal (via a Slayer sample) on the ferocious "She Watch Channel Zero" from their breakthrough album, 1988's *It Takes a Nation of Millions to Hold Us Back.* Generally, though, Public Enemy were at their best with Terminator X and the Bomb Squad at the decks, and Chuck D and Flavor Flav out front, bringing consciousness and a hint of the absurd, respectively, to the group's dynamic raps.

After a tough minimalism on their 1987 debut, *Yo! Bum Rush the Show,* it was on the richly layered *It Takes A Nation of Millions...* that Public Enemy hit their stride. A dense, delirious patchwork of furious, changing beats, siren wails, and rock-guitar samples, topped with Chuck D's anger and Flavor Flav's interjections, the album was a hip-hop milestone. The appearance of "Fight the Power"—a thrillingly strident message with barbs at Elvis and John Wayne set to a propulsive James Brown-style groove—on the soundtrack of Spike Lee's *Do the Right Thing* (1989) truly sealed the band's reputation as hip hop's most explosive act.

Beastie Boys

EMERGING IN 1986 amid a slew of headlines, these three overgrown white rap brats were, a decade later, praised as paragons of understated sonic cool. It was a remarkable turnaround for a trio whose calling card had been "Fight for Your Right," a rap 'n' rebel yell and instant high-school favorite, thanks to Adam Horovitz's nagging adolescent whine.

Starting life in 1979 as a hardcore punk band, the Beasties slimmed down to a trio by the mid-1980s and found themselves a mentor in rap producer/Def Jam boss Rick Rubin. The result was *Licensed to Ill* (1986), an unprecedented white-rap set timed perfectly to capitalize on disaffected suburban America's interest in urban black music. Crucial to its success was the rifling of samples from hard rock, apparent in the fusion of Black Sabbath and Led Zeppelin on the opening "Rhymin & Stealin."

Paul's Boutique (1989) was a denser, more sophisticated affair, but paled in commercial terms. After reprising the collage effect on 1992's *Check Your Head*, the Beasties revisited their earlier commercial highs with *Ill Communication* (1994), fronted

by a storming rock-rap hit, "Sabotage." Since 1998's woozy DJ-style "Intergalactic," the trio have become elder statesmen, the success of *To the 5 Boroughs* (2004) and 2007's instrumental set *The Mix-Up*, proof of the band's resilience and mutability.

BELOW *After their riotous arrival in 1986, the Beastie Boys have come a long way since asking audiences to fight for their partying rights, with a series of edgy and sophisticated albums.*

Beastie Boys

Formed: *Brooklyn, New York*
Years active: *1979 to present*

Definitive lineup: *Mike D, MCA, Ad-Rock*
Genres: *punk, hip hop, alternative rock*

Key singles: *"(You Gotta) Fight for Your Right (to Party!)" (1987), "Sabotage" (1994)*

Key albums: Licensed to Ill *(1986),* Paul's Boutique *(1989)*

Hall of Fame

AFTER THE industry-baiting shock of punk rock, the newly stabilized international record business followed the motion-picture industry in confirming its status as a respected art form by celebrating its own history. The establishment of the Rock and Roll Hall of Fame, a museum based in Cleveland, Ohio (where Alan Freed hosted his legendary radio broadcasts), and the institution of an annual induction ceremony, has done much to alter the wider perception of popular music.

Since 1986, when the first annual induction ceremony took place at the Waldorf-Astoria Hotel in New York City, numerous other organizations—from MTV to rock magazines, such as *MOJO* and *Rolling Stone*—have hosted their own star-studded award shows. But none is quite so prestigious as the Hall of Fame's yearly bash, which, 25 years on, is lobbied hard by aggrieved fans of acts still awaiting their call-up—Rush and Kiss among them.

The 1986 ceremony honored a long list of key founding fathers, including Elvis Presley and James Brown. The awards ceremony has since witnessed the induction of numerous acts, many reuniting especially for the event, such as Cream and Jefferson Airplane. One that didn't was the Sex Pistols, who famously refused to attend the 2006 ceremony.

Twelve years after the foundation first came up with the idea, the museum finally opened in 1995 on a site adjacent to Lake Erie in Cleveland. The seven-level building hosts numerous exhibitions and special events, including talks and movie screenings.

ABOVE *Neil Young and a spectacularly suited Chuck Berry bridge the generations at the inaugural ceremony for the Rock and Roll Hall of Fame in 1986.*

The most prestigious yearly bash...

Heritage rock

FROM ELVIS COVERING hillbilly standards and the Rolling Stones reviving rhythm and blues, there has always been an element of heritage in popular music. The arrival of the compact disc in the mid-1980s, coupled with a mild frustration that rock was losing touch with its rebellious youth, prompted a significant retreat into the sounds of the past.

The value of rare vinyl soared, as did pop memorabilia, with Madonna's bustier and Paul McCartney's handwritten lyrics finding their way to leading auction houses. Magazines catering to nostalgia boomed, bolstered by a flourishing reissue program that exhumed everything from psychedelia and prog to northern soul and garage rock. By the mid-1990s, even rock's old enemy, easy listening, was enjoying a revival. Inevitably, this fed into contemporary music, with the Britpop bands arguably the most nostalgia-led of any rock movement.

The compact disc did much to hasten this. While early 1980s test discs featured mainstream acts, such as ABBA and the Bee Gees, and Dire Straits' *Brothers in Arms* became the first million-selling CD, flagship catalogs by the Beatles and Bowie were followed by all manner of unlikely revivals.

Since peaking in 2000, the CD may have waned in favor of digital product, but the market for huge, warts-and-all anthologies, as exemplified by the ten-disc Neil Young Archives box set, confirms the rude health of rock heritage.

BELOW *Vintage guitars once used by Jimi Hendrix, John Lennon, and Kurt Cobain are merely the tip of the memorabilia iceberg that has sprung up since the early 1980s. Everything from concert programs to rare vinyl, from George Harrison's half-eaten sandwich to Marc Bolan's magnificent wardrobe, has been offered for sale.*

Thrash metal

INSPIRED BY THE AGGRESSION of hardcore punk and the New Wave of British Heavy Metal (NWOBHM), thrash—which is just about synonymous with speed metal, though there's much crossover involved in the multitude of 1980s metal styles—brought the genre closer to punk in terms of aggression and gravel-voiced attitude. For the first time metal was pushing the boundaries of energy and originality.

BELOW TOP *Anthrax performing in Nottingham in 1989, promoting their fourth album,* State of Euphoria.

BELOW BOTTOM *After being fired from Metallica in 1983, guitarist Dave Mustaine formed rival band Megadeth.*

An occasionally cited precedent is Deep Purple's furiously paced "Fireball" (1971), although Black Sabbath's "Paranoid" (1970) and Lemmy's speed-freak hyperdrone rock style (both with Hawkwind and Motörhead) anticipated the ferocity of thrash.

Though the NWOBHM-affiliated Venom are often credited as the founding fathers of thrash, courtesy of their 1982 *Black Metal* set, it was the formation of two bands in Southern California the previous year that established thrash as a genre in its own right. Those were Slayer and Metallica, both of whom played with far more attack and acceleration than their British contemporaries. And when Metallica's guitarist Dave Mustaine was booted out of the band in 1983 he formed a rival thrash-metal band, Megadeth. The emergence of Anthrax on America's East Coast completed the so-called big four of thrash.

While Anthrax and Megadeth both released strong-selling debuts in 1985, it was the already established acts that cleaned up the following year, with

Closer to punk
in terms of
aggression and
gravel-voiced
attitude...

Metallica's *Master of Puppets* breaking big commercially and Slayer's *Reign in Blood* regarded as a genre classic. The latter was highly influential, too, with various death/extreme/black-metal permutations springing up later in the decade. Meanwhile, the continued rise of thrash's big four peaked in 1991 when Metallica's self-titled set topped the U.S. chart and Anthrax, Megadeth, and Slayer all hit the Top 10.

The leading thrash-metal protagonists weathered the noisy impact of grunge far better than the hair-metal acts, though over the years even their sound has tended to soften. In 2010, the big four toured Europe together as part of the Sonisphere Festival.

5 top thrash-metal artists

Slayer: Reign in Blood *(1986)*
Metallica: Metallica *(1991)*

Megadeth: Peace Sells... But Who's Buying? *(1986)*

Anthrax: Among the Living *(1987)*
Sepultura: Arise *(1991)*

ABOVE LEFT *Slayer, led by Chilean-born vocalist and bassist Tom Araya, hit a critical peak in 1986 with* Reign in Blood.

Metallica

METALLICA BROUGHT SPEED, sophistication, and a remarkably cliché-free
approach to a metal scene that had not only survived the slate-wiping
onslaught of punk but had begun to flourish again in the new decade.
Emerging from the San Francisco underground, the band brought a new
toughness and radicalism to metal, both faster and heavier, and in the
process inspired the entire mid-1980s thrash-metal boom.

Though formed in Los Angeles in 1981, the
band had moved to San Francisco by 1983,
where they became prime movers in the Bay
Area thrash scene. Their most immediate
inspiration, as stated in the original
advertisement calling for musicians placed
by drummer Lars Ulrich, was NWOBHM.
But something of LA's hardcore scene had
rubbed off, for their 1983 debut set, *Kill 'Em
All*, sounded significantly more powerful
than those of their British counterparts.

By now guitarist Dave Mustaine had
been sacked (forming Megadeth), though
his replacement Kirk Hammett continued in
a similar buzz-saw style. At least as integral
to the band's style were bassist Cliff Burton's
subterranean sound and the roar of James
Hetfield's voice.

BELOW *Metallica mainman
James Hetfield, on stage
in Minneapolis in July
1988. The band were part
of the Monsters of Rock
tour, sharing the bill with
Scorpions, Dokken,
Kingdom Come, and
headliners Van Halen.*

ABOVE *James Hetfield (right) with bassist Cliff Burton at the Aardschok Festival in Holland, 1984, part of the Seven Dates of Hell tour with black-metal trailblazers Venom. Two years later, Burton was dead.*

Crucial to Metallica's appeal was what they were not—bubble-permed hair-metal clowns. Elektra Records, noted for its credible roster of artists, signed the band late in 1984 and gave them space to develop. The result was *Master of Puppets* (1986), an acclaimed classic that spent over a year in the U.S. chart, despite the inclusion of some intricate and lengthy instrumentals.

Tragedy struck when the band's tour bus overturned in Sweden in September 1986, killing Burton. Continuing in his honor, Metallica took their almost progressive-style riffery to an international audience with 1988's *…And Justice for All*, crowning their success in 1991 with *Metallica* (sometimes known as "The Black Album"). Louder, smoother, and boasting their theme song, "Enter Sandman," it spent four weeks at U.S. No. 1 before going multiplatinum.

Massive tours and high-charting albums followed, among them 1998's *Garage Inc.*, a disc of cover versions revealing a variety of influences from Budgie (the legendary "Breadfan") to the Misfits and Nick Cave. That Metallica can still command massive sales was proved in 2008, when the Rick Rubin-produced *Death Magnetic* became the band's fifth album to debut at No. 1 in the United States.

Metallica

Formed: *Los Angeles*

Years active: *1981 to present*

Definitive lineup: *James Hetfield, Lars Ulrich, Kirk Hammett, Cliff Burton*

Genres: *thrash metal, metal, hard rock*

Key singles: *"Enter Sandman" (1991), "Until It Sleeps" (1996)*

Key albums: *Master of Puppets (1986), Metallica (1991)*

Glam metal

NOT ALL 1980S METAL was tightly permed and brightly polished, but a fair number of its most popular practitioners rose to prominence on a combination of glam-inspired sartorial excess, recycled 1970s rock riffs, and air-punching anthemic choruses. Among them were Mötley Crüe, Hanoi Rocks, and Poison, all of whom owed far more to T. Rex and the New York Dolls, Aerosmith, Kiss, and Alice Cooper than to the old heavy-metal big guns.

BELOW Nikki Sixx and Mick Marrs of Mötley Crüe during the quartet's early 1980s heyday. The band were even more colorful off stage, with their individual careers dogged by numerous arrests and addiction problems.

Glam metal was pure Hollywood sleaze, with Mötley Crüe, Ratt, and W.A.S.P. shifting from Sunset Strip clubs to chart success during the early 1980s. Probably upstaging them all, at least in terms of excess, were Finland's Hanoi Rocks, while Poison's move from Philadelphia to LA earned them the enormously successful *Open Up and Say… Ahh!* (1988), thanks in part to the chart-topping single, "Every Rose Has its Thorn."

Glam metal's pomp and preening was hijacked by mid-1980s pop-metal phenomenon Bon Jovi for "Livin' on a Prayer" (1986), though no power ballad could touch Swedish band Europe's huge international hit, "The Final Countdown" (1986). Ironically, it was only after falling out and cleaning up that Mötley Crüe enjoyed their biggest success, *Dr. Feelgood* (1989).

The disparaging "hair-metal" sideswipes of the grunge era did it for glam metal, and when the Darkness threatened a revival with *Permission to Land* (2003), the venture was strictly tongue in cheek.

5 Top glam-metal artists

Hanoi Rocks: Two Steps from the Move *(1984)*	**Bon Jovi:** Slippery When Wet *(1986)*	**Mötley Crüe:** Dr. Feelgood *(1989)*
W.A.S.P.: W.A.S.P. *(1984)*	**Poison:** Open Up and Say…Ahh! *(1988)*	

House music

HIP HOP, SYNTH-POP, AND RARE GROOVE might have dominated the club scene during the early 1980s, but from mid-decade a new form of dance music began to emerge out of Chicago. Taking its name from the Warehouse, a largely gay club where DJ Frankie Knuckles sculpted new musical highs from a judicious blend of synthesized beats, 1970s electronic rock, and soul classics, Chicago house soon became a pan-European phenomenon.

The most distinctive Chicago cut was Phuture's "Acid Tracks." A trance beat overlaid with bassy, Roland TB-303 synth squelches, the 12-minute epic released in 1987 became the template for Euro-styled "acid house." Landing in Britain later that year via DJs Danny Rampling and Paul Oakenfold, who'd just returned from a visit to Balearic idyll Ibiza, acid house first took hold in clubs such as Shoom in London and the Hacienda in Manchester.

During 1988, it moved out from the clubs into a wider rave scene, held in out-of-town locations, such as large warehouses and open fields. Proclaimed as the Second Summer of Love, thanks to the euphoria-inducing drug ecstasy and the ubiquitous "Smiley" logo, rave culture soon prompted tabloid scares and police crackdowns. Musically, Manchester's 808 State and A Guy Called Gerald ("Voodoo Ray") were early homegrown pioneers, though it was S'Express who made the big chart breakthrough when "Theme From S'Express" hit No. 1 in spring 1988.

By the early 1990s, superclubs such as Ministry of Sound in London and Cream in Liverpool brought rave culture to heel. But the music continued to flourish, with house prompting numerous dance-music styles, from ambient to hardcore techno.

BELOW *Rave culture of the late 1980s saw clubbers lost in an ecstatic haze of visual stimulation and hands-in-the-air house music.*

Madchester

SANDWICHED SOMEWHERE between the Second Summer of Love and grunge was a domestic British phenomenon centered on Manchester in northwest England. Dubbed "Madchester," not least because of the commotion caused when a generation of soccer-mad music fans swapped beer for the "blissed-out" high of MDMA (or "ecstasy"), the phenomenon can also be seen as the missing link between the ska revival and Britpop.

As home to Buzzcocks, the Fall and John Cooper-Clarke, Manchester had been the second city of punk. During the 1980s, the rise of Factory Records and its key act New Order introduced a strong dance element to the local scene that found its most perfect realization in the two cornerstones of the "baggy" movement, Stone Roses and Happy Mondays.

Though both had been active since the mid-1980s, the catalyzing effect of the Factory-run Hacienda Club brought a new, groove-based urgency to their music later in the decade. Happy Mondays' chaotic mix of funk, psychedelia, and acid house was quintessentially "Madchester," while the Stone Roses' dance credentials were always more understated.

Fellow travelers James and Inspiral Carpets were closer to the guitar-rock end of the indie-dance spectrum, while 808 State and their renegade member A Guy Called Gerald (whose "Voodoo Ray" was Madchester's unofficial anthem) were deeply embroiled in house and techno.

When attention turned toward grunge capital Seattle during 1991, Madchester collapsed—but a new generation of Mancunian acts, notably Oasis and Chemical Brothers, soon emerged.

TOP *Happy Mondays epitomized a new age of abandon during the late 1980s, both on record and especially on stage, where most eyes were trained on the band's resident dancer, Bez.*

ABOVE *No band caught the indie-dance synergy, and the mood of the times, more perfectly than the Stone Roses. Their self-titled debut continues to poll well in "Greatest Album Ever" listings.*

5 Top Madchester artists

The Stone Roses: The Stone Roses *(1989)*
808 State: Ninety *(1989)*

Happy Mondays: Pills 'n' Thrills and Bellyaches *(1990)*

Inspiral Carpets: Life *(1990)*
James: Gold Mother *(1990)*

New Order

FEW SUSPECTED there was any future for the remaining three Joy Division members after the suicide of frontman Ian Curtis in May 1980—and debuting as New Order with the lackluster Joy Division pastiche "Ceremony" seemed to confirm it. Inspiration came in 1981 on a trip to New York where, exposed to the joys of electro-dance music, New Order found the perfect counterbalance to their instinctively morbid sound.

With their reputation assured, New Order took time out in 1993 to pursue solo projects. Returning in 1998 for a series of festival appearances, they reintroduced several Joy Division songs into the set, and continued to do so for the next decade before bassist Peter Hook's apparently terminal departure in 2007.

BELOW *The three remaining Joy Division members, fronted by Bernard Sumner after Ian Curtis's death, reinvented themselves as indie-dance pioneers, bridging the gap between post-punk and house.*

The next two singles, "Everything's Gone Green" and "Temptation," weren't too far off what electronic pioneers Cabaret Voltaire had been doing, though no one was prepared for "Blue Monday" (1983). Issued only on 12 inch, and clocking in at seven-and-a-half minutes, its blend of bored, Bernard Sumner vocals and upbeat electro beats marked an indie-dance watershed. New Order had found their niche.

Inextricably entwined with the mythology of both Factory Records and Manchester, the beats-driven band also benefited from rave and, in 1990, took the official England World Cup song, "World in Motion," to No. 1.

New Order

Formed: *Manchester, England*
Years active: *1980–93, 1998–2007*

Definitive lineup: *Bernard Sumner, Peter Hook, Stephen Morris, Gillian Gilbert*

Genres: *post-punk, indie dance, electropop*
Key singles: *"Blue Monday" (1983), "True Faith" (1987)*

Key albums: *Power, Corruption & Lies (1983), Technique (1989)*

Featuring

Nirvana • Primal Scream • Dr. Dre • Rage Against the Machine • Björk • Beck •
Nine Inch Nails • PJ Harvey • Nick Cave & the Bad Seeds • Manic Street Preachers •
Tricky • Blur • Oasis • Radiohead • The Notorious B.I.G.

1990s

1990s: Introduction

THIS WAS THE DECADE that rocked again. After the high-gloss 1980s, dictated as much by technically minded studio personnel as it was by musicians, the 1990s witnessed a revival in confidence, with artists back in the driving seat.

Music got louder, too. Hardcore was appropriated by acts that broke through into the mainstream. Hip hop continued to evolve, hitting new levels in sonic sophistication. Rock legends found their feet again thanks to a revival in songcraft. There was even room for assorted maverick talents to break through and reach an international audience. Above all, the ever-expanding world of rock sounded as if it had rediscovered its soul.

The banishment of the weak digital sound that had undermined so much work during the previous decade was largely down to the emergence of grunge, with its emphasis on a raw, visceral sound, and the growth of MTV's *Unplugged* series, which enabled musicians to step out from behind a production gloss and perform "in person." Veterans such as Neil Young, Eric Clapton, Bob Dylan, and the Rolling Stones clawed back their dignity during the 1990s with grittier, and far less perfunctory, new work.

ABOVE LEFT The decade began with a bang when grunge went global, with the arrival of acts such as Soundgarden.

LEFT Warring siblings Liam and Noel Gallagher were at the heart of Oasis's success at the height of Britpop.

Sounds of the decade

"Smells Like Teen Spirit":
Nirvana (1991)

"Nuthin' but a 'G' Thang":
Dr. Dre (1993)

"Loser":
Beck (1994)

"You Oughta Know":
Alanis Morissette (1995)

"Gangsta's Paradise":
Coolio featuring L.V. (1995)

"Wonderwall":
Oasis (1995)

The arrival of grunge during 1991 ("The year that punk broke," as claimed by its protagonists) set the tone for the decade, prompting various strands of alternative rock to enjoy mass acceptance. A proliferation of subgenres—from G-funk and jungle to black metal—were united only in a penchant for multiple tattoos and piercings.

Alongside the refreshed rock market, which drew increasingly on new initiatives in hip hop and electronic music, club culture continued to dominate weekends with the emergence of superclubs and the mass annual exodus to Mediterranean clubbing Mecca, Ibiza.

By 1999, the entrance of white rap sensation Eminem illustrated just how far hip hop had traveled. But its ability to attract headlines had, if anything, intensified, with controversies concerning sexism, gratuitous violence, and homophobia eclipsed by the shocking murders of Tupac

and the Notorious B.I.G. at the height of the so-called "rap wars." Music had come to mean something again, but surely not so much that people's lives were put in danger.

BELOW Hip hop hit the headlines for the wrong reasons, with the murders of the Notorious B.I.G. and Tupac Shakur.

"Paranoid Android":
Radiohead (1997)

"Bitter Sweet Symphony":
The Verve (1997)

"Doo Wop (That Thing)":
Lauryn Hill (1998)

"Hard Knock Life (Ghetto Anthem)":
Jay-Z (1998)

1990s: Time line

1990

Sinéad O'Connor

January 1990
Irish newcomer Sinéad O'Connor enjoys instant success with a heartbreaking version of Prince's "Nothing Compares 2 U." The single is supported by a suitably stark promo video.

April 1990
Jimi Hendrix Experience drummer Mitch Mitchell sells the Fender Stratocaster guitar that Hendrix used at his legendary Woodstock performance. It goes under the hammer for U.S.$295,000.

May 1990
The Madchester movement climaxes in a large field on Spike Island in Cheshire, where 27,000 baggily attired rock 'n' rave enthusiasts turn out for a muddy night with the Stone Roses.

July 1991
Originally conceived as a 1991 farewell tour for his band Jane's Addiction, Perrey Farrell's Lollapalooza becomes an annual fixture for most of the decade, pulling together a range of alternative acts. Arguably none could rival this first outing, which also features Siouxsie & the Banshees, Nine Inch Nails, Ice-T and Body Count, Butthole Surfers, the Rollins Band, and Living Color.

Perrey Farrell

September 1991
French singing legend and cultural ambassador Serge Gainsbourg, one half of the infamous "Je T'Aime" (1969) singing duo with partner Jane Birkin, dies of a heart attack. The nation mourns for days.

k.d. lang

March 1992
The traditionally conservative country-music market is rocked by the success of k.d. lang's second album, *Ingénue*. An alt-country milestone, the record is richly textured and free from cliché.

November 1992
The success of the self-titled debut album by Los Angeles-based rap metal band Rage Against the Machine suggests that rock audiences are ready to embrace tough, politically charged music once more.

December 1992
Dr. Dre outflanks his NWA colleagues by becoming the most influential man in hip hop. His first album, *The Chronic*, is a key record in the transition from gangsta rap to G-Funk.

1990-1993

September 1990

David Lynch's deliciously subversive *Twin Peaks* TV series spawns a similarly intriguing hit single. Cowritten by Lynch and Angelo Badalamenti, and eerily intoned by Julee Cruise, "Theme from Twin Peaks" anticipates the incoming craze for loungecore.

November 1990

Anthologizing Madonna's first decade, *The Immaculate Collection* quickly becomes the biggest-selling compilation of all time. Though confirming that the singer's chief appeal is as a singles act, later in the decade Madonna will also win critical praise as an album artist.

1991

March 1991

There had been rock biopics before, but none capture the imagination like Oliver Stone's *The Doors*, essentially a celebration of the band's charismatic frontman Jim Morrison. The surviving Doors disagree, calling the movie "a cartoon."

November 1991

Just hours after it is announced that he is battling with AIDS, Queen frontman Freddie Mercury dies at his London home. Many fans hadn't even been aware of his sexuality, let alone his illness.

1992

January 1992

While Nirvana's 1989 debut album *Bleach* won critical acclaim, the slow, steady rise of *Nevermind*, released the previous September and topping the U.S. chart at the start of 1992, takes the rock world by surprise.

Huggy Bear

February 1992

Having prompted some of the most savage record reviews ever two decades earlier, Yoko Ono's work reappears in a lavish six-CD box set, *Onobox*. But times have changed. She is now praised as one of rock's most remarkable pioneers.

1993

Elvis Presley

January 1993

In 1992, the U.S. Postal Service invited the American public to vote whether the young or Vegas Presley should appear on a forthcoming national stamp. About 75 percent voted for young Elvis, and now, well over 100 million sales later, it is the most popular postage stamp of all time.

February 1993

Initially a U.S. phenomenon, the underground feminist Riot Grrrl movement has its moment of glory in Britain, when Huggy Bear attempt to kick-start the "boy/girl revolution" on British TV show *The Word*. Their incendiary 45 "Her Jazz" hits the lower reaches of the charts, but it's "lads culture" that wins out.

March 1993

In contrast to Madchester and grunge, the glam-inspired Suede fulfill their promise with a self-titled debut that becomes an instant No. 1 hit. Their success is a clear harbinger of Britpop.

1990s: Time line

May 1993

Supporting 18 Wheeler at King Tut's Wah Wah Hut in Glasgow, Scotland, visiting Manchester band Oasis catch the eye of Creation Records boss Alan McGee. He offers them a deal immediately.

June 1993

Twenty-five years after John Cale first walked out on the group, the Velvet Underground bury their differences and kick off their reunion tour in Edinburgh, Scotland. But even before a U.S. leg is scheduled, Cale and Lou Reed fall out once more, and the unlikely venture folds prematurely.

August 1993

The black-metal wars that rock Norwegian metal reach a horrific climax when Mayhem guitarist Euronymous is stabbed to death by Varg Vikernes from rival band Burzum.

October 1993

Hole, fronted by Courtney Love, record a second album, *Live Through This*. Partly inspired by the songwriting style of Love's husband, Kurt Cobain, its release will be largely overshadowed by news of his death.

May 1994

The marriage is announced of Michael Jackson and Lisa Marie Presley—daughter of Elvis. A most extraordinary and unlikely union of pop DNA, it lasts all of 19 months. Many will later denounce the venture as a sham, vehemently denied by Lisa Marie, though she will concede it was "an unusual relationship."

August 1994

For once, a musician escapes from the glare of his rock-legend father, when the improbably gifted Jeff Buckley—son of 1960s songwriter Tim—emerges with a powerfully original debut album, *Grace*.

Alanis Morissette

May 1995

The fortunes of long-suffering indie band Pulp are transformed by the upbeat and brilliantly lyrical "Common People." The song gets a further boost when the group deputize for the Stone Roses at Glastonbury in June, turning in one of the most memorable performances in the festival's history.

Pulp's Jarvis Cocker

June 1995

Canadian singer Alanis Morissette undergoes a significant makeover and reemerges as a tough-talking grunge-inspired harpie. Her album, *Jagged Little Pill*, tops the U.S. chart for three months.

1993-1996

Beck

January 1994

It started life as a small-time independent release, but after Geffen pick it up several months later, Beck's hip-hop flavored "Loser" gives the shy musical eclectic a Top 10 U.S. hit.

April 1994

Though the warning signs—including a suicide attempt while touring Europe in March—had long been there, the announcement that a body has been found at the Seattle home of Nirvana frontman Kurt Cobain confirms every grunge fan's worst fears.

1995

October 1994

After a couple of tetchy Led Zeppelin reunions during the 1980s, singer Robert Plant and guitarist Jimmy Page patch up their differences for a 90-minute "Unledded" MTV documentary. The pair will continue to work together until 1998.

February 1995

Manic Street Preachers guitarist and inspiration Richey Edwards disappears close to a suicide spot by the Severn Bridge, which joins England and his native Wales. He is never seen again.

Richey Edwards

March 1995

Garbage, a commanding hi-tech rock band formed by three music producers and Scottish singer Shirley Manson, release their debut single, "Vow."

1996

August 1995

A brooding hip-hop song about urban breakdown becomes the biggest hit of the year in the United States. Based on a sample from an old Stevie Wonder song, Coolio's Grammy-winning "Gangsta's Paradise" is also a huge international hit.

December 1995

"Free as a Bird" becomes the first "new" Beatles single since 1970. Based on a sketchy John Lennon demo from 1977, the song is worked up in the studio by his three ex-colleagues with assistance from ELO's Jeff Lynne.

February 1996

Emerging from prison in October 1995, 2Pac—alias Tupac Shakur—heads straight for the studio to record "All Eyez on Me." His most raw and personal release, it is also his swansong, for he is gunned down seven months later.

March 1996

The Sex Pistols announce they're coming back for six months of reunion shows. Only for the money, of course—the event is playfully named the Filthy Lucre Tour.

1990s: Time line

June 1996
On the comeback trail are Kiss, who kick off their sellout tour in Detroit performing classic 1970s material in makeup and costumes. Original members Ace Frehley and Peter Criss are also back on board.

July 1996
Piggybacking the cheery Britpop revival come the Spice Girls with their hyperactive debut, "Wannabe." The single unleashes a remarkable run of hits and plenty of debate concerning the merits of "Girl Power."

David Bowie

1997

January 1997
David Bowie celebrates his 50th birthday with a show at Madison Square Garden, New York. A range of musical pals both old and new show up, including Lou Reed, Sonic Youth, Foo Fighters, and Placebo.

September 1997
Elton John sings a new version of his 1973 hit, "Candle in the Wind," at the funeral of close friend Diana, Princess of Wales. It quickly becomes the biggest-selling single in British history.

October 1997
Chris Cunningham's extraordinary promo video for Aphex Twin's latest single, "Come to Daddy," augments the song's manic postindustrial techno sound with a scary portrayal of social breakdown and urban decay.

November 1997
A U.S. Senate subcommittee on the effect of violent rock lyrics hears a father blame his son's suicide on Marilyn Manson's *Antichrist Superstar*, which is described as "vile, hateful, nihilistic, and damaging."

1998

March 1998
Fifteen years after first appearing on a home-produced cassette, Run-DMC's "It's Like That" is remixed by DJ Jason Nevins, spends six weeks at No. 1 in Britain, and becomes a huge European hit.

December 1998
"My Name Is" paves the way for white rapper Eminem's *The Slim Shady* LP, released the following February. The record introduces his Slim Shady alter ego and Eminem is poised to become the first music superstar of the twenty-first century.

Eminem

1999

January 1999
A little-known married couple duo record their debut album on basic equipment in a Detroit studio. A fusion of blues roots and punk-rock energy, *The White Stripes* provides a blueprint for the new wave of garage rock.

February 1999
Twenty years after they enjoyed their first British No. 1 hit, the reformed Blondie repeat the success with their sixth chart-topper, "Maria."

1996-1999

March 1997

In the early hours of March 9, the Notorious B.I.G. is shot dead after attending the Soul Train awards in Los Angeles. As with the shooting of Tupac six months earlier, Biggie's murder remains unsolved.

The Notorious B.I.G.

May 1997

The release of "Paranoid Android," Radiohead's extraordinary new six-minute single, anticipates the giant leap they'll take on their forthcoming album, *OK Computer*, issued weeks later.

June 1997

The success of the Verve's "Bitter Sweet Symphony" is bittersweet indeed when the copyright owners of the song's key sample later successfully sue, forcing the band to forfeit all royalties on the track.

May 1998

Frank Sinatra, the grandaddy of the teen idols, dies aged 82. His last big success is *Duets* (1993), where the old smoothie paired up with a range of singers, from Aretha Franklin and Bono to near contemporary Tony Bennett.

August 1998

The Miseducation of Lauryn Hill, the first solo album by the Fugees vocalist, is an instant success. Drawing on a range of black-music styles, the album yields several hit singles, including "Doo Wop (That Thing)."

Lauryn Hill

October 1998

Latest in a string of legendary lost recordings unearthed for the booming CD market is Bob Dylan's infamous "Royal Albert Hall" concert. Actually taped in Manchester on the same 1966 tour, it features the infamous cry of "Judas!" from a disgruntled fan.

March 1999

The appearance of Andy Williams's "Music to Watch Girls By" in the British Top 10 crowns a remarkable change in fortunes for easy-listening music, for so long consigned to the dustbin of popular music.

April 1999

Mamma Mia, a stage production based on the life and work of 1970s Swedish singing sensations ABBA, opens in London's West End. Its extraordinary success prompts a wave of productions worldwide.

July 1999

Thirty years after the original festival, Woodstock 99 is blighted by rapes, looting, and violence. A series of indiscriminate fires break out during the Red Hot Chili Peppers' set, prompting singer Anthony Kiedis to compare the event to a scene from *Apocalypse Now*.

December 1999

Paralyzed from the neck down in 1990 after stage lights fell on him at a concert in New York, Curtis Mayfield eventually succumbs to the aftereffects of his injuries, aged 57.

Grunge

ALTHOUGH THE ROOTS of grunge can be found in the mid-1980s U.S. underground, in late period Black Flag, even in the heavy-metal sludge of Black Sabbath or acid-metal power trio Blue Cheer, the "slacker" style emerged in earnest in the late 1980s. By 1992, post-Nirvana's *Nevermind*, grunge had redefined alternative rock. Metal, too, never quite sounded—or looked—the same again, as the new philosophy of sonic rawness and unfussy performance style soon rendered the "hair-metal" bands virtually obsolete.

Grunge is synonymous with "the Seattle Sound" for good reason. All the major bands came from the Pacific Northwest state of Washington, with most enjoying the early platform of the Seattle-based Sub Pop label. None was more archetypal than Mudhoney, whose frontman Mark Arm is usually credited with coining the "G" word. Mudhoney's magnificently messy, Stooges-like "Touch Me I'm Sick" had been an early grunge favorite, though it was the 1970s-flavored metal rock of Soundgarden that broke first, earning the group a major deal and a mainstream audience.

RIGHT TOP *Led by Kat Bjelland, Babes in Toyland were never more dynamic than on the 1991 To Mother mini-LP.*

RIGHT CENTER *Pearl Jam's frontman Eddie Vedder. The band popularized the grunge sound with 1991's Ten.*

RIGHT *Mudhoney, grunge pacemakers fronted by Mark Arm, never bettered their classic, "Touch Me I'm Sick."*

Contemporaries such as Alice in Chains, Screaming Trees, and latecomers Pearl Jam followed suit, all veering toward the already established hard-rock and metal market. Nirvana were different. Mining a more disobedient rock tradition, they augmented grunge's raw, distorted, rock energy with a characteristic stop/start and soft/loud style that became the group's trademark.

Nirvana inspired and radicalized a new generation of musicians, from feminist-inspired acts, such as Hole, Babes in Toyland, and the Riot Grrrl movement, to more obviously experimental bands, such as the Flaming Lips and Trumans Water.

By mid-1994, with Pearl Jam and Soundgarden playing arenas and Kurt Cobain dead, grunge collapsed as an identifiable genre. Nevertheless, its sonic grit and air of disaffection remains influential, informing everything from industrial rock to the twenty-first-century guitar-rock revival.

5 Top grunge artists

Mudhoney: Superfuzz Bigmuff *(1988)*
Babes in Toyland: To Mother *(1991)*
Nirvana: Nevermind *(1991)*

Pearl Jam: Ten *(1991)*
Hole: Live Through This *(1994)*

ABOVE *Though famously known as "the slacker generation," grunge brought a new dynamism to alternative rock, as Pearl Jam's Eddie Vedder clearly demonstrates.*

Nirvana

WITH HIP HOP AND DANCE at the frontier-bashing forefront during the 1980s, and only the more extreme forms of metal attempting to reinvent guitar-based music, rock had become cowed, almost conservative by the late 1980s. Nirvana's rude intrusion on the mainstream toward the end of 1991 altered all that.

BELOW *Kurt Cobain in concert in Italy, little over six weeks before his death in April 1994. Both gifted and troubled, the Nirvana frontman seemed to embody the grunge sensibility.*

Riding the grunge tide coming out of Seattle, Nirvana became "the band most likely to" after an endorsement from Sonic Youth landed the quietly ambitious power trio a deal with major label Geffen. Settling on a sound for September 1991's breakthrough *Nevermind* took several months and countless remixes. One thing was certain: the bleak, Black Sabbath-inspired grunginess of the 1989 debut set *Bleach* would be augmented with a melodic sensibility that was almost poplike.

If *Nevermind* prompted a mini-rock revolution, the leadoff single, "Smells Like Teen Spirit," was more iconic still. Joy, rage, a perfectly weighted riff-hook, ominous verses followed by an oblivion-chasing chorus—it was as if rock's essence had been distilled into one song. Squinting from behind his floppy blond hair, displaying an ambivalence about the band's success that verged on disdain, and visibly growing into the role of the tortured artist, frontman Kurt Cobain was the embodiment of grunge's antagonistic attitude toward the mainstream.

After a flurry of promotional activity and global tours, Nirvana spent much of 1992 out of the spotlight, as their status soared. When a follow-up album duly arrived, in September 1993, *In Utero* was an altogether more raw and rage-filled record than its predecessor—and with Steve Albini at the controls, brilliantly realized. This was rock as it was supposed to sound, you could almost hear Cobain saying, as an extraordinarily visceral song, such as "Scentless Apprentice," cranked into action.

An appearance on *MTV Unplugged* in November that year revealed Cobain's more sensitive side, which was increasingly finding expression in more damaging ways beyond the glare of the spotlight. His shotgun suicide in April 1994 brought rock's glorious, raucous, and rebellious revival to a sad and abrupt end. As if too painful to bear, the phrase "grunge" dropped from the vernacular almost overnight. Cobain's legend, of course, had only just begun.

Ominous verses and an oblivion-chasing chorus...

ABOVE AND RIGHT *Following in the footsteps of Cream and the Jimi Hendrix Experience, Nirvana (above) were one of the great rock power trios and (right) intensely explosive on stage.*

Nirvana

Formed: *Aberdeen, Washington*

Years active: *1987–94*

Definitive lineup: *Kurt Cobain, Krist Nosovelic, Dave Grohl*

Genre: *rock, pop, alternative rock*

Key singles: *"Smells Like Teen Spirit" (1991), "Come as You Are" (1992)*

Key albums: Nevermind *(1991),* In Utero *(1993)*

MTV Unplugged

IN TERMS OF OLD-STYLE songwriting, only the power ballad seemed to flourish during the 1980s, a decade that had turned instead toward the irrepressible grooves of hip hop and house, and to the programmed beats of synth-pop. In 1989, though, MTV launched a new strand that would put the focus firmly back on the song.

The premise of *MTV Unplugged* was that artists would perform their work unaided (in the main) by electronics or even electric instruments. Launching in November 1989 with acclaimed British new-wave band Squeeze, within two years *MTV Unplugged* had, with grunge, made a pincerlike attack on rock that virtually consigned the engineer-led production revolution of the 1980s to the margins.

The years 1991 to 1995 witnessed the heyday of *MTV Unplugged*, with Paul McCartney's January 1991 performance a key moment in popularizing the initiative. In its wake, the ex-Beatle took off on an "Unplugged" tour to promote a tie-in album featuring highlights from the show. When Eric Clapton did the same the following year, his "Unplugged" set sold millions and was showered with Grammys. Dylan's unadorned night of vintage classics, taped in November 1994, was similarly successful.

The high point of the series probably remains Nirvana's December 1993 broadcast, filmed just months prior to Kurt Cobain's suicide and revealing a quite different side to the band's work.

RIGHT *Bob Dylan returned to his 1960s glory days for his November 1994 MTV Unplugged set. Later released on CD, the broadcast revived Dylan's career.*

BELOW *Hitherto known for its veteran performers, Unplugged secured a huge coup when Nirvana were encouraged to tone down the electricity for their 1993 appearance.*

Primal Scream

FEW HAVE WORN their influences so clearly as Primal Scream, from the Byrds-style jangle of their mid-1980s work to an enduring fascination with the Rolling Stones at their debauched, post-psychedelia peak. Nor has a band so successfully united two seemingly conflicting genres as the Primals did in 1991 with the enormously influential indie-rock-dance hybrid *Screamadelica*.

The catalyst for this transformation from retro rock also-rans to zeitgeist act was DJ Andrew Weatherall. Prior to their meeting, Primal Scream had been little more than "that band fronted by the ex-Jesus and Mary Chain drummer." Once Weatherall had remixed "Loaded," adding some judicious samples (Peter Fonda's "We wanna get loaded and we wanna have a good time" capturing perfectly the hedonism of the acid-house dance floor), the band also recruited ex-Stones producer Jimmy Miller, and *Screamadelica* was in the bag.

In Memphis for some infamously "recreational" follow-up sessions, Primal Scream nailed perhaps the quintessential rock buff's dream fusion in "Movin' on Up," which drew on everything from Stax and the Stones to Can.

Inevitably, the high life prompted a mid-decade collapse, though the arrival of ex-Stone Roses bassist Mani in 1996 brought new impetus to the hard-living band. *Vanishing Point* (1997) was a trippier affair, radical politics reared its angry head for the rage-filled *XTRMNTR* (2000), and, less meaningfully, supermodel Kate Moss

guested on 2002's *Evil Heat*. Though hardly their best, 2006's "Country Girl" gave Primal Scream their biggest single success, hitting the British Top 5 and confirming their unpredicted resilience.

BELOW *Having built a hugely important bridge between alternative rock and dance music on 1991's Screamadelica, Primal Scream—led by Bobby Gillespie, left—began to live out their Rolling Stones fantasies.*

Primal Scream

Formed:
Glasgow, Scotland

Years active:
1982 to present

Definitive lineup:
Bobby Gillespie, Andrew Innes, Robert Young, Martin Duffy, Henry Olsen, Phillip "Toby" Tomanov

Genres: *rock, alternative rock, indie dance*

Key singles:
"Loaded" (1990), "Movin' on Up" (1992)

Key albums:
Screamadelica (1991), XTRMNTR (2000)

Dr. Dre

ONETIME TURNTABLIST with incendiary LA gangsta-rap pioneers NWA, Dr. Dre's 1990s productions changed the pulse of popular music. And as a label boss and entrepreneur, who masterminded the early careers of rap superstars Snoop Doggy Dogg, Eminem, and 50 Cent, his importance continues well into the twenty-first century.

Dre, born André Young, emerged as a street DJ during the mid-1980s. Inspired by the flamboyant funk of George Clinton and the scratch sounds of Grandmaster Flash, his talents found him by the end of the decade masterminding NWA's revolutionary rap and becoming in-house producer for the band's Ruthless label.

After his acrimonious departure in 1991, Dre cofounded Death Row Records with Suge Knight, releasing his solo debut, *The Chronic*, in 1992. With its stripped-back, slowed-down, and warmed-up grooves, overlaid with melodic synth lines and often scandalously explicit lyrics, *The Chronic* patented "G-Funk"—and introduced rap partner Snoop Dogg to the world.

Dre produced Snoop's U.S. chart-topping *Doggystyle* (1993) before falling out with Knight shortly before Death Row became embroiled in the mid-1990s rap wars. Having set up his own Aftermath Entertainment label in 1996, two releases during 1999 reaffirmed Dre's reputation. Eminem's *The Slim Shady LP*, which Dre coproduced, was groundbreaking, while Dre's own *2001* was a gangsta-inspired sequel to *The Chronic*.

Since then, Dr. Dre has launched the career of 50 Cent, worked with everyone from Nine Inch Nails to Mary J. Blige, and carved out a secondary career in movies, making him one of the most powerful individuals in contemporary music.

BELOW *Dr. Dre's production skills came to attention via his work with the provocative NWA, though it was his debut solo set, 1992's The Chronic, that slowed tempos and set the tone for 1990s hip hop.*

Dr. Dre

Born: *February 18, 1965, Compton, Los Angeles, California*

Years active: *1983 to present*

Genres: *hip hop, gangsta-rap, G-funk*

Key singles: *"Nuthin' but a 'G' Thang" (1993), "Fuck Wit Dre Day (And Everybody's Celebrating)" (1993)*

Key albums: *The Chronic (1992), 2001 (1999)*

Rage Against the Machine

NO ONE DURING THE 1990S sang of the desire for social change with such clarity and force as Rage Against the Machine. If their name said it all, Rage's music said it louder still.

Inspired by hip hop and the tougher end of rock, the LA-based RATM's self-titled 1992 debut was a ferocious mix of Black Sabbath riffery, Zack de la Rocha's rap-style roar, a booming backbeat reminiscent of Led Zeppelin, and surprisingly crystal-clear production. With accusatory songs such as "Killing in the Name," Rage were rock's social conscience, and the album's slow-burn success created much anticipation for the follow-up. It was four years before *Evil Empire* arrived, though when it did, Rage landed a U.S. No. 1 and, in the grindingly frenzied "Bulls on Parade," an international hit single too.

Another lull, during which time Korn and Limp Bizkit emerged to steal some of Rage's thunder, ended in 1999 with the Orwellian-influenced *The Battle of Los Angeles*. Again, it topped the U.S. chart, but intraband relations had reached a low, prompting the group's outspoken singer to quit in 2000. When Soundgarden's Chris Cornell stepped in, the group changed its name to Audioslave.

The original RATM reformed in 2007, and have since continued to have run-ins with the corporations. More surprisingly, a successful Facebook campaign in 2009 made "Killing in the Name" a Christmas No. 1 in Britain that year.

ABOVE *Dreadlocked RATM frontman Zack de la Rocha, whose band channeled the frustration and anger of grunge into political activism.*

Rage Against the Machine

Formed: *Los Angeles, California*
Years active: *1991–2000, 2007 to present*

Definitive lineup: *Zack de la Rocha, Tom Morello, Tim Commerford, Brad Wilk*
Genre: *rap metal, alternative rock*

Key singles: *"Killing in the Name" (1992), "Guerrilla Radio" (1999)*

Key albums: Rage Against the Machine *(1992)*, Evil Empire *(1996)*

Björk

THOUGH HER CURIOUSLY engaging vocals dominated the work of late-1980s Icelandic indie rock band the Sugarcubes, Björk's blossoming as the next decade's most cherished maverick could have been foreseen only by close friends, aware that this strong-willed progeny of hippie parents had been releasing albums since she was 12. An instinctive, restless creative, Björk's solo career has been an adventure into musical realms every bit the equal of that extraordinary, instantly recognizable voice.

Björk's first adult solo album, *Debut*, coproduced with trip-hop pioneer Nellee Hooper, was sophisticated dance music that, from the breakthrough groove of "Human Behaviour" to the tumbledown sound of "Big Time Sensuality," enraptured a hip, upmarket urban crowd. The follow-up, *Post* (1995), was more extravagant and satisfying, with "Army of Me" rivaling the Prodigy's claustrophobic dance beats, and "It's Oh So Quiet" reviving the carefree abandon of big bands. Best of all was the sublime "Hyperballad"—quintessential Björk if ever there was such a thing.

Her twenty-first-century work proves that there isn't. From the *Selmaşongs* soundtrack (2000) that accompanied her role in *Dancer in the Dark* to the celebration of the human voice (*Medúlla*, 2004) and the Timbaland-enriched *Volta* (2007), Björk continues to explore new forms of musical expression. A series of wildly imaginative tours confirms that her eclecticism and perfectionism aren't limited to the studio.

Björk

Born:
November 21, 1965, Reykjavik, Iceland

Years active:
1977 to present

Genres: *alternative rock, indie dance, art rock*

Key singles:
"Big Time Sensuality" (1993), "Hyperballad" (1996)

Key albums:
Post (1995), Medúlla (2004)

LEFT *With her outlandish fashions and quirky quotability, Björk inevitably creates headlines. But, above all, she's a ferocious talent who continues to break new musical ground.*

Beck

ARRIVING OUT OF NOWHERE in 1994 with a strange, if oddly perfect for the times, hit single "Loser," Beck seemed destined for one-hit-wonderland. Instead, like Björk, he has become an evergreen, a maverick for whom eclecticism is not a career move but part of his DNA.

"Loser"—the title says it all—nailed the Generation X/grunge ethic. Musically, though, there was plenty going on, its baggy groove, rap-style delivery, and rootsy slide guitar neatly encapsulating the new rock era's vintage-meets-modern vibe. And it's that widescreen view that has provided the bedrock of Beck's career.

Beck Hansen, once connected to the raw, antifolk movement of late-1980s New York, was a one-man cottage industry whose extraordinarily prescient song sparked a bidding war. His first major release, 1994's *Mellow Gold*, was eclipsed by the richly textured *Odelay* (1996), which drew on gospel, hip hop, funk, and country music. *Mutations* (1998) was more subdued and, establishing a pattern in his work, was followed by an irrepressible glam-funk party album (1999's *Midnite Vultures*).

In 2002 *Sea Change*, which chronicled a relationship breakup in the manner of Serge Gainsbourg's *Histoire de Melody Nelson*, pulled out another creative peak from a personal low point. Since then Beck has worked with old friends—the Dust Brothers, Radiohead producer Nigel Godrich—and new, touring with the Flaming Lips as his backing band. And his work remains rarely less than fascinating.

ABOVE *Despite his lo-fi beginnings, Beck has smartened up and ventured into some remarkably high-gloss music, notably 1999's transcendent* Midnite Vultures. *But his early reputation as a gifted eclectic still sticks—and deservedly so.*

Beck

Born: *July 8, 1970, Los Angeles, California*

Years active: *1988 to present*

Genres: *alternative rock*

Key singles: *"Loser" (1994), "Devils Haircut" (1996)*

Key albums: Odelay *(1996),* Midnite Vultures *(1999)*

Vintage meets modern...

Industrial metal

A 1990S PHENOMENON that managed to weave its influence into rock, hip hop, and electronic dance, industrial metal was spearheaded by Ministry and Nine Inch Nails, with archetypal bogeyman Marilyn Manson emerging as the figurehead later in the decade.

If the melodic, almost polite R.E.M. and the Smiths typified alternative rock during the 1980s, the underground bristled with U.S. hardcore and postindustrial music noiseniks forming part of a post-punk continuum. While industrial-music pioneers Throbbing Gristle had been defiantly antirock, the emergence of guitar-led bands, such as Big Black, Head of David, and Godflesh, all of whom reveled in industrial's "entertainment through pain" aesthetic, paved the way for a more rock-orientated mutation.

The Al Jourgensen-fronted Ministry were the first to make commercial waves when *The Land of Rape and Honey* (1988) augmented the expected Aleister Crowley and war-movie samples with a musical motor that was undeniably rock driven. The band's success prompted the emergence of an industrial-related scene in Chicago centered on the Wax Trax! label, home to Germany's KMFDM, Front 242, and Jourgensen spin-off, Revolting Cocks.

It was Ministry's 1992 album, *Psalm 69: The Way to Succeed and the Way to Suck Eggs*, that proved the breakthrough for sex, death, and magic-obsessed industrial metal. Nine Inch Nails mainman Trent Reznor took the form down a more exploratory route, first with *Broken* (1992), then with the genre

masterpiece, *The Downward Spiral* (1994). Reznor was soon being courted by David Bowie and covered by Johnny Cash (the magnificent "Hurt," 2002).

By the mid-1990s, industrial metal's almost martial beat was being successfully reworked by German controversialists Rammstein, and its shock tactics were taken to almost comical limits by Marilyn Manson. Both Manson (1998's *Mechanical Animals*) and NIN (1999's *The Fragile*) enjoyed great success until the end of the decade, before the genre faded in the face of an even more technologically advanced century.

RIGHT *Although their sound is closest to industrial metal, Rammstein also draw from punk and electronic music, overlaid with frontman Till Lindemann's aggressive vocals.*

BELOW *Marilyn Manson, a Trent Reznor protégé whose preoccupation with sex and crime made him very much the modern-day Alice Cooper—with a string of headlines to match.*

Entertainment through pain...

5 Top industrial-metal artists

Ministry: Psalm 69: The Way to Succeed
and the Way to Suck Eggs *(1992)*
Nine Inch Nails: The Downward Spiral *(1994)*

KMFDM: Xtort *(1996)*
Marilyn Manson: Antichrist Superstar *(1996)*
Rammstein: Sehnsucht *(1997)*

Nine Inch Nails

LYRICALLY MORBID and explicit, sonically abrasive yet artful, and mostly recorded in the Beverly Hills residence of Manson Family murder victim actress Sharon Tate, 1994's *The Downward Spiral* by Nine Inch Nails brought the more salacious aspects of the industrial aesthetic into the mainstream. Almost overnight, the relatively bland dramas of 1980s rock sounded decidedly dull.

Controversial and confrontational, ex-studio engineer and NIN mainman Trent Reznor is also a highly skilled multiinstrumentalist, sound sculptor, and, lest we forget, a gifted songwriter whose "Hurt" was hauntingly reinterpreted by Johnny Cash.

The virtual one-man-band's 1989 debut, *Pretty Hate Machine*, had been all theatrical vocals and concessions to synth-pop. That changed in 1992 with the *Broken* mini-album, a giant creative step darker in mood and dirtier in sound than its predecessor. Coming on the back of a long tour, *Broken* punctured the U.S. Top 10, a feat eclipsed by *The Downward Spiral* two years later.

NIN's trademark "rock-band soundscape" style soon found its way into all manner of 1990s music, although after the similarly successful *The Fragile* (1999), industrial rock collapsed. Reznor nevertheless retains a huge core audience who, in recent years, have benefited from his anticorporate, pro-download stance. *Ghosts I–IV* and *The Slip* (both 2008) were made available for free and as deluxe limited editions, while Reznor has also released songs in formats that allow fans to remix the songs.

Nine Inch Nails

Formed:
Cleveland, Ohio

Years active:
1988 to 2009

Definitive lineup:
Trent Reznor

Genres: *industrial rock, industrial metal, alternative rock*

Key singles:
"March of the Pigs" (1994), "The Day the World Went Away" (1999)

Key albums:
The Downward Spiral *(1994),* The Fragile *(1999)*

LEFT *Nine Inch Nails' mainman Trent Reznor emerged from the fringes to become one of rock's most influential creatives during the mid-1990s, thanks to the success of* The Downward Spiral.

PJ Harvey

Again like Beefheart, Harvey found in the blues a universal language and a suitably earthy vehicle for her early songs of blood, loss, and sexual prowess. Stylistically, though, Harvey's series of mutations—prompting an "indie Madonna" tag—have seen her embrace hardcore (1993's *Rid of Me*), deep-hued complexity (1995's *To Bring You My Love*), and even the romance of New York, on her most successful record, *Stories from the City, Stories from the Sea* (2000).

In recent years Harvey's stature has grown further. *Uh Huh Her* (2004) eschewed the production finesse of her previous set for a disparate collection of raw, often achingly delicate, DIY recordings. The piano-dominated *White Chalk* (2007) marked an even more significant break with tradition, while 2011's *Let England Shake* found Harvey at her most poetic and inventive.

ABOVE *The ever-artful PJ Harvey carefully conceives each individual project with both sound and visual presentation in mind.*

PJ Harvey

Born: *October 9, 1969, Dorset, England*

Years active: *1987 to present*

Genre: *indie rock*

Key singles: *"50ft Queenie" (1993), "A Perfect Day Elise" (1998)*

Key albums: Uh Huh Her *(2004),* White Chalk *(2007)*

Nick Cave & the Bad Seeds

THE TRANSFORMATION of Nick Cave from post-punk racketeer to suave balladeer has been as effortless as it once seemed improbable. Still dressing in black—albeit tailored suits rather than the torn leather of his Birthday Party days—helps. At the root of this renovation has been Cave's channeling of all that barely controlled post-punk rage and despair into more traditional and sophisticated song forms.

The Birthday Party got by on sheer sonic violence, their independent hit "Release the Bats" (1981) striking a suitably disturbed chord with the emerging goth scene. When relations with chief collaborator Rowland S. Howard collapsed in 1983 and the band disbanded, Cave formed the Bad Seeds, a five-piece featuring ex-colleague Mick Harvey and ex-Einstürzende Neubauten mainman Blixa Bargeld.

Messing with the ghosts of the old American South ("Tupelo," 1985), and patenting a continental-style swamp blues ("From Her to Eternity," 1984), the Bad Seeds presented a formidable, and hardly less intimidating, prospect. An early peak was reached with 1988's "The Mercy Seat," a terrifying, tension-wracked evocation of the tortured mind of a Death-Row prisoner, and still Cave's signature song.

Since then, the band has been most effective on ballads such as "The Ship Song" (1990) and the stark "Into My Arms" from the acclaimed The Boatman's Call (1997). From 2006 Cave has also fronted the band's garage-rocking alter ego, Grinderman.

Nick Cave & the Bad Seeds

Formed:
Melbourne, Australia

Years active:
1983 to present

Definitive lineup:
Nick Cave, Mick Harvey, Blixa Bargeld, Conway Savage, Warren Ellis, Martyn P. Casey, Thomas Wydler, Jim Sclavunos

Genres: alternative rock, rock, pop

Key singles:
"The Mercy Seat" (1988), "Where the Wild Roses Grow" (1995)

Key albums:
The Boatman's Call (1997), No More Shall We Part (2001)

LEFT Nick Cave (left) with his onetime second-in-command Bad Seed, Blixa Bargeld. Cave is one of the few artists from the punk era whose subsequent work has eclipsed that of his youth.

Manic Street Preachers

FUSING THE INDIGNANT, fist-waving attack of the Clash with an all-too-real sense of alienation that carried tragic echoes of Kurt Cobain, the Manic Street Preachers began the 1990s as small-time indie cult antiheroes. By the end of the decade, iconic guitarist Richey Edwards was missing, presumed dead, and the band's stadium-friendly anthems and enormous popularity echoed that of Queen a decade earlier.

The defining moment in the Manics' transformation from self-styled "art terrorists" into a politically conscious hit machine came on February 1, 1995, when Edwards vanished. His car was found parked close to a suicide spot on the border between Wales and England, but with no body ever recovered, the band's intense lyricist, so ferociously committed that he was once moved to carve the letters "4REAL" in his arm, was officially declared dead in 2008.

In an echo of Pink Floyd's subsequent success after the collapse of original ideas man Syd Barrett, the Manics have both carried the myth respectfully and eclipsed it with an acclaimed body of work that has far outgrown the band's original audience. Inevitably, 1994's *The Holy Bible*, the last album to feature Edwards, remains the apotheosis of the anguished, androgynous, early Manics. Most popular, though, in the collective memory is 1996's *Everything Must Go*, the band's first as a trio. With swooping strings enveloping James Dean Bradfield's impassioned vocal, the leadoff track from "A Design for Life" was a huge hit every bit as memorable as any Britpop anthem.

Entering the new decade in radical style with the riotous and chart-topping single "The Masses Against the Classes" before making a well-publicized appearance in Castro's Cuba, the band continue to refine their bombastic approach.

ABOVE *Since the disappearance of Richey Edwards in 1995, the spotlight has fallen on frontman James Dean Bradfield and glam-inspired bassist Nicky Wire.*

Manic Street Preachers

Formed:
Caerphilly, Wales

Years active:
1986 to present

Definitive lineup:
James Dean Bradfield, Richey Edwards, Nicky Wire, Sean Moore

Genre:
alternative rock

Key singles: *"A Design For Life" (1996), "If You Tolerate This Your Children Will Be Next" (1998)*

Key albums: *The Holy Bible (1994), Everything Must Go (1996)*

Politically conscious hits...

Trip hop

MOST ARTISTS DESPAIR at being boxed into a genre, though few more so than the small but influential handful that emerged during the early and mid-1990s and were saddled with the trip-hop tag. Since two of those acts, Tricky and Portishead, have gone on to produce some of the most brilliant but indefinable work in modern times, it's easy to empathize with their exasperation.

There was also a geographical dimension to their defiance. For trip hop, very much associated with the city of Bristol in England's West Country, was a phrase invented by the London media initially for a club cut ("In/Flux") by American mega-sampler DJ Shadow. But the release of three hugely distinctive and successful albums, each one falling into that electronic-atmospherics-over-slow-beats style that loosely defines trip hop, soon shifted attention westward. For the first time since the heady days of post-punk, the spotlight returned to Bristol.

TOP *The haunting voice of Beth Gibbons has led Portishead out of the trip-hop trap and toward somewhere else entirely.*

ABOVE *Massive Attack's Daddy G and Robert Del Naja pictured in suitably subterranean surroundings.*

Even before Massive Attack's *Protection* (1994), Portishead's *Dummy* (1994), and Tricky's *Maxinquaye* (1995) confirmed that Britain at last had its own peculiarly twisted and insular take on hip hop, Bristol had for years been mixing influences from across the racial spectrum. The apocalyptic dub solo work of Mark Stewart, ex-frontman with the city's maverick post-punk funkers the Pop Group, anticipated trip hop by a decade, though it was mid-1980s sound system collective the Wild Bunch that provided a training ground for the genre's early 1990s groundbreakers, Massive Attack.

With its stoner-paced beats, subtle, often whispered raps, and soulful heart, Massive's 1991 set, *Blue Lines*, had an immediate effect. And not only on the album chart, as the success of the Shara Nelson-fronted "Unfinished Sympathy" single proved. Björk absorbed the sound for *Debut*, while the band's youngest rapper, the onetime "Tricky Kid," broke out, found himself a singing partner, and reemerged a few years later with the stunningly original *Maxinquaye*.

By the mid-1990s "trip-hop" remixes were everywhere, as bands like Morcheeba and Sneaker Pimps allied themselves with the style. DJ Shadow's label boss at Mo'Wax, James Lavelle, even got in on the act with U.N.K.L.E. But toward the end of the decade, as Massive Attack grew more melancholy, Tricky more aggressive and experimental, and Portishead more anguished, the trip-hop moniker was rendered meaningless by the continued reinvention of its artists.

Electronic atmospherics over slow beats...

ABOVE *Tricky, pictured in 2003. The stoner vibe of his debut,* Maxinquaye, *is belied by the intensity of his performances.*

5 Top trip-hop artists

Massive Attack: Blue Lines *(1991)*
Portishead: Dummy *(1994)*
Tricky: Maxinquaye *(1995)*

Morcheeba: Who Can You Trust? *(1996)*
DJ Shadow: Endtroducing….. *(1996)*

Tricky

LIKE BJÖRK AND PJ HARVEY, Tricky was one of a small handful of innovators whose presence added to the overriding sense that rock and its various offshoots were on fire again during the 1990s.

Maxinquaye (1995), Tricky's breakthrough album, was a fusion of bloodshot beats, babbling electronica, and a production fog that hung heavy like smoke. With then partner Martina Topley-Bird providing the vocals, which Tricky would shadow eerily with his own heavy whisper, everything about the album seemed inverted and furtive. In the wake of its success, with the media lapping up Tricky's habit of presenting himself in makeup, wearing devil horns, and engulfed by circles of cigarette smoke, his reaction was to hide uncredited behind a collaborative project, *Nearly God* (1996).

Reverting to his name for *Pre-Millennium Tension* (1996), Tricky shattered the relative calm of trip hop with a genuinely disturbing set. "Vent" opened the set with a panic. "Tricky Kid," issued as a single, was hypnotizing post-hip hop—and the nagging grind of "Bad Dreams" was cold and chilling.

In 2001, Tricky's *Blowback* was a far more commercial affair and featured collaborations with Cyndi Lauper, Alanis Morissette, and the Red Hot Chili Peppers. It earned him a higher profile in the United States, and much of the new decade was spent exploring new territories. By 2008, a new deal with hotshot label Domino had revived his profile at home, as well as prompting his first "rock"-style vocal, for the single "Council Estate." His album *Mixed Race* (2010) gave a vaguely French slant on Tricky's continually evolving sound.

Tricky

Born: *January 27, 1968, Bristol, England*

Years active: *1987 to present*

Genres: *trip hop, art rock*

Key singles: *"The Hell EP: Hell Is Round the Corner" (1995), "Tricky Kid" (1997)*

Key albums: Maxinquaye *(1995),* Pre-Millennium Tension *(1996)*

LEFT *Like onetime collaborator Björk, Tricky has a unique sound that draws from a multitude of styles, yet eludes easy categorization. Arguably, he has never sounded so potent as on 1996's* Pre-Millennium Tension.

Loungecore

BY THE EARLY 1990S, every conceivable style of popular music, from ska to psychedelia, had enjoyed a revival of sorts—all except one: easy listening.

A vast field of music that covered everything from Bacharach & David ballads to big band bossa novas, Hammond organ instrumentals to the exotica of Yma Sumac and Esquivel, "easy"—as it was restyled in the mid-90s—had for decades been the nemesis of every young rock and pop fan. Now, stripped of its cozy, middle-aged cocktail-quaffing associations, the sound of easy was reinterpreted less as a soporific than as a gleefully illicit trip into the sonic sublime.

With rock going round in ever-more familiar circles, the rhythms and textures of the numerous easy styles sounded fresh, almost avant-garde in comparison. The near synthetic mellifluousness of Mantovani's strings, the complex Polynesian flavors of exotica king Martin Denny, and the effortless delivery of Andy Williams (whose enormous success with "Music to Watch Girls By" earned him an "Emperor of Easy" tag) left mainstream rock and pop sounding distinctly old-fashioned.

Having initially met with much critical disapproval, the easy revival soon saw Burt Bacharach celebrated on an Oasis album sleeve, Stereolab seizing its avant-garde potential, and all manner of artists reintroducing strings into their music. Remarkably, less than two decades later, easy commands at least as much respect as any other music genre.

ABOVE *Martin Denny (left), whose band were regular fixtures on the 1950s Hawaiian hotel scene. During the 1980s, he was rediscovered and hailed as the "Father of Exotica."*

LEFT *The onetime sweater-wearing epitome of 1960s Middle America, Andy Williams enjoyed a surprise comeback during the 1990s on the back of the grassroots boom in easy listening.*

Britpop

DURING THE MID-1990S, three decades after the highs of Swinging London, a feel-good vibe returned to Britain. Spearheaded by two bands, Oasis and Blur, Britpop was ignited by music but soon touched everything from art and fashion to politics. It was, parroted the headlines, the era of "Cool Britannia."

Britpop—a term minted in the late 1980s to describe guitar bands such as the La's—gathered pace in the aftermath of Kurt Cobain's suicide in April 1994. With the latest great British hopes Suede in disarray, middling indie-dance act Blur became chief beneficiaries with the widescreen English pop of *Parklife* (1994), their third album.

Later that year saw the emergence of Oasis, whose instantly successful *Definitely Maybe* debut was a more unruly affair. Unlike Blur, who came from Essex and had been typecast as middle-class bohemians, Oasis were from Manchester and were an altogether more northern, saltier bunch. Both, however, were hugely ambitious, knew

OPPOSITE TOP *Oasis songwriter and guitarist Noel Gallagher, whose uplifting songs and iconic, customized guitar did much to define Britpop.*

OPPOSITE BOTTOM *Outside "the big two," Supergrass enjoyed the era's best run of classic singles, including the joyously upbeat "Alright."*

BELOW *Pulp's Jarvis Cocker was the era's great antihero, best expressed in perhaps the finest Britpop single of all, "Common People."*

their rock history, and were on creative rolls. August 1995 witnessed "the Battle of Britpop," prompted by both bands choosing to release new singles on the same day. Blur took the immediate spoils when "Country House" topped the chart, seeing off "Roll With It" fairly convincingly. But Oasis, who disparagingly dismissed their rivals' "chimney-sweep music," eclipsed Blur in the months ahead.

Arguably, the most enduring Britpop anthems came from outside the "big two"—the irrepressibly cheery "Alright" (Supergrass) and the class-conscious "Common People" (Pulp). Elastica took the artful route; Ocean Colour Scene, Cast, and a newly invigorated Paul Weller played up to the concurrent "lads' culture"; the Spice Girls sold "Girl Power" (and the ubiquitous Union Jack) to the preteen market; while Cornershop's chart-topping "Brimful of Asha" (1998) struck a gong for multicultural Britain.

By that time, Britpop was virtually over. Triumphalism in the Oasis camp and Blur's willful dive into more esoteric sounds caused the center to collapse, while the endorsement of incoming Labour Prime Minister Tony Blair soon melted any residual "cool." In 1977, two extraordinary records, Radiohead's *OK Computer* and the Verve's *Urban Hymns*, signaled a new, rather less convivial mood.

5 Top Britpop artists

Blur: *"Girls & Boys" (1994)*
Oasis: *"Cigarettes & Alcohol" (1994)*

Pulp: *"Common People" (1995)*
Supergrass: *"Alright" (1995)*

The Verve: *"Bitter Sweet Symphony" (1997)*

Blur

FROM UNEXCEPTIONAL indie-dance beginnings, Blur tapped into retro pop for 1994's *Parklife* and saw their fortunes transform. At the forefront of Britpop, thanks largely to the "geezer-pop" appeal of the title track, the band were soon embroiled in a massive spat with rivals Oasis. Then something interesting happened.

Whereas the soul of Oasis was likely forged during guitarist Noel Gallagher's stint as roadie for Mancunian "baggies" Inspiral Carpets, Blur had formed at art school. While this gave them no special favors in terms of originality—pop culture had largely given up on that by the 1990s—it did encourage the band to pull in their influences from a wider, and not necessarily commercially driven, range of sources than their Beatles-obsessed rivals.

That was obvious as early as "Girls & Boys" (1994), a Top 5 British hit built on an angularity reminiscent of post-punk dissidents Wire. And after being trumped by Oasis during the mid-1990s, Blur switched to the raw, lo-fi energy of U.S. alternative rock for their 1997 singles,

RIGHT Blur turned out to be a more sophisticated pop machine than frontman Damon Albarn's faux-Cockney persona initially suggested.

"Beetlebum" and "Song 2." While both creatively and commercially successful, the move eventually broke the band.

The gulf between the new Blur and the Kinks-style observational pop of 1995's *The Great Escape* highlighted a growing factionalism, and after 1999's art-rock set *13* frontman Damon Albarn and guitarist Graham Coxon put their energies into solo projects. Coxon quit for good while making *Think Tank* (2003), though the band buried their differences for a series of reunion gigs in 2009–10.

A massive spat with rivals...

Blur

Formed: *London, England*
Years active: *1989–2004, 2009 to present*

Definitive lineup: *Damon Albarn, Graham Coxon, Alex James, Dave Rowntree*

Genres: *Britpop, pop, rock, alternative rock*
Key singles: *"Girls & Boys" (1994), "Song 2" (1997)*

Key albums: The Great Escape (1995), Blur (1997)

Oasis

RELEASING THEIR DEBUT SINGLE in April 1994, the month of Kurt Cobain's death, was coincidental but symbolic. By the end of the year, after a run of five increasingly successful singles and a No. 1 album, *Definitely Maybe*, the era of the grunge slacker was over. In its place came the cocky swagger of Britpop.

No one embodied the strutting, jaw-jutting surliness of the new "lads' culture" in Britain as perfectly as Oasis frontman Liam Gallagher. And no songwriter so effortlessly distilled the most potent elements of classic British pop into contemporary feel-good anthems as Noel Gallagher did.

Blur had pipped Oasis in the Britpop battle for No. 1 in August 1995, when the Mancunians' Status Quo-like "Roll with It" lost out to the Essex boys' "Country House." But newsworthy sibling rivalry (Noel is the older brother), coupled with universally acclaimed songs on their next album, *(What's the Story) Morning Glory?* (1995), earned Oasis a place at rock's top table. After a series of huge outdoor shows they became a cultural phenomenon, and while *Be Here Now* (1997) was less well received, the band's popularity was such that a collection of B-sides, *The Masterplan* (1998), could still enjoy enormous sales.

After various lineup changes (including a stint for Beatles scion Zak Starkey on drums), as well as further acclaimed records, the warring brothers endured their final backstage altercation in August 2009. Noel quit, while Liam and his remaining renegades soldier on as Beady Eye.

BELOW *The tension between the Gallagher brothers Liam (left) and Noel (right) gave an edge to the band's work and their public perception. Songwriter Noel finally quit the group in 2009.*

Oasis

Formed: *Manchester, England*
Years active: *1991–2009*

Definitive lineup: *Noel Gallagher, Liam Gallagher, Paul "Bonehead" Arthurs, Paul McGuigan, Alan White*

Genres: *Britpop, pop, rock*
Key singles: *"Supersonic" (1994), "Wonderwall" (1995)*

Key albums: Definitely Maybe *(1994)*, (What's the Story) Morning Glory? *(1995)*

Electronic dance

THE MID-1990S WITNESSED a sometimes overlooked musical revolution right at the center of popular music. Combining the disobedient rock roar of grunge with the propulsive dance-floor energy of hardcore rave, the big beats of new electronic dance acts, such as the Prodigy, Chemical Brothers, and Fatboy Slim, traversed genres and yielded some of the decade's most explosive hit records.

The Liam Howlett-led Prodigy led the charge. The British hit "No Good (Start the Dance)," lifted from their 1994 album *Music for the Jilted Generation*, raged with all the ferocity of hardcore punk or heavy metal. Two years later, and with comic frontman Keith Flint accentuating the rock band crossover, singles "Firestarter" and "Breathe" brought an almost industrial-like apocalyptic energy to the top of the British charts. The subsequent album, *The Fat of the Land* (1997), repeated the success worldwide.

For so long a marginal and often derided musical form, electronically generated sound dominated dance floors and attained rock

respectability during the mid-1990s. The emergence of rock-savvy acts, such as the Chemical Brothers—whose 1997 chart-topping British hit "Block Rockin' Beats" owed much to 1980s industrial funk band 23 Skidoo—and big-beat specialist Fatboy Slim, did much to bridge the gap. And while Underworld's riveting and relentless "Born Slippy .NUXX" was ostensibly a club anthem, its inclusion on the soundtrack of the hit drug-abuse movie *Trainspotting* alongside veterans (Iggy Pop, Lou Reed), Britpoppers (Pulp, Blur), and club trendies (Leftfield, Goldie) confirmed that the gap between rock and dance was fast closing.

RIGHT *"Big-beat" sound specialist Fatboy Slim created a series of hugely popular dance-floor anthems in the late 1990s.*

BELOW LEFT *The Prodigy's Maxim and Keith Flint bringing some dance-floor ferocity to the mid-1990s singles chart.*

BELOW *Chemical Brothers Tom Rowlands and Ed Simons. The duo were joined by Noel Gallagher for their chart-topping "Setting Sun."*

5 Top electronic-dance artists

Leftfield: Leftism *(1995)*

The Chemical Brothers: Dig Your Own Hole *(1997)*

The Prodigy: The Fat of the Land *(1997)*

Fatboy Slim: You've Come a Long Way, Baby *(1998)*

Moby: Play *(1999)*

Radiohead

FROM UNPROMISING BEGINNINGS, Radiohead became the proverbial one hit wonders with 1992's outsider anthem "Creep" before developing into the most adventurous and consistently creative major rock band since the 1970s. Everything came together for the Oxford-based combo in 1997 when their third album, *OK Computer*, was declared an instant classic by critics and audience alike.

It was true: no record in years had managed to whisk up the eclecticism of its era into one single, coherent package. Diverse enough to include programmed beats and prog-styled shifts in tempo, this highly sophisticated record was bound together by the emotional charge that was frontman Thom Yorke at the center of everything.

Few imagined the five private-school-educated musos would be able to avoid the pitfalls of superstardom after *OK Computer*, but a healthy disdain for the music biz and a genuinely inquisitive attitude toward the art of sound has since found Radiohead defying all the odds. A decade and a half later, the group's work has grown ever more subtle, and they've taken risks without losing either kudos or their core audience.

Though 1995's *The Bends* had marked a clear break with the faux-grunge of their earlier work, Radiohead's most dramatic sonic shift took place in 2000 with *Kid A*, a laptop-inspired record that ditched virtually every rockist inclination and was greeted with some shock on its release. It was, history now suggests, the first truly modern album of the twenty-first century.

Since then Radiohead have smuggled the sublime into the pop charts ("Pyramid Song"), hit a seductive new peak in 2007 with *In Rainbows*, the first "pay what you want" download from a major act and an artistic triumph, and in 2011 opted again for the download-first approach with *The King of Limbs*. It's common for classical composers and jazz musicians to peak well into their careers, but for a rock band to do so is rare.

Most adventurous and consistently creative major band since the 1970s...

Radiohead

Formed: *Abingdon, Oxfordshire, England*

Years active: *1985 to present*

Definitive lineup: *Thom Yorke, Jonny Greenwood, Ed O'Brien, Colin Greenwood, Phil Selway*

Genres: *alternative rock, experimental rock, rock*

Key singles: *"Creep" (1992), "Paranoid Android" (1997)*

Key albums: OK Computer (1997), In Rainbows (2007)

The Notorious B.I.G.

THE MURDER IN 1997 of Biggie Smalls—the alias of Christopher Wallace from Brooklyn, New York—brought a chilling end to the hip-hop wars. It has also overshadowed his reputation as a tough-talking poet of the 'hood whose fluid, distinctive delivery made him perhaps the most gifted rapper of his generation.

During the mid-1990s, Biggie made the transition from bit-part player, guesting on records such as Mary J. Blige's "Real Love" (1992), to the savior of East Coast hip hop, whose success soon began to parallel his outsize persona. At the time of his death, he was poised to unleash the presciently titled *Life After Death*, his follow-up to 1994's defining set, *Ready to Die*. He was married to rising R&B star Faith Evans, left his stamp all over protégés Junior M.A.F.I.A. and Lil' Kim, and was putting together a hip-hop supergroup, the Commission.

More ominously, trouble followed this teenage crack dealer and weapon felon, whose street experiences and rap-star lifestyle fueled his rhymes. The success of *Ready to Die* singles "Juicy" and "One More Chance" had been crucial in the renaissance of East Coast hip hop, prompting the first stirrings of a feud with the West Coast's rising star, Tupac Shakur, in 1995.

After his death, in March 1997, *Life After Death* hit No. 1 in the United States and his label boss and collaborator Puff Daddy led several tributes with the international hit "I'll Be Missing You." Since then, many—including Eminem and Usher—continue to draw on the work of the self-styled "illest" rapper of them all.

RIGHT *It's his fluid, distinctive, and abrasive style, rather than the manner of his death, that truly makes the Notorious B.I.G. a hip-hop legend.*

The Notorious B.I.G.

Born: *May 21, 1971, Brooklyn, New York*

Died: *March 9, 1997*

Years active: *1992–97*

Genre: *hip hop*

Key singles: *"Juicy" (1994), "Hypnotize" (1997)*

Key albums: *Ready to Die (1994), Life After Death (1997)*

The hip-hop wars

IN FEBRUARY 1996, four months after being released from prison, Tupac Shakur, alias 2Pac, had witnessed his fourth solo studio album, *All Eyez on Me*, debut at No. 1 in the United States. Eight months later, on September 13, 1996, the latest, and potentially greatest, of the ghetto superstars was dead.

BELOW *Tupac Shakur was the shining star of West Coast hip hop until his tragic death in September 1996.*

The murders of Tupac and the Notorious B.I.G. marked the awful climax to a long-festering beef between West Coast hip hop, which had enjoyed a successful early 1990s, and a rejuvenated East Coast, buoyed by the mid-1990s triumphs of Biggie and Puff Daddy's Bad Boy roster.

Tupac, the son of a Black Panther activist, had been destined for better things. Socially conscious, and handsome enough to win several acting roles, he saw the success of 1993's *Strictly 4 My N.I.G.G.A.Z.* eclipsed by headline-grabbing incidents, such as shooting two policemen and facing a rape charge. The night before a verdict was due, on November 30, 1994, Tupac was shot and wounded in Manhattan. He laid the blame at Bad Boy's door.

Post-prison, Tupac signed for Suge Knight's Death Row label and the rivalry intensified. A June 1996 B-side, the splenetic "Hit 'Em Up," namechecked East Coast rivals beside threats, such as "You deserve to die." On September 7, Tupac was shot, dying six days later. Within six months, Biggie too fell victim to a gunman. Neither murder has been solved—though the hip-hop wars came to an abrupt end.

Electronica

WHILE VARIOUS FORMS of electronic music had been vying for recognition since the late 1960s, it was only during the 1990s that its threatened breakthrough was made complete. A glut of hard-hitting, rock-friendly, electronic dance hits eclipsed the waning house-music scene, tearing up the singles charts with rock-enhanced abandon. But beyond the mainstream, even stranger things were happening

so much so, in fact, that a blanket term "electronica" was introduced to deal with the decade's proliferation of artists and styles—ranging from trip hop (Massive Attack) and drum 'n' bass (Goldie) to mainstream dance (Orbital), ambient chill-out (the KLF), and more maverick talents (Aphex Twin). More specifically, electronica refers to music where the primary purpose is not necessarily an inducement to dance-floor nirvana.

Perhaps the biggest boon to electronic music's post-house liberation from the tyranny of the beats-per-minute formula was the chill-out room. The early 1990s saw the emergence of DJ-led acts, such as the KLF (with the hugely influential 1990 set, *Chill Out*) and the Orb, whose sample-heavy sounds prompted comparisons with the more blissed-out edges of 1970s progressive rock. Even more eclectic were the Future Sound of London, whose acclaimed *Lifeforms* (1994) later gave way to the more dystopian electronic landscape of 1996's *Dead Cities*.

The latter half of the decade witnessed an explosion of laptop explorers, with some of the most notable congregating around the influential, Sheffield-based Warp label. Chief among them was Aphex Twin (alias Richard D. James), whose two volumes of *Selected Ambient Works* (1992 and 1994) signified the general shift from beats to ventures into the sonic beyond. A whiz kid once dubbed "the Mozart of electronic music," Aphex emerged from the electronica undergrowth in 1997 with an industrial-strength single, "Come to Daddy," augmented by a remarkable video shot by collaborator Chris Cunningham. Together, the impact was enormous, a devastating social critique couched in something akin to bleak, black comedy. Electronic music had come a long way.

OPPOSITE TOP *Richard James, alias Aphex Twin, has been described as "the Mozart of electronic music."*

OPPOSITE BOTTOM *The serene electronica of Air's Jean-Benoît Dunckel and Nicolas Godin peaked in 1998 with "Sexy Boy."*

BELOW *Alex Paterson of the Orb, ambient house pioneers often dubbed the Pink Floyd of 1990s electronic music.*

Top electronica artists

The Orb: U.F.Orb *(1992)*

Autechre: Tri Repetae *(1995)*

The Future Sound of London: Lifeforms *(1994)*.

Air: Moon Safari *(1998)*

Aphex Twin: Drukqs *(2001)*

Featuring

Eminem • The Strokes • The White Stripes • Coldplay • Muse • Arctic Monkeys • Jay-Z • Gorillaz

2000s

2000s: Introduction

COMING AFTER THE BOOM in sampling and the CD revolution, both of which reawakened interest in rock and pop's past, the all-pervading power of the internet means that past and present now coexist in ways that would have been unthinkable a decade or two earlier. The turn of the calendar might have suggested a giant leap into a twenty-first-century future, but in the realm of popular music, history now weighs more heavily than ever before.

That doesn't necessarily mean that the past decade has been an overly familiar, dust-covered affair. Far from it. Art rock, post-punk, and folk had all languished uncherished for years before a new generation of acts emerged to reinvigorate, and often reinvent, these forgotten traditions. In fact, eclecticism remains rampant, with social networking sites, such as Myspace, offering a global platform for trend-defying newcomers. In terms of range and quality, rock has never enjoyed such abundance. But that's not the whole story.

ABOVE: *The White Stripes invigorated the twenty-first-century guitar-rock boom with originality, blues-flavored passion, and a riot of red and white color.*

ABOVE RIGHT: *Having collaborated on the new century's first great single, "Crazy in Love," Beyoncé and Jay-Z became pop's First Couple, marrying in 2008.*

Sounds of the decade

"Stan":
Eminem (featuring Dido) (2000)

"Hard to Explain":
The Strokes (2001)

"No One Knows":
Queens of the Stone Age (2002)

"Seven Nation Army":
The White Stripes (2003)

2000-2011

The main obstacle to the wider success of this new generation of artists, creating ever-innovative sonic hybrids, has been the limited vision of the major labels, which in tandem with the advertising-led media increasingly back tried and tested artists and formulas. Sometimes, the early years of the twenty-first century sounded as if they were drowning under a forgettable flood of boy bands and anonymous R&B and dance flavors.

By contrast, those rock veterans who for so long had battled to retain their youthful vigor gave up the fight and emerged all the more credible for it. Arthur Lee's Love (*Forever Changes*) and the Beach Boys' Brian Wilson (*Pet Sounds, Smile*) led the way in recreating their classic albums in public; soon everyone from Iggy Pop to the Who was at it. While Led Zeppelin, Genesis, the Police, and Pink Floyd reformed to great acclaim, contemporary acts, such as Coldplay, Muse, and particularly the Strokes-inspired wave of new guitar bands, all drew heavily on the past, whether it was the bombast of Queen or the rumbling bass lines of Joy Division.

RIGHT *Having announced his arrival in 1999, Eminem soon became the first superstar of the twenty-first century. A decade on, he's still topping charts.*

"Crazy in Love":
Beyoncé (2003)

"Wake Up":
Arcade Fire (2005)

"I Bet You Look Good on the Dancefloor":
Arctic Monkeys (2005)

"Paper Planes":
M.I.A. (2008)

"Sex on Fire":
Kings of Leon (2008)

"Empire State of the Mind":
Jay-Z (featuring Alicia Keys) (2009)

2000s: Time line

2000

April 2000

Online file-sharing site Napster receives a lawsuit from Metallica claiming copyright infringement. Similar suits follow, forcing the site to close. Peer-to-peer file-sharing, even harder to police, soon takes off.

Eminem

May 2000

Eminem's second album, *The Marshall Mathers LP*, sells a record-breaking 1.76 million copies in its first week of release, becoming the fastest-selling solo album ever.

October 2000

In the United States Radiohead defy expectations after the huge success of 1997's *OK Computer* with *Kid A*, a largely laptop-prompted collection that owes as much to edgy and often sublime electronica as it does to left-field rock.

Nickelback

December 2001

Canadians Nickelback top the U.S. singles chart with a song that defines twenty-first-century mainstream rock. With its grainy vocal, agonized lyric, and air-punching chorus, "How You Remind Me" becomes one of the decade's most played radio hits.

2002

April 2002

Blues-wailing garage rockers the White Stripes enter Toe Rag studios in London to work on their album, *Elephant*, which will yield the tie-in hit single "Seven Nation Army," an instant riff-rock classic.

May 2002

After its appearance on the *Oceans Eleven* soundtrack, "A Little Less Conversation," an Elvis Presley song from 1968, falls into the hands of Dutch remixer Junkie ZL. The result appears on a Nike ad and becomes a No. 1 hit in Britain.

November 2002

On the first anniversary of George Harrison's death, ex-Beatles Ringo Starr and Paul McCartney are joined by Ravi Shankar, Billy Preston, and assorted friends for Concert for George. The night includes Indian chanting that reflects the guitarist's spirituality.

December 2002

Ex-Clash frontman Joe Strummer dies of a heart-related condition. In recent times, he had rediscovered his musical desire and political activism, performing a benefit show for striking firefighters just weeks before his death.

Joe Strummer

2003

February 2003

Phil Spector is arrested after actress Lana Clarkson is found dead at his mansion in Alhambra, California. Two lengthy trials later, in May 2009, the legendary "Wall of Sound" record producer will be found guilty of murder.

2000–2003

2001

March 2001
Sean Combs, alias Puff Daddy, spruces up his name again, changing it to P. Diddy. In four years' time the pop impresario will simplify it further by dropping the P. and keeping Diddy.

P. Diddy

May 2001
With its sharp writing and flamboyant Timbaland production, Missy Elliott's *Miss E…So Addictive* provides a kaleidoscopic take on urban groove. The spin-off singles "Get Ur Freak On" and "One Minute Man" both become huge hits.

October 2001
In the wake of the previous month's terrorist attacks on the Twin Towers, Paul McCartney assembles a stellar cast—including Rolling Stones Mick Jagger and Keith Richards, the Who, and Eric Clapton—at Madison Square Garden for the marathon Concert for New York City.

June 2002
The day before the Who are due to begin their U.S. tour, bassist John Entwistle takes a bit of cocaine, beds down with an old flame—and is found dead next morning, having suffered a heart attack.

July 2002
Two decades after debuting in Oklahoma, the Flaming Lips make their commercial and critical breakthrough with their tenth album, the woozy, electronica-enriched *Yoshimi Battles the Pink Robots*.

August 2002
For the first time in almost a decade, ex-Nirvana drummer and Foo Fighters frontman Dave Grohl picks up his sticks at the behest of Queens of the Stone Age. The resulting *Songs for the Deaf* is a scorching slab of contemporary hard rock that virtually reinvents the form.

Queens of the Stone Age

March 2003
Johnny Cash releases a version of Nine Inch Nails' "Hurt." The song, supported by a video shot at Cash's home, serves as a moving epitaph for the country-music legend (his wife June Carter will die in May and Cash will die four months later).

April 2003
Utilizing a distinctive horn sample from an old Chi-Lites record, and boasting an off-the-cuff contribution from future husband Jay-Z, Beyoncé's "Crazy in Love" rips up the charts in style on both sides of the Atlantic.

May 2003
Just yards away from Lenin's tomb in Moscow's Red Square, Paul McCartney makes his debut in the new Russia in front of a 20,000-strong crowd. He performs the Beatles' old iron-curtain rocker "Back in the USSR" twice.

2000s: Time line

December 2003

OutKast, fronted by the Atlanta-born prodigy André 3000, break big with an irresistible slice of rock 'n' soul (and much else besides) titled "Hey Ya." The song spends nine weeks at the top of the *Billboard* chart.

2004

August 2004

The troubled relationship between Carl Barât and Pete Doherty is the subject of the Libertines' biggest hit, "Can't Stand Me Now." Two months later, the band's final single, "What Became of the Likely Lads," chronicles the pair's inevitable fallout.

The Libertines

September 2004

Having been thwarted by his perfectionism back in 1967, when he shelved his "teenage symphony to God" *Smile* project, Beach Boy Brian Wilson returns to the task, and rock's greatest lost masterpiece is released to almost unanimous acclaim.

April 2005

In light of the flourishing post-punk revival, prompted by the Strokes and Franz Ferdinand, Simon Reynolds's book *Rip It Up and Start Again: Post-Punk 1978–1984* reawakens interest in the likes of the Slits, the Pop Group, and Subway Sect.

Pink Floyd at Live 8

July 2005

Marking the 20th anniversary of Live Aid, a series of Live 8 concerts is organized worldwide. The major event takes place in London's Hyde Park, where the classic Pink Floyd lineup perform together for the first time since 1981.

September 2005

After picking up the Mercury Music Prize with the Antony & the Johnsons album, *I Am a Bird Now*, golden-voiced New York cabaret-scene habitué Antony Hegarty becomes the singing sensation of the year.

September 2006

"I Don't Feel Like Dancin'," a 1970s-style retro-disco collaboration with Elton John (who plays piano on the recording), gives the Scissor Sisters their first and only British No. 1 hit single.

October 2006

Stack-haired, blue-eyed soul singer Amy Winehouse releases the autobiographical "Rehab" and writes herself into pop history on two counts—for her talent and her notoriety.

Amy Winehouse

November 2006

Queen's Return of the Champions tour, their first since Freddie Mercury's death, concludes in Japan. Ex-Free frontman Paul Rodgers is on board as frontman.

2003-2007

2005

October 2004
Having championed so much marginalized music—from psychedelia to punk, Captain Beefheart to the Fall, and reggae to death metal—trailblazing BBC radio DJ John Peel dies of a heart attack.

January 2005
Europe's 50-year copyright expiry rule now affects recordings from the rock 'n' roll era. Among those potentially affected are Bill Haley and Elvis Presley. In 2013, it will be the Beatles' turn...

March 2005
The innovative electro hip hop of M.I.A.'s debut album *Arular* is hailed on its release. However, the album's guerrilla-style rhetoric will sit awkwardly with the London bombings in July, and her breakthrough will be postponed until the less inflammatory *Kala* appears two years later.

M.I.A.

2006

October 2005
Domino Records achieves a new level of success when Franz Ferdinand's album *You Could Have It So Much Better* and Arctic Monkeys' "I Bet You Look Good on the Dancefloor" both top the British charts.

June 2006
For two nights, Rufus Wainwright recreates Judy Garland's legendary April 1961 performance at New York's Carnegie Hall. In 2007, he will take the acclaimed show to London, Paris, and Los Angeles.

Rufus Wainwright

July 2006
Syd Barrett, the iconic and prodigiously talented spearhead of the original Pink Floyd, dies at his home in Cambridge, where he had spent most of his adult life living in obscurity.

2007

Red Hot Chili Peppers

February 2007
The Red Hot Chili Peppers' *Stadium Arcadium* picks up five Grammys, including an award for best album. The set is taken on the road for a similarly vast 18-month world tour.

September 2007
After several years in relative freak-folk obscurity, Devendra Banhart's rich, acoustic eclecticism and distinctive vocal vibrato land on the *Billboard* album chart for the first time with his sixth solo set, *Smokey Rolls Down Thunder Canyon*.

October 2007
Consuming new music via the internet receives a boost when Radiohead announce that their new album, *In Rainbows*, will be a download release. Fans are invited to pay whatever they see fit. It is later revealed that the average "donation" per album was less than U.S.$8.

2000s: Time line

November 2007

Untrue, the second album by Burial, extends the dubstep producer's explorations into subterranean dance atmospheres by incorporating a range of vocal samples. It is later rewarded with a Mercury Prize nomination.

December 2007

After an absence of 19 years, Led Zeppelin reform, with drummer Jason Bonham replacing his late father, for a wildly acclaimed two-hour performance at London's O2 arena.

December 2007

From Roxy Music to founding father of ambient music, Bowie collaborator to U2 producer, Brian Eno has enjoyed a rich cultural life. To that he now adds a new role—as youth affairs adviser for Britain's third political party, the Liberal Democrats.

David Bowie, Bono, and Brian Eno

Jeff Buckley

December 2008

Despite a strong, internet-prompted surge in favor of a version by the late Jeff Buckley, the UK *X Factor* winner Alexandra Burke pips him to the top spot in Britain with her take on Leonard Cohen's 1984 song, "Hallelujah."

2009

April 2009

Black Eyed Peas enjoy a remarkable 26-week stay at the top of the U.S. singles chart with two consecutive releases. Both "Boom Boom Pow" and "I Gotta Feeling" are taken from the band's chart topping album, *The E.N.D.*

Black Eyed Peas

June 2009

Deep into rehearsals for his "This Is It" comeback tour, Michael Jackson is found dead in his bed, prompting a mass outbreak of public grief. A legend may be gone, but with cash registers doing overtime, his commercial value soars.

June 2010

Rap star Kanye West signs up to Twitter and drops in at the company's HQ to showcase material from his forthcoming album. Released in November, *My Beautiful Dark Twisted Fantasy* will become West's most successful and acclaimed yet.

July 2010

Ringo Starr celebrates his 70th birthday with a show at New York's Radio City Music Hall. Among the guests are Paul McCartney, who reprises the Beatles' "Birthday," and Yoko Ono, who joins in a rendition of "With a Little Help from my Friends."

August 2010

In his most critically acclaimed year since the start of the decade, Eminem teams up with R&B diva Rihanna for "Love the Way You Lie," a huge international hit that confirms his end of decade renaissance.

2007-2011

2008

March 2008
From their jumpy, math-rock beginnings, the Oxford-based quintet Foals bring Afrobeat and post-punk flavors to their distinctive debut set, *Antidotes*.

Foals

August 2008
Isaac Hayes, the soul legend whose career took him from Stax to *Shaft*—and more recently to *South Park* (he was the voice of Chef)—suffers a second stroke in two years. This time, he doesn't pull through.

September 2008
Having made their mark with 2006's *Return to Cookie Mountain*, the David Sitek-led, Brooklyn-based sound collective TV on the Radio return with *Dear Science*. Another critics' favorite, on this occasion the enthusiasm is matched by strong sales.

Kings of Leon

September 2009
Just months after shaving off their trademark beards, Kings of Leon top charts worldwide with the hyperactive "Sex on Fire," the first single from their fourth album, *Only by the Night*.

December 2009
Another internet crusade hoists the reunited Rage Against the Machine to the top of the British charts with their signature song, "Killing in the Name." The campaign was inspired by the desire to prevent a fifth UK *X Factor* winner from taking the Christmas No. 1 spot.

2010

May 2010
The Rolling Stones' sprawling two-disc set, *Exile on Main St.*, is reissued in a luxury edition. Confirmation that it has clawed its way into the "legendary album" category comes with tie-in television documentaries and impressive chart placings.

2011

November 2010
Apple, the Beatles' parent company, finally authorizes the digital release of the band's catalog via iTunes. A reported two million singles and 450,000 albums are shifted in the first week.

December 2010
Despite Captain Beefheart's withdrawal from the music industry in 1983, his reputation as a peerless rock original has continued to grow. News of his death, after a long battle with multiple sclerosis, is a reminder of the absence of idiosyncratic visionaries in the contemporary rock world.

January 2011
The new decade begins with another "Rock is Dead" story, based on an analysis of the British singles charts, which is clearly dominated by R&B, pop, and hip hop. In the album charts, and online, the picture that emerges is quite different.

Eminem

ANY INITIAL DISTRUST that he was merely the overwhelmingly white American music industry's latest stooge in its attempt to hijack the dynamic and overwhelmingly black hip-hop form was immediately dispelled the moment you heard Eminem. His rhymes were comic, complex, and of course controversial, his delivery brattish, sardonic, and compelling—and he came with the endorsement of Dr. Dre.

Irreverent, rage-filled, and offensive, Eminem's rhymes were a meticulously worked barrage of invective and worldly insight. On top of that, his never-ending howl of discontent matched his surly, brat-boy look and Loony Toon voice perfectly. As "the artist most likely to" at the end of 1999, Eminem became the first and thus far only genuine musical and cultural phenomenon of the twenty-first century, following in the footsteps of Elvis, Jimi Hendrix, and Johnny Rotten.

There was, as has been common in rap, an element of Alice Cooper-like exaggerated persona and movie-style playing out of good versus evil in his work. But Eminem was no white rapper cash-in. A creation of "Trailertown," East Detroit, and nurtured by West Coast rap guru Dr. Dre, this onetime Beastie Boys fan, who freestyled with the neighborhood black kids, hit on his own style in 1997 with the independently released "The Slim Shady EP." Dre's subsequent involvement on *The Slim Shady LP* helped create a suitably cracking sonic backdrop for Eminem's tight and incredibly fast-paced raps concerning death, celebrities, and his wife.

Surly brat-boy look and Loony Toon voice

The breakthrough was *The Slim Shady LP* (1999), which with its effervescent tie-in single, "My Name Is," announced Eminem loudly to the world. *The Marshall Mathers LP* (2000) extended his reach, with the huge international hit "Stan" boasting a serenely melodic sample from British singer Dido, while "Kim" was an industrial-strength sonic assault on his estranged wife. Both she and Mathers's mother filed lawsuits against the singer during the early months of his fame.

It all made great headlines, and by 2002 Eminem was starring in *8 Mile*, a movie loosely based on his life, discovering and producing new acts (D12, 50 Cent) and, in mid-decade, battling the trappings of superstardom. His album *Recovery* (2010) suggests that he is winning the personal battle, even if he has passed the high watermark of his career.

Eminem

Born: *October 17, 1972, Saint Joseph, Missouri*

Years active: *1995 to present*
Genre: *hip hop*

Key singles: *"My Name Is" (1998), "Stan" (2000)*

Key albums: The Slim Shady LP *(1999)*, The Marshall Mathers LP *(2000)*

Guitar-rock revival

DESPITE THE ADVANCES in technology, guitar-based rock has never really gone away. Even during the 1980s, with hip hop and synth-pop in the driving seat, there were always endless indie strummers and metal virtuosos keeping the trusty six-string in view.

By the end of the twentieth century, guitar bands once again seemed to sound tired and orthodox in the face of hip hop's continued advance and a new teen-pop revival prompted by the success of Britney Spears, Christina Aguilera, and numerous identikit boy bands. In 2001, the guitar evangelists in the rock press had found their cause—New York-based power poppers, the Strokes. Despite the group's near bubblegum approach to a sound clearly inspired by the Clash and Iggy Pop, the phrase "post-punk" was plucked from its 1980 heyday, reclaimed, reinvented, and was soon everywhere.

For the next few months, it was silly season in the press. When even British tabloids started acclaiming bands such as the White Stripes with "Is This the Future of Rock 'n' Roll?" headlines, it shows how far removed

5 Top guitar-rock revival artists

The Strokes: Is This It (2001)
The White Stripes: Elephant (2003)

Franz Ferdinand: Franz Ferdinand (2004)
The Libertines: The Libertines (2004)

Arctic Monkeys: Whatever People Say I Am, That's What I'm Not (2006)

Edgy and vintage post-punk

the whole thing was from the original underground and politicized post-punk movement. The Hives, the Vines, and Yeah Yeah Yeahs quickly followed, prompting a second rash of bands—Franz Ferdinand, the Libertines, the Rapture, and the Killers. By mid-decade the guitar revival was in full swing. Wire, Gang of Four, and—later—the Pop Group all reformed, while Joy Division bathed in a posthumous reputation that made them the Doors of their time.

While most twenty-first-century post-punk was sexed-up new-wave garage rock, and all the more successful for it, a handful of bands ran with the more edgy, angular direction of vintage post-punk: and thus math rock was born. Steve Albini's Shellac, a regular fixture of the genuinely alternative All Tomorrow's Parties festivals, remain leading lights, while Battles—from fashionable New York and recording for the ever-imaginative Sheffield-based Warp label—are probably the most intriguing. The most successful sponsor of twenty-first-century guitar rock, though, has been the similarly eclectic Domino Records, home of Franz Ferdinand, the Kills, and Arctic Monkeys.

LEFT *The Strokes' Nick Valensi strikes a classic, low-slung rock 'n' roll pose, reminiscent of Led Zeppelin's Les Paul-playing Jimmy Page.*

TOP *Karen O of the Yeah Yeah Yeahs, 2009. The New York-based band's full-length debut, 2003's Fever to Tell, was a more twisted take on guitar rock.*

ABOVE *White Stripes' frontman Jack White taking the duo's contorted garage rock to a mass audience at New York's Madison Square Garden in 2007.*

The Strokes

POST-GRUNGE, post-Britpop, post-Green Day fun-punk, post-twentieth century, the once clearly demarcated lines between alternative rock and the mainstream blurred to become almost meaningless. The music industry certainly didn't like the idea of another uncompromising Sex Pistols or even a Nirvana that would take the market by surprise and force them to adapt accordingly. It simply wanted a peppy young band with bags of attitude and feel-good tunes that would revitalize the industry and disprove the fashionable notion that guitar rock was on the way out.

Enter the Strokes, hyped to the hilt and yet delivering on all counts. These scions of the exclusive Dwight School in Manhattan emerged with a studied sound—grainy vocals over a bouncy, new-wave-style backing—and a look cut to fashion-magazine perfection. The cover photo for their hugely successful debut set, *Is This It* (2001), showing a gloved hand on a model's bare backside, was suitably iconic and obvious. And two tie-in hit singles, "Last Nite" and "Someday," were no less than effervescent pop in the great tradition of the Pretenders and the Monkees.

The trademark insistent guitar riffs, draped with the electronically processed voice of Julian Casablancas, was diluted for 2003's *Room on Fire*, which earned them belated success at home. *First Impressions of Earth* (2006) was less critically acclaimed yet sold better still. Since then the Strokes have virtually retired from view.

BELOW *After 2006's First Impressions of Earth, the Strokes took a lengthy break. Frontman Julian Casablancas toured solo during 2010 in anticipation of their fourth album,* Angles.

The Strokes

Formed: *New York City*

Years active: *1998 to present*

Definitive lineup: *Julian Casablancas, Albert Hammond Jr., Nick Valensi, Nikolai Fraiture, Fabrizio Moretti*

Genres: *alternative rock, garage-rock revival, post-punk revival*

Key singles: *"Hard to Explain" (2001), "Last Nite" (2001)*

Key albums: *Is This It (2001), Room on Fire (2003)*

The White Stripes

ALTHOUGH THIS ARTFUL, minimalist duo from Detroit emerged amid a tide of hype in the wake of the Strokes, the White Stripes had far more in common with rock's disobedient spirit, drawing as they did from the Delta blues, smash-bash garage rock, and edgy post-punk.

Jack and Meg White—who initially claimed to be siblings but were in fact a divorced couple—enjoyed their optimum moment in 2003 with their fourth album, *Elephant*. Recorded on vintage analog equipment at Toe Rag Studios in London, the record retained the band's early DIY aesthetic, was raw like dusty rock 'n' roll, but kicked like Led Zeppelin. It also included "Seven Nation Army," as explosive as anything released during the decade, with a riff to rival classics by Deep Purple or Nirvana.

The White Stripes' pocket-sized Zepp ambition first manifested itself on *White Blood Cells* (2001), though after the critical and commercial acclaim heaped upon

Elephant, the pair adopted a more textured approach on the 2005 follow-up, *Get Behind Me Satan*.

A deal with Warner Brothers resulted in *Icky Thump* (2007), marking a return to the blistering ramshackle attack of their earlier work. However, in recent years, Jack White has been testing the limits of the four-piece rock band with two ancillary projects, the Raconteurs and the Dead Weather. The White Stripes announced their split in February 2011.

ABOVE *Employing a minimal lineup – consisting of drummer Meg White and guitarist and frontman Jack White—served the White Stripes well, helping to differentiate their sound from more orthodox guitar-rock revivalists.*

The White Stripes

Formed: *Detroit, Michigan*
Years active: *1997 to 2011*

Definitive lineup: *Jack White, Meg White*
Genres: *alternative rock, garage-rock revival, blues rock*

Key singles: *"Fell in Love With a Girl" (2002), "Seven Nation Army" (2003)*

Key albums: White Blood Cells *(2001),* Elephant *(2003)*

Coldplay

IN TERMS OF BOTH their celestial, epic soundscapes and the enormous commercial success they've enjoyed since 2000's breakthrough single "Yellow," Coldplay inhabit a realm way beyond that of their more earthed guitar revivalist contemporaries.

One of a clutch of what were termed "post-Radiohead acts," this university quartet eschewed the revivalist tendencies of most of their contemporaries and instead patented their own sound. Unveiled on *Parachutes* (2000) and perfected on *A Rush of Blood to the Head* two years later, that highly distinctive creation has been lampooned by some, though the band's mainstream melancholia has certainly caught the flavor of the times.

Essentially placid and inoffensive, in the manner of a rock-relaxation tape, Coldplay's music nevertheless connects hugely in the twenty-first century—not only with the public but with makers of television dramas, too. However, Coldplay—who also quietly support all manner of progressive and humanitarian causes—are impressively mindful not to allow their music to be used to endorse consumer products. Of course, with 2005's *X&Y*, which came with more acoustic textures, confirming their top-ranked status in the United States, they

ABOVE *Chris Martin on stage and screen at London's Wembley Stadium in September 2009 at the climax of Coldplay's worldwide Vida la Vida tour. The tour was undertaken in partnership with Oxfam, reinforcing the band's reputation as one of the most socially conscious acts around.*

can afford to be. But any band prepared to admit, as Coldplay did when they called on Brian Eno to help produce their 2008 album *Vida la Vida*, that they hoped he'd compel them to be more adventurous, has to be applauded as refreshingly honest in a market thick with charlatans.

Coldplay

Formed:
London, England

Years active:
1996 to present

Genre:
alternative rock

Definitive lineup:
Chris Martin, Jonny Buckland, Guy Berryman, Will Champion

Key singles:
"Yellow" (2000), "Speed of Sound" (2005)

Key albums:
Parachutes (2000), A Rush of Blood to the Head (2002)

Muse

MUSE EMERGED in the aftermath of Radiohead's *OK Computer* (1997), although no less influential on their future sound was the soaring voice of the late, gifted Jeff Buckley. More than a decade later, while Radiohead have largely withdrawn from view, Muse continue to grow both in sound and stature.

If the band's 1999 debut, *Showbiz*, revealed their influences a little too transparently, the Devon trio's next effort, *Origin of Symmetry* (2001), brought a new flamboyance to their work. "You make me sick," sang Matt Bellamy in his trademark style, "because I adore you so." It's a line from the epic "Space Dementia" that neatly encapsulates the band's trademark doomed romanticism.

Rather less willing to play the game than many of their PR-obsessed contemporaries, Muse have commanded a wide-ranging respect through a combination of diverse, progressively inclined albums and their enormous reputation as a live act, which grew immeasurably after their acclaimed 2004 performance at Glastonbury.

Of course, there's an overblown aspect to Muse that's sometimes oddly reminiscent of Queen in all their pomp, but as the band proved with their daring 2001 cover of Nina Simone's "Feeling Good," Muse seem to be big enough to defy the prevailing here today, gone tomorrow ethos and flirt dangerously with the possibilities of sacrilege. They emerge all the stronger for it.

ABOVE AND BELOW
Matt Bellamy enjoys a reputation as a latter-day guitar hero as he spearheads the trio to ever more adventurous work.

Muse

Formed:
Devon, England

Years active:
1994 to present

Genres:
alternative rock, progressive rock

Definitive lineup:
Matt Bellamy, Chris Wolstenholme, Dom Howard

Key singles: *"Plug in Baby" (2001), "Uprising" (2009)*

Key albums: *Origin of Symmetry (2001), Absolution (2003)*

The rise of online

THE PACE OF CHANGE in the music industry during the new century has been phenomenal. No development has been of greater consequence than the internet, which opened up the market for artists, whether signed or not, and offered an alternative route to accessing music. By the end of the new decade, digital downloads, both legal and otherwise, had become the norm—sounding the death knell for the record store and all but the most resilient megastores.

ABOVE *Apple co-founder Steve Jobs, the man behind the iPod, which transformed the consumption of music after its launch in 2001.*

BELOW *After incurring the wrath of record companies, Napster shut down in 2001. It has since reopened as a legitimate service.*

Concern over piracy early in the decade resulted in the closure in 2001 of file-sharing site Napster (which later reopened as a paid-for service), as well as highly publicized cases where individuals were prosecuted for illegally downloading songs. The April 2003 launch of iTunes, which worked in tandem with the industry, was instrumental in changing perspectives, so much so that, by the end of the decade, revenues from digital sales were easily eclipsing losses suffered by the old formats.

Artists have played their part too. Both the Beastie Boys and Nine Inch Nails embraced the potential of the internet positively, and when Radiohead released their album *In Rainbows* as a "pay what you like" digital download in October 2007, there was no turning back.

"It is piracy...which is our main competitor"

Steve Jobs

Arctic Monkeys

HYPED UP as the first rock band to benefit from the publicity-generating power of the internet, the young and dynamic Arctic Monkeys from Sheffield made a brilliant transition from Myspace to the summit of the British charts in a matter of months between 2004 and 2005. But on this occasion, unlike similarly feted acts, such as the Libertines, Arctic Monkeys justified their worth.

Unusually for an act swept along by the tide of guitar-prompted revivalism, Arctic Monkeys managed to imprint a distinctive style onto their work, which displayed little of the derivativeness of their contemporaries. There was no doubting the Buzzcocks-like energy of their debut single, "I Bet You Look Good on the Dancefloor," which went straight to No. 1. But as the head-turning 2005 first album *Whatever People Say I Am, That's What I'm Not* confirmed, an intelligent approach to rhythm and song dynamics, coupled with Alex Turner's wryly observational lyrics, confirmed that Arctic Monkeys warranted the media hoopla that followed their every move.

The pace of success, also felt in the United States, was maintained for a second album, *Favourite Worst Nightmare* (2007), but a greater intricacy, exemplified by the

ABOVE *The British music press hype machine got to work on the Arctic Monkeys months after an internet frenzy on Myspace. In this instance, the hoopla seemed to be justified, with frontman Alex Turner in particular singled out for the originality of his contributions.*

leadoff single "Brianstorm," saw a recession in the band's power as a singles act. By 2009, the decade's favorite cult rockers were playing arenas, while at the same time toughening up their sound with the help of Queens of the Stone Age guitarist Josh Homme, part-producer of their riffier, though noticeably less hyperactive third album, *Humbug*.

Arctic Monkeys

Formed:
Sheffield, England

Years active:
2002 to present

Genres:
alternative rock, post-punk revival

Definitive lineup:
Alex Turner,
Jamie Cook,
Andy Nicholson,
Matt Helders

Key singles: "I Bet You Look Good on the Dancefloor" (2005), "When the Sun Goes Down" (2006)

Key albums:
Whatever People Say I Am, That's What I'm Not (2006), Favourite Worst Nightmare (2007)

Freak folk

GUITARS, MACHINES, and—more recently—computers had dominated the musical landscape for years. While *MTV Unplugged* focused attention back on songcraft and unamplified instruments, the project inevitably centered on established and superstar artists. But, as the twenty-first century began, a new generation of folk-inspired artists emerged, breaking through the rattle and hum of the guitar bands and impacting on the wider musical soundscape.

BELOW LEFT *Sierra "Rosie" Casady of New York duo CocoRosie with just one of the weird and wonderful instruments they have utilized.*

BELOW *Heard it all before? No one says that once they've tuned into Californian harpist Joanna Newsom's wavelength.*

Only it wasn't folk as the rock mainstream had always understood it. As artists such as Devendra Banhart, Joanna Newsom, and CocoRosie released a series of richly tapestried, often spellbinding albums, audiences struggled to find a handle for it—hence "New Weird Folk" or "Freak Folk." Certainly, the heroes of the new iconoclasts were less likely to be Joan Baez or Bob Dylan than less celebrated acts, such as Vashti Bunyan, the Incredible String Band, and even Tyrannosaurus Rex-era Marc Bolan.

Banhart, the force behind the 2004 folk compilation, *The Golden Apples of the Sun*, certainly echoed Bolan's distinctive warble, which lent a further otherworldliness to work already marked by alternate tunings and songs about growing his beard. Sister duo CocoRosie utilized tablas, toy pianos, and loops of animal noises in their magical work. Later, Fleet Foxes wove elements of new folk into their own harmony-rich recordings. Most distinctive of all was and remains harp-player Joanna Newsom, whose expressive voice, penchant for lengthy song cycles, and unquenchable thirst for staking out new musical territory has gifted the twenty-first century with one of its most extraordinary musical talents.

5 Top freak-folk artists

Devendra Banhart: Rejoicing in the Hands *(2004)*
CocoRosie: Noah's Ark *(2005)*

Joanna Newsom: Ys *(2006)*
Fleet Foxes: Fleet Foxes *(2008)*
Grizzly Bear: Veckatimest *(2009)*

Emo

EMO IS A DIFFICULT genre
to classify. Both a style and a
subculture, it has mutated much
since its origins in U.S. hardcore
punk in the mid-1980s, and it is as
much defined by the whims of its
audience as anything else.

In its initial incarnation, "emo" was an
unloved term used to describe a small
group of acts that congregated on the
Washington, DC-based Dischord label,
formed by Ian MacKaye. Eschewing the
political dimension of the hardcore acts,
emerging bands such as Rites of Spring
patented a new "emotional hardcore" sound
that augmented the trademark sonic attack
with a melodic sensibility and lyrics of a
more personal dimension.

It was during the 1990s that emo as we
know it really took off, gaining credence in
the press and witnessing bands such as
Seattle-based Sub Pop band Sunny Day
Real Estate and Jawbreaker from San
Francisco breaking through. An emo culture
also developed around this time, loosely
characterized by skinny-jeans-sporting
teenagers adrift in their private thoughts.

ABOVE Three members of
Weezer, who broke big
in 1996 with Pinkerton,
wore specs. Frontman
Rivers Cuomo wrote lyrics
that connected with a
midteen audience, and
the emo tag stuck.

Since then, most bands have been
eager to distance themselves from the
emo tag, though numerous acts—from
Placebo to Weezer—that specialize in
confessional lyrics, emotionally wrought
power chords, and a hopelessly devoted
fan base have at one time or another been
described as emo bands.

ABOVE Ex-Minor Threat
frontman Ian MacKaye
fronting hardcore legends
Fugazi. A proponent of the
"no drugs, careful sex"
philosophy, U.S. hardcore
luminary MacKaye is also
regarded as the first man
of "emotional hardcore."

5 Top emo artists

Sunny Day Real Estate: Diary *(1994)*
Weezer: Pinkerton *(1996)*
Placebo: Without You I'm Nothing *(1998)*

Jimmy Eat World: Bleed American *(2001)*
My Chemical Romance: The Black Parade *(2008)*

Jay-Z

BRIDGING THE GAP between hip hop's troubled mid-1990s and the more integrated, corporate, and successful era in the decade that followed, Jay-Z has risen from hustling on the streets of Brooklyn to become one of the most powerful figures in popular music.

A gifted, instinctive rapper, and a hugely successful record company mogul with an ever-expanding portfolio of business interests, Jay-Z also makes cameos in movies, sits on various company boards, and works with virtually anyone he wants to. And, as the partner of R&B queen Beyoncé, he's also one half of the American music industry's First Couple. No surprise, then, that his extraordinary feat of scoring 11 U.S. No. 1 albums sometimes gets overlooked.

Like friend and contemporary Notorious B.I.G., Jay-Z started out entering rap contests and guesting on other people's records, before breaking through with his U.S. Top 30 debut, *Reasonable Doubt*, in 1996. It was the refreshingly original and chart-topping "Hard Knock Life" (1998) that made him a major player, and by 2001 his acclaimed sixth album, *The Blueprint*, featured both Eminem and superstar-in-waiting Kanye West.

Collaborations with Beyoncé and Linkin Park, Rihanna, and U2, an exploration of his "hard-knock" years on *American Gangster* (2007), a successful crossover appearance at the notoriously guitar-heavy Glastonbury Festival, and, more recently, a pairing with Alicia Keys for 2009's affectionate tribute to New York, "Empire State of Mind," have only served to confirm Jay-Z as a twenty-first-century phenomenon.

Jay-Z

Born: December 4, 1969, Brooklyn, New York

Years active: 1988 to present

Genre: hip hop

Key singles: "Hard Knock Life (Ghetto Anthem)" (1998), "Empire State of Mind" (2009)

Key albums: Vol. 2... Hard Knock Life (1998), The Blueprint (2001)

BELOW Contemporary music's First Couple performing at the Yankee Stadium in September 2010.

Gorillaz

SADDLED WITH a "Little
Englander" reputation thanks
to Blur's pivotal role during the
Britpop era, frontman Damon
Albarn took a flight from
familiarity with his next project.

Cooked up with artist Jamie Hewlett, cocreator of the comic *Tank Girl*, Gorillaz were designed as a "virtual" band made up of cartoon characters, for whom music would be but one aspect of their artistic endeavors. At once playful and cutting edge, Gorillaz have also defied the cynics by enjoying some remarkable musical successes amid the attendant "multimedia band" hype. Four singles were lifted from *Gorillaz*, the first, the dub-influenced "Clint Eastwood," setting out the band's nonrock stance. Subsequent remixes, guest DJs, and collaborations with Eminem's Detroit pals D12 all confirmed Albarn's desire for distance from white-boy rock—as did Gorillaz' globally sourced sonic mashups.

There was more genre hopping on 2005's *Demon Days,* presaged by the up-tempo "Feel Good Inc.," a U.S. Top 20 hit, and followed by the warm electro-dance of "Dare," a No. 1 in Britain. Less successful were the band's thwarted plans for an animated movie and a tour fronted by the Gorillaz aliases. But there have been designer figurines, books, and a game issued in conjunction with a third album, *Plastic Beach* (2010). Recent appearances, including a mildly downbeat performance at Glastonbury, have featured a more conventional lineup—including ex-Clash men Mick Jones and Paul Simonon.

ABOVE *Blur frontman Damon Albarn surprised many when he ditched all evidence of his Britpop past in favor of an nonrock sound with his virtual band Gorillaz. Recently, though, the guitars have been creeping back—as evidenced in this shot from 2010.*

Gorillaz

Formed: *London, England*
Years active: *1998 to present*

Genres: *alternative, dance, pop*
Definitive lineup: *Damon Albarn, Jamie Hewlett*

Key singles: *"Clint Eastwood" (2001), "Feel Good Inc." (2005)*

Key albums: Gorillaz *(2001),* Demon Days *(2005)*

Six decades on...

IN RECENT TIMES, a rash of "Death of Rock" headlines has appeared in the press announcing the passing of the old world order. The evidence? It had been noted that guitar-oriented songs were conspicuous by their absence in the singles charts. In contrast, hip hop, R&B, pop, and dance accounted for an overwhelming slice of the market.

But in the album charts, across the internet, and in performance, rock music still flourishes. There is greater crossover with hip hop and electronic music than ever before, but its core elements—rhythm, electric guitars, the verse-chorus-verse format—continue to beat loudly. While the enduring appeal of metal and the garage/punk hybrid is obvious, the new millennium has seen a plethora of bands—Elbow, Queens of the Stone Age, Kings of Leon, and Arcade Fire among them—that continue to blur genres and reinvigorate rock music.

What has changed is that rock can no longer claim its once pivotal, battering-ram role at the heart of contemporary Western culture, while the major labels desire to invest only in formula-driven, TV tie-in "stars" aimed largely at the young teenage market. There is no doubt that rock will survive—though it may be the packaging and the selling of its personalities that we learn to admire most.

RIGHT *Canadian septet Arcade Fire are routinely joined by further musicians when they tour, which illustrates the intricate nature of the band's richly textured music. Multiinstrumentalist Régine Chaussagne holds a hurdy-gurdy during the band's appearance at London's O2 Arena in December 2010.*

LEFT *Guy Garvey of Elbow, whose passionate, sophisticated sound has brought them critical acclaim and real commercial success.*

Glossary

ACID ROCK Popular between 1966 and 1968 thanks to the influence of LSD. Synonymous with psychedelia.

AFROBEAT Exuberant blend of Ghanaian highlife, jazz, funk, and Nigerian rhythms, named and nailed by Fela Kuti.

ALTERNATIVE DANCE 1980s/1990s dance nexus with rock attitude. Also known as indie dance.

ALTERNATIVE ROCK Ignited by the late 1970s independent scene, known as indie rock in Britain during the 1980s. Still regarded as a key alternative to pop.

ART ROCK A product of the Beatles' *Sgt Pepper*, sometimes synonymous with progressive rock. Usually signifies music that has some conceptual ambition.

BLUES African-American style originating in the Mississippi Delta, developed by soloists (Son House, Robert Johnson) and the primary inspiration for rock 'n' roll.

BLUES ROCK The result of late 1960s bands (Cream, Fleetwood Mac, Jimi Hendrix) mashing blues with acid rock.

BRITPOP Mid-1990s phenomenon in Britain that saw many guitar bands (Oasis, Blur) move into the mainstream to a backdrop of national enthusiasm.

BUBBLEGUM A 1960s phenomenon that applied a "hit factory" approach to pop, still very much in evidence today.

COUNTRY Previously known as hillbilly music, country music was a key influence on Elvis Presley in the 1950s.

COUNTRY ROCK The Byrds, Bob Dylan, and the Band revived "the people's music" during the late 1960s.

DANCE Since house and techno, dance has been used as a catchall for numerous floor-filling subgenres.

DISCO A slick, ecstatic, 1970s mutation of funk that revitalized the Bee Gees and introduced Donna Summer as the world's first dance diva.

DUB A studio-enhanced variant of reggae characterized by vocalless remixes and added sound effects.

ELECTRONICA A 1990s variant of electronic dance that refers to electro music not necessarily aimed at the dance floor.

ELECTROPOP Coined during the early 1980s to describe emerging electronic pop acts, such as the Human League.

EMO An offshoot of the 1980s U.S. hardcore scene, this grassroots movement closely identifies with lyrically expressive alternative rock bands.

EXPERIMENTAL ROCK A catchall term for rule-breaking acts ranging from Captain Beefheart & His Magic Band to contemporary acts such as Battles.

FOLK Popularized during the 1940s by Woody Guthrie, who was the key inspiration for Bob Dylan.

FOLK PROTEST A Dylan-inspired subgenre that helped give mid-1960s pop a purpose.

FREAK FOLK A twenty-first-century development that marked a return to mysticism and acoustic instruments.

FUNK An intensely rhythmic African-American descendant of gospel, patented by James Brown and at its peak during the early 1970s.

GANGSTA RAP Hard-hitting hip hop that reflected the dark side of the African-American urban lifestyle.

GARAGE ROCK The United States' mid-1960s answer to the British beat boom, revived on numerous occasions.

GLAM METAL 1980s hybrid of metal guitars and glam rock's visual excess. Also known as hair metal.

GLAM ROCK Early 1970s British pop phenomenon based on big beats, rock 'n' roll revivalism, and starry personas, such as Marc Bolan, Elton John, and David Bowie.

GOSPEL Sacred music secularized during the 1950s by Ray Charles, and a forerunner of soul.

GRUNGE Seattle-based, alternative-rock phenomenon of the late 1980s that eschewed high-gloss 1980s production in favour of fuzzed-up guitars and loud/soft dynamics.

HARD ROCK Tough rock riffs, virtuoso musicianship, and macho posing characterized this 1970s genre.

HARDCORE A belated U.S. response to punk rock, this 1980s underground movement later fed into grunge.

HEAVY METAL Hard rock without the blues, but with more emphasis on pace and 1980s-style showmanship.

HIP HOP Vibrant black music and cultural form based on repetitive beats, often sampled, and "rap"-style vocals.

HOUSE Minimal electronic club music nurtured in Chicago during the 1980s and subsequently a Europewide phenomenon.

INDUSTRIAL METAL Late 1980s and 1990s genre combining the shock aesthetic of late 1970s industrial music with robust metal riffs.

JAZZ Twentieth-century African-American development, characterized by an improvisatory, intellectual attitude toward popular music.

JAZZ ROCK Where jazz met the exploratory progressive rock instinct. Miles Davis's 1970 set, *Bitches Brew*, was the catalyst, the early 1970s the heyday.

KRAUTROCK A distinctly German response to acid rock that also drew on the repetitive beats of funk and the radicalism of the classical avant-garde.

LATIN ROCK Late 1960s fusion of Hispanic beats and post-*Sgt Pepper* rock ambition, best exemplified by Santana.

LOUNGECORE 1950s and 1960s easy listening music given a 1990s makeover to entice a new generation.

MOR An acronym for "middle of the road" used during the 1960s and 1970s to describe crooner ballads and soothing orchestral music. The enemy of rock and pop.

NEW ROMANTICISM Early 1980s style-obsessed offspring of new wave that, in the form of Duran Duran, lent itself well to the new MTV era.

NEW WAVE Originally synonymous with punk, new wave soon widened to embrace both more artful and more pop-orientated late 1970s newcomers.

POP Hijacked from the Pop Art movement, the word is forever synonymous with music. Pop was and remains the epitome of the instant, modern, cheaply reproduced commodity.

POST-PUNK Taking punk's DIY principles and venturing far beyond the limitations of its proverbial three chords, this late 1970s/early 1980s development was exhumed by revivalists during the early 2000s.

PROGRESSIVE ROCK Hugely popular during the early 1970s, prog marked the high point of pop's ambition to achieve a grandeur usually reserved for classical music.

PSYCHEDELIA *see* ACID ROCK.

PSYCHEDELIC SOUL The techniques and ambition of psychedelia had a profound influence on Motown (Temptations, Marvin Gaye) and Sly & the Family Stone during the late 1960s.

PUNK ROCK A noisy, iconoclastic reaction to prog rock, 1970s punk originally centered on the Sex Pistols, before its DIY aesthetic rang loud around the globe.

R&B Electrified blues centered on urban cities such as Chicago—1940s rhythm and blues was the main ingredient in the rock 'n' roll of the 1950s.

RAGA ROCK The dronelike intensity of Indian music, first noted by Beatles guitarist George Harrison, left its mark on much psychedelic rock during the late 1960s.

RAP METAL During the mid and late 1980s, metal became adept at connecting with other genres. The alliance of Run-DMC and Aerosmith opened the possibilities for rap metal after the success of "Walk This Way."

REGGAE After the hyperactive ska, and the mildly less manic rocksteady, the slowed-down, bass-heavy rhythms of reggae became Jamaica's most famous musical export, gaining popularity in the 1970s thanks to Bob Marley.

ROCK A catchall term first coined in the mid-1960s as a way to differentiate "serious," album-orientated pop artists from singles-chart entertainers.

ROCKABILLY 1950s rock 'n' roll with the emphasis on the hillbilly beat.

ROCK 'N' ROLL The hybrid of blues, R&B, and country music that came together in the person of Elvis Presley and ushered in the rock 'n' roll era.

SINGER-SONGWRITER The singer-songwriters of the late 1960s and 1970s utilized an intimate, usually acoustic backing, accompanied by lyrics detailing highly personalized, adult themes.

SOUL A hybrid of gospel and R&B, soul gained currency during the mid-1960s when Otis Redding and later Aretha Franklin found success with a mix of up-tempo belters and cathartic heartbreaker ballads.

SURF Initially an instrumental, guitar-led scene, the early 1960s California surf music boom was turned on its head when the Beach Boys recast it as a genre fit for exquisite harmony pop.

SYNTH-POP A synthesizer-led, mainly British pop boom of the early 1980s, closely allied to the new romantic scene.

THRASH METAL Inspired by the New Wave of British Heavy Metal earlier in the decade, thrash took off during the mid-1980s as a dynamic counterbalance to the more sanitized sounds of mainstream metal.

TRIP HOP A distinctively British take on hip hop characterized by slowed-down beats and hypnotic, stoner atmospherics.

2-TONE Initially a record label set up by ska revivalists the Specials, 2-Tone soon became a genre in its own right and a more dance-friendly alternative to post-punk.

Index

Main entries appear in **bold** type.

ABBA, 103, 120, 241, 259
AC/DC, **194**, 228
Ace, Johnny, 13
Adverts, 183
Aerosmith, 133, 206, 219, 246
Afrika Bambaataa, 219
Air, 291
Albini, Steve, 232–33, 263, 305
Amon Düül II, 161
Animals, 47, 58, **67**, 72, 79
Anka, Paul, 17
Ant, Adam, 202, 237
Anthrax, 238, 242, 243
Antony and the Johnsons, 298
Aphex Twin, 258, 291
Arcade Fire, 295, 316
Arctic Monkeys, 295, 299, 304, 305, **311**
Autechre, 291
Avalon, Frankie, 11, 38

B-52's, 190, 191
Babes in Toyland, 260, 261
Bad Brains, 233
Baez, Joan, 74–5, 236
Baker, Ginger, 181
Band, The, 101, 121, 137, 172
Banhart, Devendra, 299, 312
Battles, 305
Beach Boys, 27, 47, 52, 53, **54–55**, 94, 121
Beastie Boys, 219, **239**, 310
Beat, 210, 211
Beatles, 16, 24, 37, 42–43, 44, 45, 46, 47, 48, 58, 59, **60–63**, 64, 69, 79, 81, 85, 94, 98, 101, 102, 105, 116, 118, 126, 127, 129, 205, 241, 257, 299, 301
Beck, 18, 252, 257, **269**
Beck, Jeff, 69
Bee Gees, 123, 188, **189**, 241
Beefheart, Captain, 30, 32, **113**, 273, 301
Berry, Chuck, 21, **26–27**, 29, 35, 38, 45, 54, 118, 207, 240
Beyoncé, 294, 295, 297, 314
Big Black, 197, 232–33, 234, 270
Big Bopper, 16, 37
Big Brother & the Holding Company, 91, 107
Björk, **268**, 277, 278
Black Eyed Peas, 300
Black Flag, 225, 232–33, 260
Black Sabbath, 132, 133, **135**, 242, 260

Blondie, 191, **193**, 232, 258
Blood, Sweat & Tears, 140
Blue Cheer, 132, 260
Blues Brothers, 203
Blues Incorporated, 45
Blur, 280, 281, **282**, 283, 284, 315
Bolan, Marc, 150, 151, **152**, 241, 312
Bon Jovi, 229, 246
Booker T. & the M.G.'s, 86
Boomtown Rats, 190
Bowie, David, 120, 150, 151, **154–55**, 156, 167, 201, 202, 215, 216, 241, 259, 270
Brenston, Jackie, 13, 19, 21
Brown, Arthur, 84
Brown, James, 17, 24, 44, 48, **50–51**, 86, 87, 121, 166, 167, 220, 240
Brown, Roy, 21
Brown, Ruth, 28
Buckley, Jeff, 256, 300, 309
Buckley, Tim, 79, 121, 144
Buggles, 148, 203, 212
Burial, 300
Burning Spear, 176, 177
Bush, Kate, 215
Butthole Surfers, 197, 234, 254
Buzzcocks, 123, 157
Byrds, 78, 79, **80**, 81, 94, 137

Cabaret Voltaire, 197, 216, 249
Cale, John, 97, 163, 202, 256
Can, 160, 161, 166
Cash, Johnny, 14, 19, **36**, 44, 129, 137, 270, 272, 297
Cassidy, David, 150
Cave, Nick, 145, 245, **274**
& the Bad Seeds, **274**
Charles, Ray, 24, **33**, 50, 86
Cheap Trick, 123, 191
Checker, Chubby, 45
Chemical Brothers, 248, 284, 285
Chic, 167, 188
Chicago, 140
Chords, 13
Clapton, Eric, 46, 98, 100, 101, 121, 128, **172**, 179, 252, 264, 297
Clark, Petula, 68, 69
Clash, 123, 177, 180, 182, 183, 195, 196
Cliff, Jimmy, 118, 177
Clinton, George, **169**, 266
Clovers, 12
Coasters, 16
Cobain, Kurt, 95, 241,

256, 257, 261, 262–63, 264
Cochran, Eddie, 17, 20, 21, 44
Cocker, Joe, 110, 111, 119
CocoRosie, 312
Cohen, Leonard, 144, **145**
Coldplay, 295, **308**
Cole, Nat "King," 14, 29, 33
Collins, Judy, 145
Collins, Phil, 149, 172
Conley, Arthur, 87, 88
Cooke, Sam, 16, 87, 88
Coolio, 252, 257
Cooper, Alice, 135, 151, 156, 162, 163, 246
Cornershop, 281
Costello, Elvis, 123, 191, **192**
Count Five, 82, 83
Country Joe & the Fish, 91, 111
Cream, 43, 46, **100**, 133, 172, 240
Creedence Clearwater Revival, 136, 137
Crosby, Stills, Nash & Young, 111, 137, **138**
Crow, Sheryl, 208
Crystals, 57
Cure, 197
Curtis, Ian, 197, 203, 205

D12, 303, 315
Daft Punk, 216
Dale, Dick, 53
Damned, 163, 183
Darin, Bobby, 17
Darkness, 246
Dave Clark Five, 58, 59, 68, 69
Davis, Miles, 11, 17, 49, 119, 140, 141, **142–43**, 166
De La Soul, 207, 219
Dead Kennedys, 232–33
Deep Purple, 117, 121, 132, 133, **134**, 205, 242
Def Leppard, 212, 228, 229, 230
Dekker, Desmond, 118, 176
Denny, Martin, 16, 279
Depeche Mode, 200, 216, **217**
Diddley, Bo, 28, 29, **32**
Dire Straits, 197
Dixon, Willie, 28, 30, 31
Domino, Fats, 12, 14, 20, 21, 24, 28, 38
Dominoes, 13
Donegan, Lonnie, 16, 58
Donovan, 75, 79, 94, 106
Doors, 49, **95**, 118, 119, 255
Dre, Dr., 252, 254, **266**, 302
Drifters, 12
Duran Duran, 212, **213**, 216

Dury, Ian, 129, 190
Dylan, Bob, 18, 45, 46, 61, **72–73**, 74, 78, 79, 80, 101, 121, 128, 129, 137, 144, 237, 252, 259, 264
Eagles, 137, **139**
808 State, 248
Elastica, 281
Elbow, 316
Electric Prunes, 82, 83
Elliott, Missy, 297
Emerson, Lake & Palmer, 120, 147
Eminem, 219, 253, 258, 266, 288, 294, 295, 296, 300, **302–3**, 314
Eno, Brian, 153, 222, 300, 308
Epstein, Brian, 58, 85
Europe, 206, 246
Everly Brothers, 17

Faces, 173
Fairport Convention, 137, 145
Fall, 113, 197
Fatboy Slim, 284, 285
Faust, 161
Feelgood, Dr., 190
50 Cent, 266, 303
Flaming Lips, 261, 269, 297
Fleet Foxes, 312
Fleetwood Mac, 118, 122, **170**
Floyd, Eddie, 87
Foals, 301
Foo Fighters, 259
Fontana, Wayne, & the Mindbenders, 68
Four Tops, 47
Frampton, Peter, 120
Frankie Goes to Hollywood, 204
Franklin, Aretha, 48, 87, 88, **89**, 259
Franz Ferdinand, 197, 225, 298, 299, 304, 305
Freddie & the Dreamers, 58
Free, 133
Freed, Alan, 10, 12, 13, 14, 20, 21, 38, **39**, 240
Front, 242, 270
Funkadelic, 167, 169
Future Sound of London, 291

Gabriel, Peter, 149, 207
Gaga, Lady, 212, 226
Gang of Four, 197, 305
Garbage, 257
Gaye, Marvin, 76, 77, 86, 87, **130–31**
Geldof, Bob, 236, 237
Genesis, 147, **149**, 156, 295

Gerry & the Pacemakers, 58
Gil, Gilberto, 108
Godflesh, 270
Goldfrapp, 216
Goldie, 284, 291
Gordy, Berry, 16, 50, 76, 77, 131, 208
Gorillaz, 103, **315**
Grandmaster Flash, 200, 203, 218, 219, 266
& the Furious Five, 200, 203, 219
Grateful Dead, 47, 90, 91, **93**, 107, 111, 123
Grizzly Bear, 312
Guns N' Roses, 207, 229, 231
Guthrie, Woody, 11, 45, 72, 74

Haley, Bill, 13, 18, 299
& His Comets, 14, 15, 34–5
Hancock, Herbie, 140, 167, 204
Hanoi Rocks, 246
Happy Mondays, 248
Harris, Wynonie, 28
Harrison, George, 81, 128, 241, 296
Harvey, P.J., 233, 273
Havens, Richie, 111
Hayes, Isaac, 87, 167, 301
Head of David, 270
Hendrix, Jimi, 30, 31, 42, 48, 49, 91, 94, **98–99**, 106, 110, 111, 116, 119, 142, 221, 241, 254
Experience, 43, 91, 98–99, 133
Herman's Hermits, 58, 68
Hill, Lauryn, 253, 259
Hole, 254, 256, 261
Holiday, Billie, 17
Hollies, 58
Holly, Buddy, 16, 37
Hooker, John Lee, 13, 28, 32
Howlin' Wolf, 19, 28, **30**, 44
Human League, 200, 216
Hüsker Dü, 225, 232

Ice-T, 254
Idol, Billy, 205
Inspiral Carpets, 248, 282
Iron Butterfly, 84
Iron Maiden, 228, 229
Isley Brothers, 98, 166, 167

Jackson 5, **104**, 150
Jackson, Michael, 76, 104, 204, 205, **208–9**, 212, 256, 300
Jagger, Mick, 50, 64, 82, 119, 206, 237, 297

Jam, 190, 191
James, 248
Jan & Dean, 45, 52, 53
Jay-Z, 253, 294, 295, **314**
Jefferson Airplane, 79, 81, 91, **92**, 94, 240
Jefferson Starship, 92, 120
Jethro Tull, 121, 147, 156
Jett, Joan, 203
Jimmy Eat World, 313
Joel, Billy, 204
John, Elton, 150, **171**, 202, 258, 298
Johnny Burnette Trio, 35
Jones, Brian, 48, 64, 81, 106
Jones, Grace, 188
Jones, Quincy, 104, 204, 208
Joplin, Janis, 49, 94, 106, **107**, 111, 116, 119
Jordan, Louis, 28
Joy Division, 197, 203, 205, 249, 295, 305

Keys, Alicia, 295, 314
Killers, 197, 305
Kills, 305
King, Carole, 144
Kings of Leon, 295, 301, 316
Kingsmen, 44, 66, 82, 83
Kinks, 47, **66**, 68, 81, 132, 156
Kiss, 133, 164, 240, 246, 258
KLF, 291
KMFDM, 270, 271
Korn, 267
Korner, Alexis, 45
Kraftwerk, 161, 202, 216
Kuti, Fela, **181**

La's, 280
lang, k.d., 254
Lauper, Cyndi, 278
Led Zeppelin, 30, 31, 35, 49, 117, 122, **124–25**, 132, 133, 237, 257, 295, 300
Lee, Arthur, 295
Lee, Brenda, 15
Leftfield, 284, 285
Lennon, John, 16, 23, 26, 48, 118, 119, **126**, 202, 241
Lewis, Jerry Lee, 14, 19, 20, **25**, 38, 118
Libertines, 298, 304, 305
Limp Bizkit, 267
Linkin Park, 314
Little Richard, 20, 21, **24**, 28, 38, 50, 86, 98, 118, 166
Live Aid, 201, 205, 226, 236, 298
Living Color, 254
Lollapalooza, 254
Love, 79, 295

Love, Courtney, 207, 226, 256
Lovin' Spoonful, 79
Lydon, John, 197, 203, and see Rotten, Johnny

M.I.A., 295, 299
Madness, 210, 211
Madonna, 204, 206, 208, 212, **226–27**, 237, 241, 255
Mamas & the Papas, 78, 79, 94
Manfred Mann, 68
Manic Street Preachers, 257, 275
Manson, Marilyn, 258, 270, 271
Marley, Bob, 122, 176–77, **178–79**, 180
Marvelettes, 44, 76
Massive Attack, 276, 277, 291
Mayall, John, 46
  Blues Breakers, 100, 172
Mayfield, Curtis, 87, 166, 167, 259
Maytals, 118
McCartney, Paul, 16, 37, 118, 119, **127**, 192, 202, 205, 207, 236, 237, 241, 264, 296, 297, 300
McGuire Sisters, 13
McLaren, Malcolm, 85, 118, 182, 186
Meat Loaf, 122
Meek, Joe, 45, 62
Megadeth, 242, 243, 244
Melanie, 111, 144
Melodians, 118
Metallica, 204, 229, 242, 243, **244–45**, 296
MGMT, 316
Michael, George, 171, 206
Millie, 84
Million Dollar Quartet, 14
Ministry, 270, 271
Mink DeVille, 191
Minogue, Kylie, 216
Minutemen, 232
Miracles, 76
Misfits, 245
Mitchell, Joni, 101, 138, 144
Moby, 285
Monkees, 49, **102**, 103
Monterey Pop Festival, 49, 70, 88, 94, 98 107
Moody Blues, 58, 144
Moonglows, 12, 13
Morcheeba, 277
Morissette, Alanis, 252, 256, 278
Morrison, Jim, 95, 106, 116, 118, 255

Mothers of Invention, 46, 112, 140
Mötley Crüe, 204, 246
Motörhead, 203, 228, 242
Motors, 190
Mott the Hoople, 150
Mountain, 133
MTV Unplugged, 264, 312
MTV, 135, 203, 204, 208, **212**, 213, 252
Mudhoney, 260, 261
Muse, 147, 295, **309**
Music Machine, 84
My Bloody Valentine, 234
My Chemical Romance, 313

Napalm Death, 207, 229, 233
Nash, Johnny, 179
Nelson, Ricky, 11, 38
Neu!, 161
New Order, 197, 205, 248, **249**
New York Dolls, 150, 151, 182, 246
Newsom, Joanna, 312
Nice, 146
Nickelback, 296
Nico, 96–7
Nine Inch Nails, 36, 254, 266, 270, 271, **272**, 297, 310
Nirvana, 206, 212, 225, 233, 234, 252, 255, 260, 261, **262–63**, 264
Notorious B.I.G., 219, 253, 259, **288**, 289, 314
Numan, Gary, 216
NWA, 219, 266

O'Connor, Sinéad, 254
Oasis, 248, 252, 256, 280, 281, 282, **283**
Ochs, Phil, 75
Ohio Express, 103
Oldfield, Mike, 120, 147, 157
Oldham, Andrew Loog, 85
Ono, Yoko, 48, 126, 255, 300
Orb, 291
Orbison, Roy, 19, 47
Orbital, 291
Orioles, 13
Osbourne, Ozzy, 135, 203
Osmonds, 150
Otis, Johnny, 13, 28, 29
OutKast, 298

Page, Jimmy, 124, 157
Parker, Graham, 191
Parliament, 169
Parsons, Gram, 136, 137
Patton, Charley, 30
Paul Revere & the Raiders, 82
Paul, Les, 12
Pearl Jam, 229, 260, 261
Peel, John, 49, 197, 299

Pere Ubu, 191, 197, 232
Perkins, Carl, 14, 19, 35
Perry, Lee "Scratch," 177, 179, **180**
Pet Shop Boys, 216
Peter & Gordon, 68
Phillips, Sam, 12, 13, 14, 19, 39
PIL, 177, 197, 203
Pink Floyd, 91, 116, 119, 147, **158–59**, 160, 205, 295, 298, 299
Pixies, 206, 225, 233
Placebo, 259, 313
Platters, 14
Poison, 246
Police, 191, **214**, 295
Pop Group, 113, 143, 197, 298, 305
Pop, Iggy, 155, 156, 163, 284, 295
Portishead, 276, 277
Prado, Pérez, 14
Presley, Elvis, 10, 13, 14, 15, 18, 19, 20, 21, **22–23**, 35, 38, 39, 44, 49, 119, 122, 129, 240, 241, 255, 256, 296, 299
Pretenders, 123
Pretty Things, 68
Primal Scream, **265**
Prince, 143, 167, 188, **220–21**
Procul Harem, 146
Prodigy, 284, 285
Public Enemy, 207, 219, **238**, 51
Puff Daddy, 288, 289, 297
Pulp, 256, 280, 281, 284

Quatro, Suzi, 150
Queen, 123, 133, 165, 237, 255, 295, 298
Queens of the Stone Age, 294, 297, 316
Quicksilver Messenger Service, 32, 81, 90, 91
Quiet Riot, 204

Radiohead, 147, 225, 253, 259, 281, **286–87**, 296, 299, 310
Rage Against the Machine, 254, 267, 301
Rammstein, 270, 271
Ramones, 183, **185**, 191, 232
Ray, Johnnie, 12
Red Hot Chili Peppers, 278, 299
Redding, Otis, 24, 49, 87, **88**, 94
Reed, Jimmy, 28, 29
Reed, Lou, 97, 256, 259, 284
R.E.M., 225, **235**, 270

Revolting Cocks, 270
Richard, Cliff, 58, 202
Richards, Keith, 64, 119, 122, 207, 237, 297
Righteous Brothers, 56
Rihanna, 300, 314
Robinson, Smokey, 76, 77
Rodgers, Jimmie, 18, 30, 35
Rolling Stones, 12, 24, 26, 28, 29, 31, 37, 44, 46, 47, 48, 58, 59, **64–65**, 68, 68, 79, 85, 94, 98, 101, 106, 129, 137, 184, 201, 206, 241, 252, 301
Rollins Band, 254
Ronettes, 57
Ronstadt, Linda, 139
Ross, Diana, 47, 76, 77, 104
Rotten, Johnny, 123, 183, 186, and see Lydon, John
Roxy Music, 150, 151, **153**
Run-DMC, 206, 218, 219, 258
Runaways, 191
Rush, 147, 240

Sainte-Marie, Buffy, 75, 144
Salt-N-Pepa, 206
Sam & Dave, 87
Santana, **109**, 111
Saxon, 228
Scissor Sisters, 298
Screaming Trees, 261
Searchers, 58, 79
Seeger, Pete, 80, 74
Selecter, 210, 211
Sex Pistols, 85, 116, 122, 123, 163, 182, 183, **186–87**, 190, 195, 210, 240, 257
S'Express, 247
Shadow, DJ, 276, 277
Shadows, 37
Shadows of Knight, 82, 83
Shakur, Tupac, 253, 257, 288, 289
Shankar, Ravi, 49, **81**, 94, 128, 296
Shapiro, Helen, 58
Shellac, 305
Shoes, 191
Shoom, 247
Simon, Paul, 206
Simon & Garfunkel, 79, 118, 144
Simple Minds, 207
Sinatra, Frank, 10, 259
Siouxsie & the Banshees, 196, 197, 254
Slade, 118, 150
Slayer, 242, 243
Slick, Grace, 92, 168
Slits, 123, 177, 197, 226, 298

Sly & the Family Stone, 48, 87, 111, 142, 166, 167, **168**
Small Faces, 173
Smith, Patti, 174, 182, 183, **184**
Smiths, **224**, 225, 270
Sneaker Pimps, 277
Snoop Doggy Dogg, 266
Snow, Hank, 12
Soft Cell, 200, 202, 216
Soft Machine, 91, 140, 141
Sonic Youth, 197, 225, 232, **234**, 259, 262
Sonny & Cher, 79
Soundgarden, 229, 252, 260, 261
Spears, Britney, 208, 304
Specials, 203, 210, 211
Spector, Phil, 17, 47, **56–57**, 76, 145, 185, 296
Spice Girls, 103, 258, 281
Springsteen, Bruce, 116, 120, **174–75**, 184, 237
Squeeze, 264
Staple Singers, 87
Starr, Ringo, 119, 136, 296, 300
Status Quo, 237
Steel Pulse, 177

Stewart, Mark, 277
Stewart, Rod, 120, 150, **173**
Sting, 122, 207, 214
Stone Roses, 248, 254
Stooges, **163**, 182
Strokes, 225, 294, 295, 298, 304, **306**
Strong, Barrett, 16
Strummer, Joe, 182, 296
Subway Sect, 123, 196, 298
Suede, 255, 280
Sugarhill Gang, 123, 218
Summer, Donna, 123, 188, 216
Sun Records, **19**, 25, 30, 35
Sunny Day Real Estate, 313
Supergrass, 280, 281
Supremes, 47, 76, 77
Surfaris, 53
Survivor, 204
Sweet, 150, 230

T. Rex, 119, 150, 151, **152**, 246
Talking Heads, 190, 191
Tangerine Dream, 161
Taylor, James, 144
Teenage Jesus, 232

Television, 121, 190, 191
Temptations, 76, 86
Terrell, Tammi, 130
Them, 58, 68, 82
Thomas, Rufus, 12, 87
Thornton, Big Mama, 13, 28
Throbbing Gristle, 196, 216, 270
Tony Williams Lifetime, 141
Tornados, 45, 62
Townshend, Peter, 70–71, 96, 105
Trash Talk, 233
Trashmen, 53
Tricky, 276, 277, **278**
Trumans Water, 261
Tubby, King, 177, 180
Turner, Big Joe, 12, 15, 20, 28
Turner, Ike, 13
Turner, Ike & Tina, 56, 57
Turner, Tina, 205, 237
Turtles, 79
TV on the Radio, 301
23 Skidoo, 197, 284
Twitty, Conway, 16
Tyrannosaurus Rex, 91, 151, 152

U2, 206, 207, **222–23**, 237, 314
Underworld, 284
Upsetters, 176, 180

Valens, Ritchie, 16, 37
Van Halen, 212, 229
Velvet Underground, 46, **96–97**, 120, 155, 160, 182, 204, 234, 256
Venom, 242
Verve, 253, 258, 281
Vincent, Gene, 15, 35

W.A.S.P., 204, 246
Wailers, 176, 177, 178, 179, 180
Wainwright, Rufus, 299
Walker, T-Bone, 28
Walker Brothers, 48
Waters, Muddy, 28, **31**
Watson, Johnny "Guitar," 12
Weather Report, 141
Weavers, 74
Weezer, 313
Weller, Paul, 190, 281
West, Kanye, 300, 314
White Stripes, 258, 294, 296, 304, 305, **307**

Author acknowledgments

The author would like to thank Bernard Doherty, Lois Wilson, Sofia Mikaelsson, and Justyna Franuszkiewicz.

Picture acknowledgments

All photographs are reproduced courtesy of Getty Images; details of archives and photographers are as follows. Key: a = above, b = below, c = center, l = left, r = right, t = top.

AFP, pp 48b, 120b; /Robyn Beck 290b; /Carl de Souza, p 298b; /Jim Watson, p 310b; /Thomas Wirth, p 277

Archive Photos/Steve Eichner, p 289; /Scott Harrison, p 272; /Hulton Archive, pp 67, 93; /Catherine McGann, p 295; /Pictorial Parade, pp 36, 119t

Bob Thomas Sports Photography/Bob Thomas, p 85a

CBS Photo Archive, pp 10, 15t

FilmMagic/Jeff Kravitz, p 303; /Chiaki Nozu, p 308a

Getty Images Entertainment/Ray Avery, pp 57a, 57b; /Brad Barket, p 299c; /Bob Berg, p 286; /Morena Brengola, p 309a; /Georges DeKeerle, pp 165l, 198–9, 236b, 237a; /Graham Denholm, p 312l; /Jim Dyson, p 317; /C. Flanigan, p 306; /Mike Flokis, p 312r; /Jo Hale, p 154r; /Scott Harrison, p 301l; /Dave Hogan, pp 65, 227b, 237b; /Samir Hussein, p 316b; /Nick Laham, p 285; /Frank Micelotta, pp 209l, 258b, 264a, 264b; /Tim Mosenfelder, p 258a; /Christopher Polk, p 298l; /Jim Pozarik, p 202a; /Jeff Scheid, p 259b; /Michael Tullberg, p 27; /Lyle A. Waisman, p 313a

Getty Images News/National Archives, p 75b; /Spencer Platt, pp 241, 310a; /Mario Tama, p 50r

Hulton Archive, p 38a; /BIPS, p 61a; /Blank Archives, pp 44bl, 72a, 189a, 205b; /Central Press, p 106; /Hulton Archive/Richard Chowen, pp 75a, 85b; /Debi Doss, p 150a; /Epics, p 118a; /Evening Standard, pp 62, 71; /Express Newspapers, pp 14l, 46t; /Mark and Colleen Hayward, p 64; /Charles Hewitt, p 11b; /Dave Hogan, pp 201r, 222; /Keystone, p 49b, 122b, 140; /Frank Micelotta, p 220a; /David Montgomery, p 195a; /Leon Morris, p 249; /Oliver Morris, p 218

New York Daily News Archive, p 226

Michael Ochs Archives, pp 11t, 12b, 13t, 14t, 14r, 15c, 15t, 16b, 17r, 18, 20a, 21, 22, 23l, 23c, 23r, 24b, 25, 26, 29a, 30, 31, 32t, 32b, 35r, 37, 39, 44br, 45b, 47bl, 47br, 48a, 49a, 50l, 52a, 52b, 53a, 54a, 54b, 55, 63b, 68, 69r, 73, 77b, 78, 79al, 79b, 81b, 82, 83a, 83b, 86, 87a, 87b, 88, 89, 92, 94r, 98a, 102, 103a, 107, 108, 109, 113, 116c, 116b, 118b, 119b, 120t, 120c, 128, 130, 131a, 135a, 147, 156, 157, 159, 162, 165, 166a, 169, 170r, 172, 188, 191c, 194, 204t, 208, 220b, 221, 229l, 229r, 230, 238a, 246, 279a; /Robert Altman, p 163l; /Jim Britt, p 131b; /Tom Copi, pp 13c, 51, 79ar, 163r; /David Corio, pp 176r, 200, 279a; /Colin Escott, p 12r, 19b; /Anne Fishbein, p 233a; /Lisa Haun, p 225a; /Richard McCaffrey, pp 114–15, 116t; /Alice Ochs, p 45t; /Al Pereira, p 123b; /Paul Ryan, pp 70l, 90a; /Jim Steinfeldt, pp 244, 257a, 269

Popperfoto, pp 8–9, 16t, 63a

Premium Archive/Barry Z Levine, p 110r

Redferns/Richard E. Aaron, pp 121t, 170l, 174r, 182b, 191b, 204c, 235b; /Fiona Adams, p 70; /Jorgen Angel, pp 122t, 132a, 132b, 183, 184; /Ray Avery, p 56; /Roberta Bayley, pp 190, 193a; /Paul Bergen, pp 250–51, 261, 263l, 268, 283; /Marc Broussely, p 309b; /Tony Buckingham, p 239; /Clayton Call, p 254b; /Raffaella Cavalieri, p 262; /Collexxx – Lex van Rossen, p 185; /Brian Cooke, p 153l; /David Corio, pp 233b, 273, 288; /Fin Costello, pp 117, 121c, 122c, 134, 135b, 148, 174l, 196l, 212, 213, 216a, 221r; /Pete Cronin, pp 224, 245; /Phil Dent, pp 214l, 247; /George De Sota, p 124; /Peter Francis, p 84b; /Patrick Ford, p 281a; /Ian Dickson, pp 178, 181b, 196c; /Erica Echenberg, pp 182a, 191l, 255a; /Echoes, p 181a; /David Warner Ellis, pp 138, 146, 150b, 158; /GAB Archive, pp 12l, 17tl, 19a, 20b, 24a, 29b, 40–41, 42t, 42c, 42b, 44a, 46c, 58–9, 59a, 69l, 80b, 90b, 98b, 103b, 105a, 112r, 123a, 129a, 129b, 168; /Gems, p 160; /Suzie Gibbons, p 207b, 217, 238b; /Charlie Gillett Collection, p 97b; /Mick Gold, pp 96, 125; /William Gottlieb, p 17b; /Gijsbert Hanekroot, pp 70r, 101, 105b, 133, 139b, 155, 214r; /Ron Howard, pp 84a, 126, 152; /Mick Hutson, pp 243, 248a, 256b, 257b, 260t, 265, 270, 274, 276b, 281b, 282, 284l, 284r, 290a, 298c; /Sal Idriss, p 266; /JMEnternational, p 275; /K & K Ulf Kruger OHG, pp 60, 95l, 144; /Ivan Keenan, p 46b; /Bob King, pp 196b, 228; /John Lynn Kirk, p 149; /Michel Linssen, pp 235a, 248b, 252b, 300c;

/Robin Little, p 291; /McEvoy, p 177; /Ha[...] p 203ar; /Steve Mor[...] /Estate of Keith Mor[...] p 271; /Niki, pp 232[...] /Martin O'Neill, p 19[...] p 189b; /Jan Persso[...] Petard, pp 13b, 28, [...] Pitcher, p 35l; /Prem[...] pp 53b, 77a, 104, 1[...] pp 34, 43, 66, 81a, [...] 215, 279b; /Max Re[...] /Ebet Roberts, pp [...] 240, 254c, 260b; /[...] pp 223, 26f, 308b; [...] p 45c; /Gus Stewar[...] 202b, 216b, 308b; [...] pp 187, 195b, 211 [...] pp 223, 267; /Des [...] /Andrew Whittuck, [...] 301a

Sony BMG Music [...]

Sony Music Archi [...]

Terry O'Neill, pp 1 [...]

Time & Life Pictur [...] /Kimberly Butler, p [...] p 38b; /Bill Epprid[...] Kagan, p 76; /Dav[...] /Eric Schaal, p 74 [...] p 11c

WireImage/M. C[...] pp 299b, 311b; /[...] 300b; /Steve Jen[...] /Stephen Lovekin[...] p 287b; /Leslie M[...] 231a, 231b, 258 [...] Natkin, p 203al; [...] p 298t; /Bob Rif[...] /Marty Temme, p [...] 296c; /Chris Wa[...]

Jam, 190, 191
James, 248
Jan & Dean, 45, 52, 53
Jay-Z, 253, 294, 295, **314**
Jefferson Airplane, 79, 81,
    91, **92**, 94, 240
Jefferson Starship, 92, 120
Jethro Tull, 121, 147, 156
Jett, Joan, 203
Jimmy Eat World, 313
Joel, Billy, 204
John, Elton, 150, **171**, 202,
    258, 298
Johnny Burnette Trio, 35
Jones, Brian, 48, 64, 81,
    106
Jones, Grace, 188
Jones, Quincy, 104, 204, 208
Joplin, Janis, 49, 94, 106,
    107, 111, 116, 119
Jordan, Louis, 28
Joy Division, 197, 203, 205,
    249, 295, 305

Keys, Alicia, 295, 314
Killers, 197, 305
Kills, 305
King, Carole, 144
Kings of Leon, 295, 301, 316
Kingsmen, 44, 66, 82, 83
Kinks, 47, **66**, 68, 81, 132,
    156
Kiss, 133, 164, 240, 246,
    258
KLF, 291
KMFDM, 270, 271
Korn, 270
Korner, Alexis, 45
Kraftwerk, 161, 202, 216
Kuti, Fela, **181**

La's, 280
lang, k.d., 254
Lauper, Cyndi, 278
Led Zeppelin, 30, 31, 35, 49,
    117, 122, **124–25**, 132,
    133, 237, 257, 295, 300
Lee, Arthur, 295
Lee, Brenda, 15
Leftfield, 284, 285
Lennon, John, 16, 23, 26, 48,
    118, 119, **126**, 202, 241
Lewis, Jerry Lee, 14, 19, 20,
    25, 38, 118
Libertines, 298, 304, 305
Limp Bizkit, 254
Linkin Park, 314
Little Richard, 20, 21, **24**, 28,
    38, 50, 86, 98, 118, 166
Live Aid, 201, 205, 226, 236,
    298
Living Color, 254
Lollapalooza, 254
Love, 79, 295

Love, Courtney, 207, 226,
    256
Lovin' Spoonful, 79
Lydon, John, 197, 203, and
    see Rotten, Johnny

M.I.A., 295, 299
Madness, 210, 211
Madonna, 204, 206, 208,
    212, **226–27**, 237, 241,
    255
Mamas & the Papas, 78, 79,
    94
Manfred Mann, 68
Manic Street Preachers, 257,
    275
Manson, Marilyn, 258, 270,
    271
Marley, Bob, 122, 176–77,
    178–79, 180
Marvelettes, 44, 76
Massive Attack, 276, 277,
    291
Mayall, John, 46
    Blues Breakers, 100, 172
Mayfield, Curtis, 87, 166,
    167, 259
Maytals, 118
McCartney, Paul, 16, 37,
    118, 119, **127**, 192, 202,
    205, 207, 236, 237, 241,
    264, 296, 297, 300
McGuire Sisters, 13
McLaren, Malcolm, 85, 118,
    182, 186
Meat Loaf, 122
Meek, Joe, 45, 62
Megadeth, 242, 243, 244
Melanie, 111, 144
Melodians, 118
Metallica, 204, 229, 242,
    243, **244–45**, 296
MGMT, 316
Michael, George, 171, 206
Millie, 84
Million Dollar Quartet, 14
Ministry, 270, 271
Mink DeVille, 191
Minogue, Kylie, 216
Minutemen, 232
Miracles, 76
Misfits, 245
Mitchell, Joni, 101, 138, 144
Moby, 285
Monkees, 49, **102**, 103
Monterey Pop Festival, 49,
    70, 88, 94, 98 107
Moody Blues 58, 146
Moonglows, 12, 13
Morcheeba, 277
Morissette, Alanis, 252, 256,
    278
Morrison, Jim, 95, 106, 116,
    118, 255

Mothers of Invention, 46,
    112, 140
Mötley Crüe, 204, 246
Motörhead, 203, 228, 242
Motors, 190
Mott the Hoople, 150
Mountain, 133
MTV Unplugged, 264, 312
MTV, 135, 203, 204, 208,
    212, 213, 252
Mudhoney, 260, 261
Muse, 147, 295, **309**
Music Machine, 84
My Bloody Valentine, 234
My Chemical Romance, 313

Napalm Death, 207, 229, 233
Nash, Johnny, 179
Nelson, Ricky, 11, 38
Nelson, 190
Neu!, 161
New Order, 197, 205, 248,
    249
New York Dolls, 150, 151,
    182, 246
Newsom, Joanna, 312
Nice, 146
Nickelback, 296
Nico, 96–7
Nine Inch Nails, 36, 254, 266,
    270, 271, **272**, 297, 310
Nirvana, 206, 212, 225, 233,
    234, 252, 255, 260, 261,
    262–63, 264
Notorious B.I.G., 219, 253,
    259, **288**, 289, 314
Numan, Gary, 216
NWA, 219, 266

O'Connor, Sinéad, 254
Oasis, 248, 252, 256, 280,
    281, 282, **283**
Ochs, Phil, 75
Ohio Express, 103
Oldfield, Mike, 120, 147, 157
Oldham, Andrew Loog, 85
Ono, Yoko, 48, 126, 255, 300
Orb, 291
Orbison, Roy, 19, 47
Orbital, 291
Orioles, 13
Osbourne, Ozzy, 135, 203
Osmonds, 150
Otis, Johnny, 13, 28, 29
OutKast, 298

Page, Jimmy, 124, 157
Parker, Graham, 191
Parliament, 169
Parsons, Gram, 136, 137
Patton, Charley, 30
Paul Revere & the Raiders, 82
Paul, Les, 12
Pearl Jam, 229, 260, 261
Peel, John, 49, 197, 299

Pere Ubu, 191, 197, 232
Perkins, Carl, 14, 19, 35
Perry, Lee "Scratch," 177,
    179, **180**
Pet Shop Boys, 216
Peter & Gordon, 68
Phillips, Sam, 12, 13, 14, 19,
    39
PiL, 177, 197, 203
Pink Floyd, 91, 116, 119,
    147, **158–59**, 160, 205,
    295, 298, 299
Pixies, 206, 225, 233
Placebo, 259, 313
Platters, 14
Poison, 246
Police, 191, **214**, 295
Pop Group, 113, 143, 197,
    298, 305
Pop, Iggy, 155, 156, 163,
    284, 295
Portishead, 276, 277
Prado, Pérez, 14
Presley, Elvis, 10, 13, 14, 15,
    18, 19, 20, 21, **22–23**, 35,
    38, 39, 44, 49, 119, 122,
    129, 240, 241, 255, 256,
    296, 299
Pretenders, 123
Pretty Things, 68
Primal Scream, **265**
Prince, 143, 167, 188,
    220–21
Procul Harum, 146
Prodigy, 284, 285
Public Enemy, 207, 219, **238**,
    51
Puff Daddy, 288, 289, 297
Pulp, 256, 280, 281, 284

Quatro, Suzi, 150
Queen, 123, 133, 165, 237,
    255, 295, 298
Queens of the Stone Age,
    294, 297, 316
Quicksilver Messenger
    Service, 32, 81, 90, 91
Quiet Riot, 204

Radiohead, 147, 225, 253,
    259, 281, **286–87**, 296,
    299, 310
Rage Against the Machine,
    254, 267, 301
Rammstein, 270, 271
Ramones, 183, **185**, 191, 232
Ray, Johnnie, 12
Red Hot Chili Peppers, 278,
    299
Redding, Otis, 24, 49, 87, **88**,
    94
Reed, Jimmy, 28, 29
Reed, Lou, 97, 256, 259, 284
R.E.M., 225, **235**, 270

Revolting Cocks, 270
Richard, Cliff, 58, 202
Richards, Keith, 64, 119,
    122, 207, 237, 297
Righteous Brothers, 56
Rihanna, 300, 314
Robinson, Smokey, 76, 77
Rodgers, Jimmie, 18, 30, 35
Rolling Stones, 12, 24, 26,
    28, 29, 31, 37, 44, 46, 47,
    48, 58, 59, **64–65**, 68, 68,
    79, 85, 94, 98, 101, 106,
    129, 137, 184, 201, 206,
    241, 252, 301
Rollins Band, 254
Ronettes, 57
Ronstadt, Linda, 139
Ross, Diana, 47, 76, 77, 104
Rotten, Johnny, 123, 183,
    186, and see Lydon, John
Roxy Music, 150, 151, **153**
Run-DMC, 206, 218, 219,
    258
Runaways, 191
Rush, 147, 240

Sainte-Marie, Buffy, 75, 144
Salt-N-Pepa, 206
Sam & Dave, 87
Santana, **109**, 111
Saxon, 228
Scissor Sisters, 298
Screaming Trees, 261
Searchers, 58, 79
Seeger, Pete, 80, 74
Selecter, 210, 211
Sex Pistols, 85, 116, 122,
    123, 163, 182, 183,
    186–87, 190, 195, 210,
    240, 257
S'Express, 247
Shadow, DJ, 276, 277
Shadows, 37
Shadows of Knight, 82, 83
Shakur, Tupac, 253, 257,
    288, 289
Shankar, Ravi, 49, **81**, 94,
    128, 296
Shapiro, Helen, 58
Shellac, 305
Shoes, 191
Shoom, 247
Simon, Paul, 206
Simon & Garfunkel, 79, 118,
    144
Simple Minds, 200
Sinatra, Frank, 10, 259
Siouxsie and the Banshees,
    196, 197, 254
Slade, 118, 150
Slayer, 242, 243
Slick, Grace, 92, 168
Slits, 123, 177, 197, 226,
    298

Sly & the Family Stone, 48, 87, 111, 142, 166, 167, **168**
Small Faces, 173
Smith, Patti, 174, 182, 183, **184**
Smiths, **224**, 225, 270
Sneaker Pimps, 277
Snoop Doggy Dogg, 266
Snow, Hank, 12
Soft Cell, 200, 202, 216
Soft Machine, 91, 140, 141
Sonic Youth, 197, 225, 232, **234**, 259, 262
Sonny & Cher, 79
Soundgarden, 229, 252, 260, 261
Spears, Britney, 208, 304
Specials, 203, 210, 211
Spector, Phil, 17, 47, **56–57**, 76, 145, 185, 296
Spice Girls, 103, 258, 281
Springsteen, Bruce, 116, 120, **174–75**, 184, 237
Squeeze, 264
Staple Singers, 87
Starr, Ringo, 119, 136, 296, 300
Status Quo, 237
Steel Pulse, 177

Stewart, Mark, 277
Stewart, Rod, 120, 150, **173**
Sting, 122, 207, 214
Stone Roses, 248, 254
Stooges, **163**, 182
Strokes, 225, 294, 295, 298, 304, **306**
Strong, Barrett, 16
Strummer, Joe, 182, 296
Subway Sect, 123, 196, 298
Suede, 255, 280
Sugarhill Gang, 123, 218
Summer, Donna, 123, 188, 216
Sun Records, **19**, 25, 30, 35
Sunny Day Real Estate, 313
Supergrass, 280, 281
Supremes, 47, 76, 77
Surfaris, 53
Survivor, 204
Sweet, 150, 230

T. Rex, 119, 150, 151, **152**, 246
Talking Heads, 190, 191
Tangerine Dream, 161
Taylor, James, 144
Teenage Jesus, 232

Television, 121, 190, 191
Temptations, 76, 86
Terrell, Tammi, 130
Them, 58, 68, 82
Thomas, Rufus, 12, 87
Thornton, Big Mama, 13, 28
Throbbing Gristle, 196, 216, 270
Tony Williams Lifetime, 141
Tornados, 45, 62
Townshend, Peter, 70–71, 98, 105
Trash Talk, 233
Tricky, 276, 277, **278**
Trumans Water, 261
Tubby, Kind, 177, 180
Turner, Big Joe, 12, 15, 20, 28
Turner, Ike, 13
Turner, Ike & Tina, 56, 57
Turner, Tina, 205, 237
Turtles, 79
TV on the Radio, 301
23 Skidoo, 197, 284
Twitty, Conway, 16
Tyrannosaurus Rex, 91, 151, 152

U2, 206, 207, **222–23**, 237, 314
Underworld, 284
Upsetters, 176, 180

Valens, Ritchie, 16, 37
Van Halen, 212, 229
Velvet Underground, 46, **96–97**, 120, 155, 160, 182, 204, 234, 256
Venom, 242
Verve, 253, 258, 281
Vincent, Gene, 15, 35

W.A.S.P., 204, 246
Wailers, 176, 177, 178, 179, 180
Wainwright, Rufus, 299
Walker, T-Bone, 28
Walker Brothers, 48
Waters, Muddy, 28, **31**
Watson, Johnny "Guitar," 12
Weather Report, 141
Weavers, 74
Weezer, 313
Weller, Paul, 190, 281
West, Kanye, 300, 314
White Stripes, 258, 294, 296, 304, 305, **307**

Who, 46, 49, 68, **70–71**, 80, 94, 105, 111, 119, 122, 123, 295, 297
Wilcox, Toyah, 122
Wilde, Marty, 58
Williams, Andy, 279
Williams, Hank, **18**
Wilson, Brian, 47, 52, 53, 54–55, 121, 295, 298
Winehouse, Amy, 298
Wings, 123, 127
Wire, 197, 282, 305
Wonder, Stevie, 76, 77, 167
Woodstock, 48, 71, 99, 109, **110–11**, 129, 168, 236, 259
Wu-Tang Clan, 219

Yardbirds, 35, 68, 81, 124, 172
Yeah Yeah Yeahs, 305
Yes, 147, **148**
Young, Neil, 79, 101, 138, 144, 240, 241, 252

Zappa, Frank, 46, 140, **112**, 188, 220
Zé, Tom, 108

Author acknowledgments

The author would like to thank Bernard Doherty, Lois Wilson, Sofia Mikaelsson, and Justyna Franuszkiewicz.

Picture acknowledgments

All photographs are reproduced courtesy of Getty Images; details of archives and photographers are as follows. Key: a = above, b = below, c = center, l = left, r = right, t = top.

AFP, pp 48b, 120b; /Robyn Beck 290b; /Carl de Souza, p 298b; /Jim Watson, p 310b; /Thomas Wirth, p 277

Archive Photos/Steve Eichner, p 289; /Scott Harrison, p 272; /Hulton Archive, pp 67, 93; /Catherine McGann, p 295; /Pictorial Parade, pp 36, 119t

Bob Thomas Sports Photography/Bob Thomas, p 85a

CBS Photo Archive, pp 10, 15t

FilmMagic/Jeff Kravitz, p 303; /Chiaki Nozu, p 308a

Getty Images Entertainment/Ray Avery, pp 57a, 57b; /Brad Barket, p 299c; /Bob Berg, p 286c; /Morena Brengola, p 309a; /Georges DeKeerle, pp 165l, 198–9, 236b, 237a; /Graham Denholm, p 312l; /Jim Dyson, p 317; /C. Flanigan, p 306; /Mike Flokis, p 312r; /Jo Hale, p 154r; /Scott Harrison, p 3012 /Dave Hogan, pp 65, 227b, 237b; /Samir Hussein, p 316b; /Nick Laham, p 285; /Frank Micelotta, pp 209r, 258b, 264a, 264b; /Tim Mosenfelder, p 256a; /Christopher Polk, p 296t; /Jim Pozarik, p 202a; /Jeff Scheid, p 259b; /Michael Tullberg, p 27; /Lyle A. Waisman, p 313a

Getty Images News/National Archives, p 75b; /Spencer Platt, pp 241, 310a; /Mario Tama, p 50r

Hulton Archive, p 38a; /BIPS, p 61a; /Blank Archives, pp 44bl, 72a, 189a, 205b; /Central Press, p 106; /Hulton Archive/Richard Chowen, pp 75a, 85b; /Debi Doss, p 150a; /Epics, p 118a; /Evening Standard, pp 62, 71; /Express Newspapers, pp 14l, 46t; /Mark and Colleen Hayward, p 64; /Charles Hewitt, p 11b; /Dave Hogan, pp 201r, 222; /Keystone, pp 122b, 140; /Frank Micelotta, p 220a; /David Montgomery, p 195a; /Leon Morris, p 249; /Oliver Morris, p

New York Daily News Archive, p 226

Michael Ochs Archives, pp 11t, 12b, 13t, 14t, 14r, 15c, 15r, 16b, 17tr, 18, 20a, 21, 22, 23, 23c, 23r, 24b, 25, 26, 29a, 30, 31, 32t, 32b, 35r, 37, 39, 44br, 45b, 47bl, 47br, 48a, 49a, 50l, 52a, 52b, 53a, 54a, 55b, 63b, 68, 69r, 73, 77b, 78, 79al, 79b, 81b, 82, 83a, 83b, 86, 87a, 87b, 88, 89, 92, 94r, 98a, 102, 103a, 107, 108, 109, 113, 116c, 116b, 118b, 119b, 120t, 120c, 128, 130, 131a, 135a, 147, 156, 157, 159, 162, 165, 166a, 169, 170r, 172, 188, 191c, 194, 204t, 208, 220b, 221, 229r, 229r, 230, 238a, 246, 279a; /Robert Altman, p 163l; /Jim Britt, p 131b; /Tom Copl, pp 13c, 51, 79ar, 163r; /David Corio, pp 176r, 200, 219; /Colin Escott, p 12r, 19b; /Anne Fishbein, p 233a; /Lisa Haun, p 225a; /Richard McCaffrey, pp 114–15, 116t; /Alice Ochs, p 45t; /Al Pereira, p 123b; /Paul Ryan, pp 70l, 90a; /Jim Steinfeldt, pp 244, 257a, 269

Popperfoto, pp 8–9, 16t, 63a

Premium Archive/Barry Z Levine, p 110r

Redferns/Richard E. Aaron, pp 121t, 170l, 174r, 182b, 191b, 204c, 235b; /Fiona Adams, p 70; /Jorgen Angel, pp 122t, 132a, 132b, 183, 184; /Ray Avery, p 56; /Roberta Bayley, pp 191, 193a; /Paul Bergen, pp 250–51, 261, 263l, 268, 283; /Marc Broussely, p 309b; /Tony Buckingham, p 239; /Clayton Call, p 254b; /Raffaella Cavalieri, p 262; /Collexxx – Lex van Rossen, p 185; /Brian Cooke, p 153l; /David Corio, pp 203b, 273, 288; /Fin Costello, pp 117, 121c, 122c, 134, 135b, 148, 174l, 196l, 212, 213, 216a, 228r; /Pete Cronin, pp 224, 245; /Phil Dent, pp 214l, 247; /Deborah De Sota, p 124r; /Peter Francis, p 84b; /Patrick Ford, p 281a; /Ian Dickson, pp 178, 181b, 196c; /Erica Echenberg, pp 182a, 191t, 255a; /Echoes, p 181a; /David Warner Ellis, pp 138, 146, 150b, 158; /GAB Archive, pp 12l, 17b, 19a, 20b, 24a, 29b, 40–41, 42t, 42c, 42b, 44a, 46c, 58–9, 59a, 69l, 80b, 90b, 98b, 103b, 105a, 112, 123a, 129a, 191b; /Gems, p 160; /Suzie Gibbons, pp 207b, 217, 238b; /Charlie Gillett Collection, p 97b; /Mick Gold, pp 96, 125; /William Gottlieb, p 17b; /Gijsbert Hanekroot, pp 70r, 101, 105b, 133, 139b, 155, 214r; /Ron Howard, pp 84a, 126, 152; /Mick Hutson, pp 240, 248a, 248al, 256b, 257a, 265b, 260t, 265, 270, 274, 276b, 281b, 282, 284t, 284r, 290a, 298c; /Sal Idriss, p 266; /JMEInternational, p 275; /K & K Ulf Kruger OHG, pp 60, 95l, 144; /van Keeman, p 46b; /Bob King, pp 196b, 228l; /John Lynn Kirk, p 149; /Michel Linssen, pp 235a, 249b, 252b, 300c,

/Robin Little, p 291; /Jim McCrary, p 136; /Vincent McEvoy, p 177; /Hayley Madden, p 297b; /Chris Mills, p 203ar; /Steve Morley p 154l; /Chris Morphet, p 186a; /Estate of Keith Morris, pp 119c, 179l; /Bernd Mueller, p 271; /Niki, pp 232b, 313b; /Peter Noble, p 160–1; /Martin O'Neill, p 197; /Peter Pavlis, p 316a; /Ed Perlstein, p 189b; /Jan Persson, pp 72b, 100, 112l, 137, 142; /Gilles Petard, pp 13b, 28, 47t; /Martin Philbey, p 311a; /Sylvia Pitcher, p 35l; /Premium Archive/Elliott Landy, p 110l; /RB, pp 53b, 77a, 104, 121b, 139a, 153r, 186b; /David Redfern, pp 34, 43, 66, 81a, 99, 143, 151, 167, 176l, 193b, 206a, 215, 279b; /Max Redfern, p 173; /Adam Ritchie, p 97a; /Ebet Roberts, pp 180, 205c, 209a, 211b, 225b, 236a, 240, 254c, 260b; /Kerstin Rodgers, pp 205t, 232a; /John Rodgers, p 210; /Frans Schellekens, p 234; /Brian Shuel, p 45c; /Gus Stewart, p 192; /Peter Still, pp 127, 201l, 202b, 216b, 308b; /Steve Thorne, p 315; /Virginia Turbett, pp 187, 195b, 211a; /Michael Uhl, p 242b; /Rob Verhorst, pp 223, 267; /Des Willie, pp 276a, 280; /Val Wilmer, p 58b; /Andrew Whittuck, p 91; /Gary Wolstenholme, p 278, 301a

Sony BMG Music Entertainment, pp 80a, 141, 166b

Sony Music Archive/Terry Lott, p 203b

Terry O'Neill, pp 171, 207a, 254t

Time & Life Pictures, p 255b; /Dave Allocca, p 260c; /Kimberly Butler, p 253; /Ilan Cook, p 145; /Ralph Crane, p 38b; /Bill Eppridge, p 111; /Yale Joel, p 95r; /Steve Kagan, p 76; /David McGough, p 204b; /Bill Ray, p 33; /Eric Schaal, p 74; /Ted Streshinsky, p 94l; /Stan Wayman, p 11c

WireImage/M. Caulfield, p 292–3; /Shirlaine Forrest, p 299b, 311b; /Ron Galella, p 227a; /Chris Gordon, p 300b; /Steve Jennings, p 164; /Rowen Lawrence, p 242a; /Stephen Lovekin, pp 294b, 308c; /Soren McCarty, p 287b; /Leslie McGhie, p 304; /Kevin Mazur, pp 206b, 231a, 231b, 258a, 259a, 294r, 300t, 314; /Paul Natkin, p 203al; /Janette Pellegrini, p 301b; /J. Quinton, p 298t; /Bob Riha Jr, p 175; /John Shearer, pp 296b, 299t; /Marty Temme, pp 252a, 263r; /Theo Wargo, pp 287a, 296c; /Chris Walter, pp 179r, 209b; /Anna Webber, p 305a